DEDICATIONS
To Greil Marcus and Hunter S. Thompson

WHITE WOLF ENTERTAINMENT
Martin "Elricsson" Ericsson – LEAD STORYTELLER | Karim "Beach" Muammar – EDITOR IN CHIEF |
Dhaunae "Eternally Bonded" De Vir – BUSINESS DEVELOPER | Tomas "The Old One" Arfert – ARTIST AND EDITOR |
Jason "By Night" Carl – COMMUNITY AND MARKETING

DESIGN
DEVELOPED BY – Kenneth Hite, Juhana Pettersson, and Martin Ericsson
STORY & CREATIVE DIRECTION – Martin Ericsson

WRITTEN BY – Juhana Pettersson and Matthew Dawkins
ADDITIONAL WRITING BY – Martin Ericsson, Ariel Celeste, and Karim Muammar

EDITED BY – Freja Gyldenstrøm
ADDITIONAL EDITING BY – Karim Muammar

ART
ART DIRECTION – Tomas Arfert, and Martin Ericsson
BOOK DESIGN AND LAYOUT - Tomas Arfert
COVER – Tomas Arfert
INTERIOR ART AND ILLUSTRATIONS – Jer Carolina, Mary "TwistedLamb" Lee, Tomas Arfert, Sarah Horrocks,
the CCP Atlanta art team directed by Reynir Harðarson, Anders Muammar, and Mark Kelly

CLAN SYMBOLS, SECT ANKHS, CLAN FONTS, AND VAMPIRE: THE MASQUERADE LOGOS – Chris Elliott, Tomas Arfert |
LORESHEET ART – Tia Carolina Ihalainen, Christopher Shy, D. Alexander Gregory, Michael Gaydos, and Guy Davis |
CLAN FASHION DESIGN AND PHOTOSHOOTS – Mary "TwistedLamb" Lee

PHOTOGRAPHY: Viktor Herak, Derek Hutchisson, Sequoia Emanuelle, and Julius Konttinen
MODELS: MINISTRY – Ty Tugwell, Veronica Löfdal, Maria Krylova, and Emmelie Mohlin Z | BRUJAH – Grace Rizzo, Jackie Penn,
Jacqueline Roh, Lee Dawn, Marcus Natividad, Mario Ponce, Mila Dawn, Nate Kamm, Paul Olguin, Daphne Von Rey,
and Casey Driggers | GANGREL – Zoe Jakes, Pixie Fordtears, Aram Giragos, Allesandro Giuliano, and Hal Linton |
TOREADOR – Indhi Korth | TREMERE – Aidin Fanni and Marcus Söderström | ADDITIONAL MODELS – Ida-Emilia Kaukonen

VAMPIRE: THE MASQUERADE CREATORS – Mark Rein•Hagen with Justin Achilli, Steven C. Brown, Tom Dowd, Andrew
Greenberg, Chris McDonough, Lisa Stevens, Josh Timbrook, and Stewart Wieck.

SPECIAL THANKS TO
Justin Achilli for "Anarchs Unbound", Poppy Z Brite, 6104, Bassiani, Berghain, Cloak & Dagger, Stefan Bergmark,
Johan Persson, Ossian Reynolds, J. Gerdin, Dima Brodin, Anders Davén, Gösta Kamp, and Marcus Engstrand.

VISIT WHITE WOLF ENTERTAINMENT ONLINE AT WWW.WHITE-WOLF.COM AND WWW.WORLDOFDARKNESS.COM

TABLE OF CONTENTS

This is a work of speculative horror fiction, set in a dark reflection of our own world. Thus it contains graphic depictions of sex, blood-drinking, drugs, violence, abuse, political oppression, coercion, occultism, heresy and many other potentially upsetting themes. Recommended for mature readers and players. For advice on considerate play and how to handle sensitive themes in tabletop roleplaying games, see the section "Considerate play" in the PDF version of the "Vampire: The Masquerade" rulebook.

The Blood is too good to waste on eternity. You live, you die, you live again, exploding into the night as a newly created animal desperately seeking to hide among its former human peers.

You learn to lie, to hurt and to hunt.

You learn the bliss of tasting blood.

You learn to see every human being as a living mechanism keeping your blood warm for you.

You want to exist in the here and now. You want to feel everything the night can give you. You want to see what's out there. Maybe you even want to belong.

The Anarchs

The old have the power, the knowledge and the resources to keep running things to their advantage. The young have nothing but their fearlessness, numbers and an understanding of the modern world.

And that's just mortals. For vampires, it's much worse. The aged will never die. They will hold on to their positions and advantages forever and ever, crushing everyone who might one day threaten their privileges.

The War of Ages is the organizing principle of vampire society. Established power has organized itself into the Camarilla, seeking to limit the very concept of what a vampire can be. They seek to control the existence of every single vampire on earth and to keep both the mortals and the undead in an eternal stasis where power never changes hands.

The Anarch Movement stands arrayed against the Camarilla. It consists of an endless variety of ideologies and theories of power, brought together by an unwillingness to spend an eternity in a static tyranny.

The very first edition of Vampire: the Masquerade from 1991 has this quote on the back cover: "No one holds command over me. No man. No god. No Prince. What is a claim of age for ones who are immortal? What is a claim of power for ones who defy death? Call your damnable hunt. We shall see who I drag screaming to Hell with me."

That's the core experience of playing an Anarch vampire, right there. You're a young revolutionary fighting to destroy an immortal tyranny of blood. You're just a nobody, someone off the streets who got caught up in the War of Ages and trying to survive. You're an idealist torn between your dreams for a better world and the bloodlust tainting everything you touch.

There is no place for you in the Camarilla's Ivory Tower. Your story will be about blood and fire, sacrificing your eternity for a struggle as old as the world.

The Unbound

Beyond the Anarch Movement lie the Unbound. Who knows how many vampires there are out there, unconnected to the bigger society of undead? These vampires belong to families, cults or gangs, their own little societies just trying to survive the night.

The Unbound present an infinite variety of ways to experience Vampire: the Masquerade. For many Unbound, the Camarilla is just a distant shadow, a repressive force that would shut them down if it only knew about them. The truth is that there can be a vast variety of different, small vampire communities living hidden among the teeming billions populating the planet.

If you want to play a game about recently Embraced vampires still pretending to be the humans they used to be, the Unbound are your choice. Perhaps you want to tell the story of a vampiric infestation of a local crime syndicate or a strange blood cult formed around a charismatic leader. In these cases the wider framework of vampire politics could just get in the way of the human horror story you're planning.

Most of all, the Unbound keep the World of Darkness full of surprises. No Camarilla Prince can ever truly know what's happening in her city, despite her best efforts. That's an idea for another Unbound chronicle: Perhaps your characters think they're the only vampires in the world, until after ten or twenty sessions, they suddenly come into contact with the local Camarilla.

A World of Darkness

The World of Darkness stretches from ocean to ocean, continent to continent. Monsters stalk the night in Tokyo, New York, Lagos and your hometown. This is reflected in the vast variety of the Anarch experience and political projects. The Anarch revolution that created the Free States in California was animated by very different ideas than those of the Brujah who fought with Lenin in the early nights of Communism. A lot of Anarchs speak of Carthage, but they don't always mean the same thing by it.

An Anarch chronicle is connected to the mortal world, to the here and now. It will have humans driving their own agendas, terrors created by mortals worse than those perpetrated by any vampire. In an Anarch game, the characters are part of the world's social fabric and they can embrace their nature as parasites or fight against it.

For an Anarch character, the horrors of being a vampire are visited on their friends and family, people they know, people they've lived with. Vampire concepts like the hunt are not an abstraction, but a necessity forcing the vampire to consider her true nature every night.

This holds true whether your game is set in Cape Town or Montreal. The specifics of local vampire culture change and the politics evolve and mutate, but the core nature of the blood animating each vampire remains the same. And with the blood, the basic activities the characters can do in your game: Hunt, hide, fight, steal, lie, cheat, argue, infiltrate, seduce.

The Experience

This book seeks to lay out a wide variety of Anarch experiences, from the leather jacketed biker Anarchs of the Free States to the Duskborn party scene in Reykjavik. In all of these cases, the vampire lives in the now. Eternal life is but a distant dream in the nightly fight for survival, and many of the vampires who make up the Anarch scene would probably have lived longer if they had never become vampires at all.

Vampire life among the Unbound is fast and deadly. You learn to take risks, fight for what you want and die rather than submit. The concepts and ideas in this book are tools for you to use when you make a game of your own. Use them, change them, ignore them as you wish. Once you start running your own game, it's your World of Darkness.

Monsters of the Recent Past presents the history of the Anarch Movement from Carthage to the present day as told by a variety of voices among the Unbound.

Walk Among Us s all about unlife in the modern nights. What are the different kind of communities Anarchs organize themselves into?

It s Time to See Who s Who details famous figures, political positions, ideologies and scenes among the modern Anarch Movement and beyond.

What Is To Be Done? All talk and no action makes for a bad revolutionary. This is all about the practical possibilities of fighting the Anarch fight, from tips on how to disappear to the many benefits of a liberal approach to Diablerie.

This panoply of Anarch experiences across the world is followed by a look into how the different vampire clans function in the world of the Unbound. This is followed by the Loresheets expanding on specifically Anarch topics referred through this book.

Invisible Monsters

So welcome to Planet Unbound. It's a world where the sun is always setting somewhere, ready to unleash the hidden monsters living everywhere among us, as neighbors, friends, co-workers, lovers and random people on the street.

Life on Planet Unbound goes on night to night while the Camarilla watches it go by from the windows of their Ivory Tower. This is a truth known to every Anarch: If you think the hunt is somehow separate from your nightly existence, you've already became terminally lost in the modern world. For an Anarch vampire, the hunt is life, whether they're meeting an old school friend to assess if they could be forced to become a blood addict or in a desperate fight to escape the fangs of a murderous Camarilla Archon. It is no accident that among the Kindred, the prettiest ideals of humanity are held by those who don't really live among humans anymore.

This night is your night. The plane is populated by a feast of human beings, their flesh crisscrossed by veins carrying sweet blood waiting for you. It doesn't matter if you relish the hunt or view it as a horrible necessity. The blood doesn't give a damn about your morality. It's all around you, calling for you to have a taste.

Put on your best party song, wear your favorite jacket, apply some eyeliner, forget you're less than human and dance into the nightt. ∎

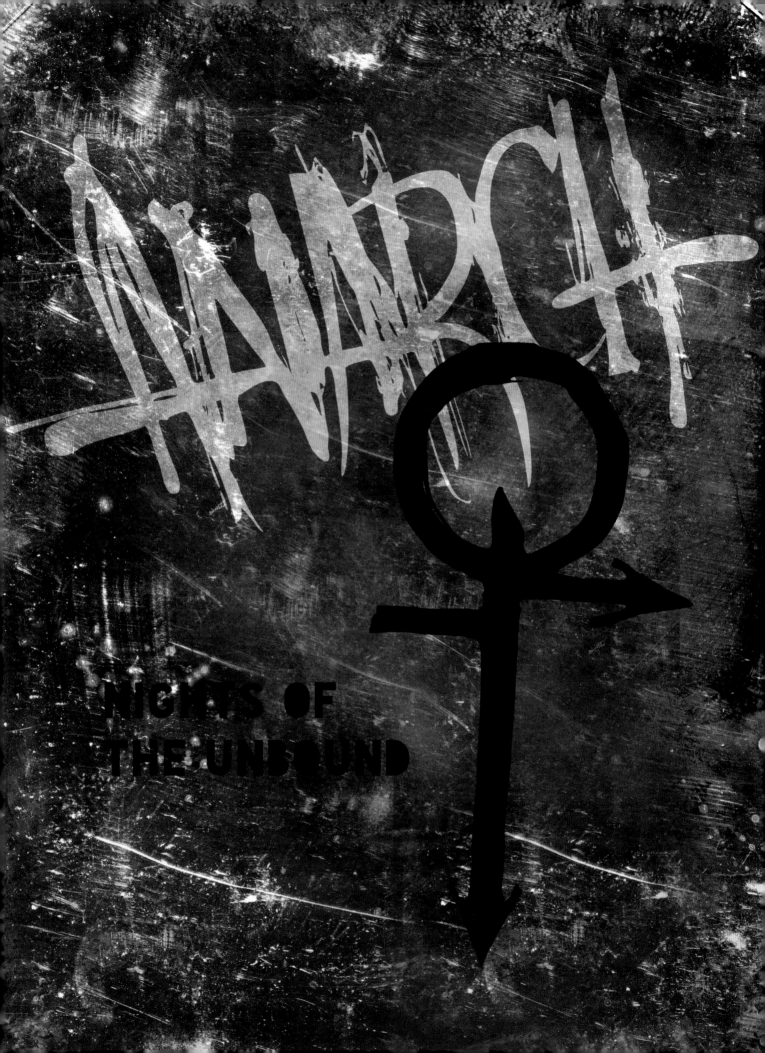

WHAT ARE WE

Okay, get ready. I'm going to explain the real truth behind our kind. You've read about alien bacteria found on the Antarctic ice, right? That's where we come from. Those bacteria infected scientists, and it spread, and here we are. It's the only explanation that makes sense.

We're a disease, nothing more. A disease that transforms the host into a perfect vehicle for spreading the plague. When you feel the hunger for blood rising, that's the virus pushing you to seek new victims. It's like those ants in the Amazon getting infected with fungi which hijacks the entire organism and starts directing it towards its own goals.

Every one of us is a demon, and every one of us is a true rebel. This is our glory and our burden. Lucifer started as a rebel but soon became the thing he despised the most, the tyrant of Hell. Only we are the true free thinkers, the demons who rejected Lucifer and came to Earth. This is our real purpose: To spread the message of true freedom among humanity.

We've always been here, from the dawn of history to the present day. We're a parallel species evolved to live in symbiosis with humanity. They provide us with sustenance, and we provide direction and purpose.

I'm pretty sure vampire blood is radioactive and we're all mutants. That's how we have all these powers.

You must discard human morality like a snake sheds its skin and learn to listen to the voice of the divine within you. You're God's chosen instrument, gifted with a fragment of divinity to show you the true way. That's our purpose and our destiny. There's no escaping our inherent holiness: Your every kindness and every cruelty is an act of God.

If you wish to understand our condition, you must study the works of the Theosophists. We all begin the cycle as inanimate minerals, and through virtuous acts, progress to plants, animals and finally human consciousness. The traditional literature often suggests that the term for the next stage is Bodhisattva, but we can also use another word with mythical connotations: Vampire. The Bodhisattva/Vampire's purpose is to guide humanity to the next stage in its cycle of reincarnation through the spiritual act of ingesting blood.

This is the simple truth that Christianity, Judaism and Islam seek to deny: Caine was the first Messiah rebelling against a tyrant God, the true visionary showing us the real power and potential we all have within us. We are Caine's true angels, bringing his judgement on Earth.

I'm a materialist. I don't believe in supernatural explanations, but I do believe in the broad sweep of history. This is the real purpose of our kind as immortal beings. To direct the curve of human events. After all, immortality is enlightenment.

Who cares if there's a big story behind all this? I call it like I see it. We're predators, exploiting humanity in the night. Nothing more.

What Are Humans

I like humans a lot, what can I say. I never get tired of the hunt. They make such funny noises when they're trying to escape, and at the moment of death they all have this endearing belief that they're unique. I've tried to explain how hilarious that is to some of them, but they never get it.

Humanity has been placed in our charge, and we are responsible for guiding and protecting them. We must fulfil the responsibility we have towards our weaker brothers, even as they fulfil their responsibility to feed us.

Lot of licks see humans as nothing but food. For them, humanity is a big blood farm giving us what we need to survive. This always makes me feel sad. Humanity can be so much more than mere nutrients! They can provide a real culinary experience.

There's a vast difference between the blood of an elderly policeman wasting away in a ramshackle geriatric ward and a plump scion of a successful family planning a wedding in the Maldives. There's no such thing as bad blood. Every human brings their own flavor to the table, and we should learn to appreciate it!

The humans are us and we are the humans. It's nothing but vanity to imagine we're somehow better, stronger, crueler or smarter than they are. We may live longer and hunt for blood, but in the end we're all just assholes trying to survive through another night.

I see every human essentially as a proto-vampire. They just need a little push and they become us. I know it feels kinda gross, but this is how our biology works. We're an organism that subsists on eating its larvae, allowing the strongest and most viable individuals to develop into the adult stage of the species. Now, here's the real question: Are we the final stage or do we develop into something more?

We're predators, night animals, hunters designed to kill fast and quiet. We're cheetah, not elephants. We need our camouflage, our hiding places, lairs from which to strike. The best defense we have is to hide among humanity like a big cat hides among tall grass.

We should never forget what it was to be human. Becoming one of us is a fall from grace, and our only hope of salvation is to return to humanity. We are not more than human. We are less, and we should always strive to return to what we were.

I don't care about humanity. A lot of us do, but in truth they're just a distraction from the real shape of the world. Sure, humanity generates a lot of noise, but in the end it's as meaningful as the crackle on an empty radio wavelength.

Humanity is loss. That's a lesson we all learn eventually. You grow attached, you fall in love, you make enemies, you hate, but in the end humanity always withers and disappears. For a lick, relying on the living is like building a sandcastle on a beach before the tide comes in.

What Is Wise

You want to gorge yourself, feel the power of the blood in your body, burn through everything you drink and become a superhuman monster capable of anything. And sure, you can do that. But if you want to live longer, maybe don't. Drink sparingly, use the blood with purpose, and you'll survive.

A lot of us detest the Hunger that always keeps us focused on the delicious red stuff coursing through the veins of mortals. For me, the Hunger is a blessing. Its purpose is to keep us alert, on our toes, ready for anything. Because of the Hunger, we're always thinking of what we need to survive. Everything beyond that is luxury.

Rule number one of a successful unlife is to nest among mortals. Exist as one of them. Look like them, behave like them, talk like them. Don't let yourself be separated from humanity. Don't give in to the idea that we

somehow live apart from human culture and civilization. The closer you are to humanity, the more successful you'll be as a hunter and harder to detect for your enemies.

Blood is the focus of your existence. Keep a stash in your fridge. Learn how to suck animals dry. (I know they taste horrible, but better than starving, right?) Make sure you always have more blood around you than you really need. This way, you'll be able to feast if you need to heal after a fight. And once bad times come around, you'll be able to roll with the punches.

A vampire is a lonely hunter. Don't rely on others, don't trust and don't reveal your secrets. In the end, the only person who really cares about your survival is you. Make sure that nobody knows where you sleep, who your blood slaves are and how you hunt.

Trying to survive alone is a fool's errand. A lot of us descend into pointless paranoia, fearing everyone and assuming ill intent behind friendly gestures. Learn to hunt in a pack. You'll find it's easier, safer and if you fuck up, someone's there to save your ass. And another thing: We get lonely too. Just because you're undead doesn't mean you can't use someone to talk to.

The Camarilla sucks, but they have one good idea: the Masquerade. If you think about their Traditions, you'll realize that most of them are geared for preserving elite power. The Masquerade is an exception. It's designed to protect all of our kind, and that's why everybody should follow it. The reality is that you might think yourself as the apex predator on a moonlit night, but at high noon you're just another fool getting burned to a crisp.

The Camarilla likes to define what being a lick is all about. They want to tell you about Caine, the Traditions, the Prince and all that bullshit. If you're not careful, you'll start believing them. You'll think their way is the only way for our kind to exist. But it isn't. There's a simple remedy to their lies: Eat the rich. Once you have a taste of a Camarilla vampire, there's no going back.

What Now

Immortality is bullshit. It's a lie designed to keep you docile and afraid. Sure, we can live forever, but is it worth it if it means an eternity of bowing to a Prince? Live fast and hard and make sure that when you die, you take those assholes with you.

You've been brought into a world where every advantage, every scrap of power and every drop of blood is already in the hands of hoary ancient creatures who will never, ever give it up. For humanity, there's at least the hope that old power dies. For us, that will never happen. Instead, we must tear it from the hands of our elders and rip them apart so they can never build their vile system again.

You've been given the powers of the blood and a deathless existence. It's time you put all that into a good use and fight for a better world. Any asshole can fight for themselves, but if you want real immortality, fight to change the world. Fight for something bigger than yourself. Only before you do that, ask yourself this question: A better world for who?

The Camarilla is a massive edifice built to preserve the power of ancient monsters who were Embraced in centuries past. They present themselves as the most powerful, the wisest, the best deserving of all of our kind, but don't fall for their lies. They're nothing but old fools holding onto their power with every ounce of their being. Your job is to demolish the Camarilla and create space for something better to be born. Something built on principle, not just to maintain existing privilege.

I didn't become undead just to get caught in someone else's wars. The Camarilla, the Anarch Movement, Caine, humanity... Who cares about any of that? I live for myself. This is my life, the only life I will ever have. I will not waste it in service of a slick sleazebag with a line he wants to sell me.

We're monsters, and nothing good can come of us. We can't build a better world, because in a better world we don't exist. The best way a lick can improve the society around him is to commit suicide. Otherwise, we poison everything, especially mortals who are trying to do something good. No human political movement has been improved by contact with our kind.

There are so many lies. Caine, Antediluvians, Golconda. All of these stories are there to keep us in our place, and they need to be demolished. I believe we can find the truth of our condition, but first we must dispel the darkness of all these medieval myths purporting to show us how to live our unlives.

There is hope for us. Far from the political games of the Camarilla and the toxic games played by our elders, we can still be redeemed. Perhaps that is Golconda, perhaps something else. There's still a chance for something better in this sordid mess. ∎

Monsters of the Recent Past

There is no single history of the Anarch Movement or the Unbound. History is always political, after all, interpreted and reinterpreted to suit the needs of the moment. Vampire society may play host to those who remember ancient times from the Roman Empire to New York in the Eighties, but only a fool would trust the version of events told by an immortal bloodsuckerr.

The truth is that vampires lie. They lie to serve their own interests, stroke their egoes and spite their enemies. In this they're no different from ordinary mortals, but the Masquerade makes it even harder to write an objective history. Reliable written sources of information on the history of the undead are scarce.

What does this mean for a young Anarch seeking to make sense of the world? How can she know where she came from and what it means to be a vampire?

You have to choose which lies you like the best.

Consider one of the most famous moments of recent Anarch history, the death of the Prince of Los Angeles Don Sebastian in 1944. Anarch legends tells how the Spanish anarchist Salvador Garcia fought his way into Don Sebastian's haven and killed him after a desperate, bloody battle.

For this and for writing the Anarch Manifesto Salvador Garcia became one of the legends of the Anarch Movement.

Did he really kill Don Sebastian all by himself?

Maybe, maybe not. Nevertheless, when he was alive Don Sebastian was nothing but the Camarilla Prince of a young, new city. In death, he became the symbol of everything wrong with the Camarilla, from autocratic practices to sheer cruelty. Even the Camarilla bought into the myth, abandoning his legacy and refusing to try to salvage the rule of a Prince who seemed so degenerate and useless.

Was Don Sebastian really worse than so many other Camarilla Princes? Probably not. But he was weak, and that was enough.

When you listen to stories about Anarch history, apply the same basic rules you should follow when you read the newspaper. Who's telling the story and what's their agenda? How is the issue being framed? Who benefits from this narrative? And of course, we always tend to believe those with power and distrust those without power. If you're a young vampire, try to keep this impulse in check. Power is never on your side.

– Rudi, Brujah ideologue

The City On the Sea

If you hang out in Anarch circles, and particularly with political Anarchs, for any length of time, there's one word you're bound to hear: Carthage. So what does a North African city state whose glory days were two thousand years ago have to do with our struggle today?

Carthage is sometimes called the Third City, after the First and Second Cities of vampire legend. Most of those legends don't get a lot of traction in Anarch circles, but Carthage does. As the story goes, it was the best and most successful attempt at creating a society where humans and vampires could live together openly and in harmony. Although created long before the birth of the modern Anarch Movement, it was our paradise on earth, and its fall still resounds through vampire history. For the Camarilla, Carthage is a symbol of the impracticality of our ideas and the supremacy of their vision for our existence, but for us it means precisely the opposite.

Let's face it: The very existence of Carthage flies in the face of centuries of Camarilla orthodoxy about the Masquerade. It calls into question the most basic conception have of ourselves. After all, the Princes tell us that we're parasites who hide among humanity, piggybacking on their successes. Their dogma states that secrecy is safety and only fools dream of radical change in human society to improve our lives.

So how did they do it? How did these ancient, mainly Brujah Kindred manage something that has rarely been even attempted since?

This is where things become difficult. There are very few written sources and our elders are notorious liars when it comes to history. It's hard to say how Carthage was really organized, but a lot of Movement Anarchs have their own ideas of how it was done.

For some, Carthage was a peaceful utopia in which humans and vampires lived as equals. We weren't predators or parasites, but rather enjoyed the blood of our human brethren consensually. We ruled our city together, sharing the power and privilege without regard to who was a vampire and who wasn't.

For others, Carthage was a benevolent vampire dictatorship. We took care of our human brothers and sisters, ruling over them benevolently and only taking the blood we needed to survive. Our immortality meant that we could exist among them openly as a privileged, trusted elite.

There are darker versions of the story as well. We're vampires after all, and the humans are a mere herd. In this vision of Carthage, the city was a utopia for Kindred, a metropolis with a captive, controlled population which understood its place. This Carthage was a place of enlightenment and peace, as long as you were one of us.

So which of these is true? Usually what you believe depends on what kind of a world you want to build. You choose the Carthage that works for you.

All three versions share two ideas: Vampires living openly among humans, and using our power to create the society we want to live in. From the charity of those who believe us equal to humans to the brutality of those who believe humans to be a mere resource our common trait is ambition. We believe we can make the world anew. We don't have to accept the current conditions like the Camarilla cowards do.

This is the true meaning of Carthage. The exact historical reality doesn't matter. The point is that a better world is possible.

This is also the truth that the Camarilla desperately seeks to suppress. Both mortal and Kindred history tells of a violent Carthaginian blood cult. Children were sacrificed in mad rituals, their bones collected in deranged ossuaries. You can ask the question, is this true? Was Carthage actually a city of violent terror, with its Brujah masters feasting on the blood of babies?

Mortal historians of Carthage have long struggled with a lack of proper records from Carthage itself. Their sources of information are second-hand, usually Roman. And who waged a bitter war against Carthage, ultimately destroying it?

That's right, Rome.

These stories of baby murder are nothing but Roman war propaganda, taken as fact by gullible historians. Indeed, recent scholarship on Carthage has disputed the Roman narrative. The ossuaries are there, but they have a more mundane explanation than mad rites: They're simply a graveyard. After all, children died of disease and hunger in Carthage the same as all across the ancient world.

Still, it's no wonder the Camarilla still tries to tarnish the reputation of Carthage. The idea of the city has always been dangerous. Two thousand years ago, it was Brujah idealists in Carthage versus Ventrue conservatives in Rome. The Ventrue understood the potential of the Carthaginian idea to create a new revolutionary society. They realized that they had no place in this new world Carthage represented and decided they had to destroy it.

From human history, it's hard to say why Carthage really fell. Maybe Roman military might supported by Ventrue wealth and power was enough. Or maybe Carthage had run into trouble on its own. Corruption is no stranger to us, so it's possible the Brujah of that time grew complacent and caused their own fall. Whatever the truth, Carthage laid the foundation for a pattern that would be repeated many times in our history. The city fell, but the idea became immortal.

Sometimes we become so enamored of the story that we forget its basis in reality. In the grand legend of Carthage it was destroyed for all eternity, but in actuality it still exists, just in a different form. After being conquered by Rome, Carthage became a Roman provincial capital. Today, it's a town in the orbit of Tunis, the capital of Tunisia. 24,000 people live there.

It's a good reminder of the fact that while we dream of our utopias, humanity doggedly barrels on with its own history.

– SALVADOR GARCIA,
AUTHOR OF THE ANARCH
MANIFESTO

LOOKING FOR TYLER

I didn't think she was anything special. Sure, she was charismatic, knew how to play a crowd. But that's not rare among Anarch Brujah. I figured she was just another recently Embraced punk girl having fun among the dead.

We were hanging at our usual place, like we did pretty much every night, when the Sheriff decided to drop by with his flunkies. She wasn't there when it started. The Sheriff told us that until the lick who was feeding in the Prince's private hunting ground was caught, he'd execute one of us every week, starting tonight.

Sure, we talked tough, but in the end we were a bunch of losers. We liked to think we were badass, but we didn't have the courage to go against the Sheriff and all he represented. He crushed my childe's head under his boot in front of me, and I didn't have the guts to do anything about it.

But she did. She came into the bar, this girl I thought was just a nobody. She had a tattered Misfits shirt and Doc Martens, but when I saw her face as she witnessed the execution, all that seemed to melt away.

She didn't make a sound, but somehow the Sheriff realized things had gotten serious. Maybe he saw it on our faces. We were no longer looking at him. He turned, and she thrust a cue stick straight through his heart as if she'd done it a thousand times before.

The Sheriff's friends started edging away. She smiled at them and said: "Say hello to the Prince. He already knows my name."

The next morning, the Sheriff burned in the sunrise. We never saw her again, but something big changed in the city that night.

– Lena, a German Anarch

Many of us regard Tyler as the first Anarch, although that's probably not strictly speaking true. What we do know is that in life, she was a 14th century English peasant rebel, a follower of Wat Tyler from whom she later took her name. In death, she fought against the Camarilla even before it was officially formed and played a key role in the original Anarch Revolt. She went to the Convention of Thorns in 1493 and was present at the newly formed Anarchs' capitulation to the Camarilla.

These are the largely undisputed historical facts about Tyler. After Thorns, she disappeared as an Anarch leader, perhaps disappointed in the way the nascent movement had betrayed its ideals in the name of a servile peace with the Camarilla. Some say that she participated in the formation of the Sabbat, but it's hard to be sure.

Perhaps it's for the best. For centuries after Thorns, the legend of Tyler has been much more important than reality. She's the first true rebel, the one who refused to capitulate. She hasn't soiled herself in the power games of the Camarilla or the brutalities of the Sabbat. She hasn't taken her place as a leader like Salvador Garcia or Jeremy MacNeil, so we can project all of our hopes and dreams onto her without having them tested by reality. We don't know her true beliefs, so she can be everything to all people.

We just know that she's out there, somewhere, and when the need is greatest she will appear to save the day.

– CHINASA ADEYEMI,
AN ANARCH CHRONICLER

I used to be jealous of Tyler. I knew her, back in the day, and sure she was impressive. But so were many others. In the centuries since, some of us have have fought on the front lines of the Movement. What has she done? Hidden in the shadows, playing Robin Hood?

I bust my ass off trying to lead this community, yet she's the real hero.

Tell you the truth, I've made my peace with it. You don't realize the real power Tyler has until you go to a meeting with the Camarilla. Sit down with an Archon or two and see how they like hearing her name.

Sure, I'm tough. I can probably take out any of those wimpy little snots the Camarilla likes to send our way. Yet they still don't fear me the way they fear a story. That's what she is, a story.

The best part is, most folks don't even know the real stuff about her. If you want to see a Prince squirm, ask him about Tyler and Hardetstadt, the mighty Ventrue Founder of the Camarilla. Only be prepared for a long interrogation about how you knew to ask that question.

- Jeremy MacNeil, an Anarch leader

I don't expect you to believe me. I'm just a nobody, a bag lady, a vagrant. You walk past me every day.

Later, they told me some well-meaning person had called the cops and insisted they take care of me. I'd passed out on the street and they were afraid I was dying.

The cops were pissed off. They arrested me and took me to a holding cell. They figured they'd had enough of me. People die in holding cells all the time, and I was half dead already. I just needed a little push and they wouldn't have to see me again.

I saw her. She was like a red angel, tearing those cops apart like it was nothing. The drunken one pissing on me, the angry one trying to rape the girl in the next cell, the scared one who tried to resist. They were all meat to her. Just bones and organs in uniform, waiting to be taken apart and spread on the linoleum floor.

You want me to confirm your story of how meth-crazed junkies assaulted and murdered all your officers. And I will. But in my heart, I will always have my angel, looking out for me.

First Anarch Revolt

Even today you hear some Anarchs saying we should talk with the Camarilla. We need a common response to the Second Inquisition. We need to make peace after the catastrophic results of the Conclave of Prague.

Anybody who knows anything about our history can tell you this is all bullshit. Let's take a look at the first Anarch Revolt. The roots of the Revolt are in the 15th century Inquisition campaign to destroy all creatures they saw as the spawn of the Devil. Although human in origin, the Inquisition was not to be fucked with: They swept across Europe destroying our kind in town after town. They were successful because they had momentum, faith and organizing behind them. We'd relied on fear for a long time to keep the mortals in check, and it had made us lazy and complacent. When the fear dissipated, we had nothing.

So how did the ancient monsters, the supremely powerful creatures leading our kind respond to this threat? The same way an Elder always survives to live another night: By running away and hiding.

It's important to understand that the Kindred society of that time was extremely authoritarian, even compared to today. Our kind were taught to follow the example of our elders in all things. A young lick had no freedom, but at least the society built by the elders was stable and secure. Right?

The first Anarchs were born in the fires of the Inquisition. They learned to survive and to fight a war against the worst foe to ever threaten our kind until the present day. Many died in the betrayal of the elders, but many more learned they could take charge of their own lives.

After the Inquisition, they were not content to bow down after the cowardly Princes returned from hiding to demand allegiance. They figured that if they could survive the Inquisition, they could depose a tyrant.

The Anarch Revolt swept across Europe, and it had some spectacular successes. In every city and every town, there were young vampires ready to take up the torch of the revolution. You must remember that in those times, our gerontocracy was even more brutal than today. Executions, torture, sadistic games of mind control... A young vampire was basically property, a toy to be used and abused by his sire any way she saw fit. The idea of a new free and just society for our kind grew in a field long tilled and cultivated by the tyrant elders themselves.

Although stories of the first Anarch Revolt often revolve around the mythic deaths of the Tzimisce and Lasombra Antediluvians in the hands of revolutionary warbands, it's important to remember that the Revolt was a true mass movement with momentum across the European continent and beyond.

Before the Revolt, the elders had felt secure in their power. They had everything set up in their favor and could afford to treat their childer like slaves. After the Revolt, every small town Princeling knew what it felt like to be afraid of your own progeny.

So how did the Camarilla fight back? Very cleverly, as befits a vampire. Those sneaky motherfuckers realized that they'd never beat back the revolution using violence. Instead, they capitulated and corrupted us from within, vampire style.

The stage for this grand maneuver was the Convention of Thorns, a peace summit held in England in

1493. The Anarchs and the nascent Camarilla sent representatives to the town of Thorns to negotiate. This was the first mistake the Anarchs made. There is no negotiating with the Camarilla. You can't win against political manipulators who've spent centuries perfecting their craft.

In Thorns, the Camarilla eviscerated our movement. Our leaders betrayed us, seduced by token concessions and personal favors. The Camarilla elders made a pretense of humility, giving us a feeling of achievement so we'd fail to realize how they were destroying us. The Camarilla played the long game, trusting in the fact that a treaty would steal away the momentum of the Revolt, giving them the time to slowly reassert their power.

Some of us understood this even at the time. Individual Anarchs dissented at the Convention, the most famous among them the Anarch folk hero Tyler. A radical wing of the Revolt staged a walkout and went on to form the extremist mystery cult Sabbat.

Still, to our eternal shame, most Anarchs accepted the deal the Camarilla offered, thus destroying any chance of a successful revolution in the centuries to come.

So what does this have to do with tonight? Well, let's see. The Second Inquisition is rooting out and murdering our kind across the world. At the same time, elders in many Camarilla cities are becoming less and less accessible, often outright disappearing. In the light of history, it's clear they're taking their lessons from the first Inquisition. Disappear, and let their childer deal with the danger.

The thing is, they're not the only ones to learn from history. We can do it too. If the elders abandon us, we can take control of the power and resources they leave behind. What's more, the Conclave of Prague was something you rarely get in Anarch history: A freebie. We got a massive boost through no effort of our own. The Camarilla managed to alienate the Brujah to such a degree they left it as a clan.

I have no idea what that means in practice, and I doubt Brujah elders are going to be any less dangerous than before. But as a symbolic act, its message was clear. The Camarilla doesn't represent the great majority of this world's licks. The Anarch Movement does.

This is the simple rule we must always remember when fighting for our freedom: It's never achieved by appealing to the conscience of the king. The Princes will never give us our freedom of their own volition. We must take it, and take it by force. We must resist every offer at compromise, because it will be an attempt to neutralize us through negotiations, as the Camarilla did in Thornss.

– DALIA NAKACHE,
A FRENCH ANARCH
REVOLUTIONARY IDEOLOGUE

Reign of Terror

The only problem with the French Revolution was that it ended unfinished. Because of that tragedy, aristocrats still infest our societies. In a just world, the revolution would have spread and every last king would have been executed for crimes against the people.

I'm not prone to envy, but I would've liked to have been there. A lot of Anarchs of a certain generation say they were, but I think that's like a hippie who says he was at Woodstock. Take it with a grain of salt.

Paris is one of the great bastions of the Camarilla, a true city of the heartland of elder power. Because of this, the two periods in which Paris became temporarily an Anarch town are much loved in our circles. The first was the Revolution, and the second May '68. In both cases, events instigated by mortals caused Anarchs to flock into the city and force the local Camarilla into hiding. Eventually the Camarilla recovered and we had to leave the city, but the memory remains.

In the case of the Revolution, political change utterly inimical to the Camarilla swept Europe. In France, feudalism was abolished, the monarchy fell and dozens of Camarilla vampires who had lived among the aristocracy died, sometimes dragged out of their havens during the day by the new revolutionary authorities.

What's more, the relatively new Prince of Paris, Francois Villon, had a hard time trying to combat the revolution despite the fact that he was absolutely on the side of the Ancién Regime. The reasons for this were twofold:

1. Villon's city was in chaos, and full of Anarchs who'd come to join the revolution.

2. He was a fucking coward, fleeing the city instead of risking personal danger.

With Villon in exile, the city's new Anarch masters had free rein with the new revolutionary government. Some of the old Anarchs like to downplay their involvement, but I think we all know what the Kindred contribution was: To make it as bloody as possible!

I bet there were some good times to be had. Just imagine the scene: The havens of old Toreador suddenly ripped open, the confused elders emerging to face crowds armed with torches. It must have been Anarch heaven. Assisted by the mortal chaos, you could have done anything, forced the Camarilla establishment to suffer any indignity.

(A lot of Anarchs are all about killing the enemy, but I advocate for the occasional ritual humiliation. It's a lot of fun!)

And even without the elders, there's still humanity. The guillotine. The line of simpering nobility waiting to die. That's what being a bloodsucker is all about. I wish I could have just laid down right next to the guillotine and let the blood from each decapitation flow into my mouth.

Unfortunately, all good things must come to an end. For the mortals, the Revolution ushered in all kinds of new ideas that took root in France and elsewhere. For us, the Revolution was an early flowering of the Anarch sentiment, successfully crushed by Villon once he returned to the city at the cusp of the 19th century.

– Agata "guillotine fangirl" Starek

'68

If you hang with Movement Anarchs long enough, you'll hear about Paris in '68. The romance, the excitement, there's always some old dude who had the time of his life on the barricades and who's never experienced anything better. Unlike the French Revolution, '68 is recent enough that many of us actually were there.

And you know what? It was pretty great. This is one of those classic uprisings that people remember, and the first one I'm old enough to have participated in.

The stage: The post-war France of Charles De Gaulle.

The issues: Capitalism, consumerism, authoritarianism and American imperialism.

The participants: Students occupying institutions of learning. 11 million workers striking.

The result: President De Gaulle is forced to secretly flee the country for a short time, and calls for a new general election upon return.

(The depressing part: De Gaulle's party won the election, although De Gaulle's personal career went into decline.)

I got to Paris a little late, and it was like an Anarch festival. Everybody who was anybody in the Movement was there. Keep in mind that I was recently Embraced, so I was super impressed with all these dudes of the revolution like Jeremy McNeil and Salvador Garcia. But there were others too. You can laugh at me, but I'm pretty sure that a girl I shared a night with on the barricades was Tyler.

Like during the French Revolution, the Camarilla went into hiding. Some of them were old enough to remember the trauma of the first Anarch occupation of Paris. Prince Francois Villon disappeared for a week, leaving his flunkies to try to deal with the massive influx of Anarchs eager for a replay of the Revolution.

Personally, I had good times. Embraced my first three childer.

One of them even survived the chaos! Drank my first Camarilla twit dry. He was lovely, a dashing little aristocrat. He begged me not to kill him. It was pretty heady stuff for a young Anarch!

This is the real generational experience of '68 for us: Rioting, partying, debating, feeding and fucking on the streets and barricades. No wonder '68 is fondly remembered among Anarchs. But there's something more. This is my personal theory: Everything moved so fast, we didn't have time to poison it.

I love a good riot as much as the next girl, but looking at the mortals, things tend to get bad when our kind is involved. This is why I always tell my compatriots we should let the humans organize their political movements in pace and get into banking or something.

Except banking is boring. Riots are fun.

– Agata "the problem" Starek

Ten Nights That Shook the World

For the duration of a single human lifetime, the Soviet Union existed as paradise on earth. Before you object to that statement, I ask you to consider *paradise for whom?*

The Camarilla and its Kindred like to see themselves as separate from human history and society. This view of themselves makes it hard for Camarilla Kindred to understand other ways of relating to humanity. They imagine that their framework is universal, when in reality it's only shared by a small minority of aged vampires.

This is important if you wish to understand who we really were, the Brujah who participated in the October Revolution.

Simply put, we were ordinary people. We were young, recently Embraced vampires, none older than ten years undead. The Embrace doesn't erase who you are. Your history, values, analysis of the world, class background. All of this survives intact. The only difference is that when the world starts to shake, you're better equipped to fight for what you believe in.

The People

There was a lot of blood in the revolution, and it fueled a cleansing of society that would have been unimaginable before. For the mortals, the blood they spilled gave them faith they could succeed. For us, it sustained us as we tore apart the lairs of monsters so ancient, even a Camarilla elder would tremble at the mention of their names.

The individualists of the Camarilla do not grasp the power of collective action. What chance a methuselah has when the masses dismantle its tomb stone by stone in the cold October sunlight? The mortals might think they're searching for provisions hidden away by corrupt aristocrats, but the effect on the body of the vampire is the same. It will burn.

In those early nights, we were all united by the common purpose of destroying the rule of the Tsar and the vampire Princes reigning in the night. We wanted to build something better, something more, a beautiful new world by the people and for the people.

Perhaps the seeds of our division had already been planted, or perhaps our ideas diverged only later. It doesn't really matter. In the beginning, we were fired up by the knowledge we were doing something the old establishment had always told us was impossible. For the vampiric scholars among us, this was our Carthage, not as a city but as a vast country stretching from Europe to Asia.

Many say that the true nature of the vampire will always assert itself. Maybe so. Personally, I think it was more about the added perspective of experience and age. Some among us never let go of the belief that we should build a place where humans and vampires could live together in open harmony, as equals.

Others, myself among them, eventually understood that a true immortal paradise would be something we built for those of our own kind. I'm not against treating humans well. I was a human once. But we have to be realistic and accept that humans are nothing but our food and larval form. Kindness is a virtue, but it doesn't make sense to advocate for full rights to mortals any more than it does to grant them to cows or dogs.

The Schism

This ideological conflict came to a head in the aftermath of the death of Lenin. In 1926 at the 4th Congress of the Revolutionary Council (colloquially known as the Brujah Council), the goal of open co-existence between our kind and humans was formally abandoned. The decision was followed at the 5th Congress in 1929 by the formal definition of the purpose of the Council as the creation of a perfect state for vampires. The pro-human universalist faction managed to push through a motion on our responsibility to treat the mortals in a spirit of equality, but it didn't stick.

In the next ten years, internal purges successfully eradicated this faction by sentencing them to death for sedition or forcing them to exile.

So did the Brujah Council control the Soviet Union? Yes and no, depending on who you ask and how you define control. To understand this, we need to go back to the Camarilla idea of our kind as separate from humanity. This is not how the Council worked. We existed as part of the larger Party structure, working together with our human colleagues.

To put this bluntly, the environment we fostered was such that if you could only have a meeting with Comrade Domasheva in the Lubyanka at night, would you really ask questions? Or would you just keep silent? Terror and censorship are wonderful tools for the protection of our privileges and keeping the Masquerade.

We were not separate from the Party. Instead, we were a part of a bigger machine, subtly nudging it so that our goals were met. Our influence was from within, not from without.

The End of the Dream

This is my only regret, that so few now understand what we did: Our society was a success, as long as it lasted. The gulags provided bountiful hunting, the Masquerade held automatically and mortals who threatened us heard a knock on their doors at three AM.

Unfortunately we were brought down by useless sentimentality and individual greed. Some of us started to dream of the Princely domains of old, and others kept up their useless prattle about the role of humans in our grand experiment. Because of these weaknesses, we were unable to defend and maintain the Soviet Union when it started to crumble.

Personally, I never gave up on the dream. There are still places on Earth where an efficient system of repression keeps the mortals in check. I couldn't stomach the new Russia so I left for Central Asia.

Still, those living in the ruins of our magnificent design must remember that for a few glorious decades, Carthage was real on a massive scale. A paradise for vampires, a cattle pen for humans. A place where we could truly flourish without fear of the depredations of the Camarilla or terrors like the modern Second Inquisition. Now that young vampires flock to build their own domains in the former Soviet territories, they'd do well to honor those who paved the way for them.

– Oksana Dimitrovna Domasheva, a former member of the Brujah Council

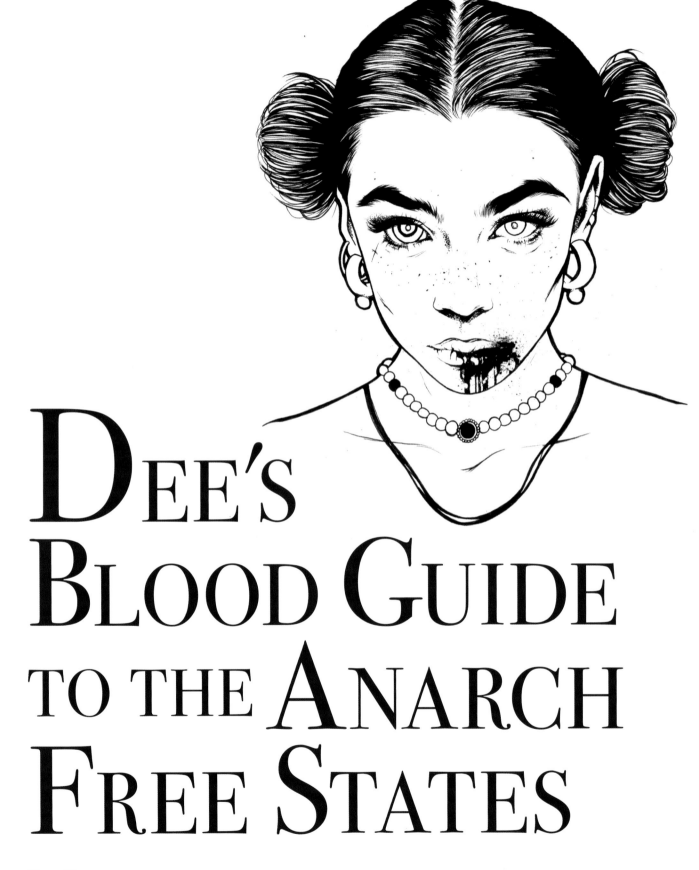

Dee's Blood Guide to the Anarch Free States

By: Dee

A lot of porn gets made in the San Fernando Valley, so much that sometimes they call it the Porn Valley. I'll tell you something about porn and being a vampire that will make you a happier person, if you can accept it.

A lot of people think that they must want to fuck what society tells them to. A dude must want to fuck blonde porn girls. If deep in his heart he actually wants to fuck something else, he needs to suppress that feeling because otherwise his identity and self-worth become confused.

A lot of vampires do this as well. They too think they need the blonde porn girls, to feed from them. They think that's what you must do as a vampire: Seek out conventionally attractive, clean humans to feed from.

But you know, the heart wants what it wants. And usually what it wants is the most fucked up inappropriate thing.

Like, I know a Brujah tough guy, we went to hunt together. There was a porn shoot, one of those "World's Biggest Gangbang" things. There was a woman on all fours getting fucked. For a lot of folks, she would have been the obvious victim.

But my friend is a modern man. He's in tune with his desires.

On a shoot like that, there's a dude whose job is to keep the star clean. He has a towel he uses to wipe sperm and other fluids off her body. Not a lot of folks are paying attention to him. This is the man my friend wanted to taste. The sperm toweler..

The Free States

If you want to read about how to suck blood from porn stars, you don't need me. But if you want to know where to find the sperm-cleaners, Dee's here for you.

The answer to that question is the Anarch Free States. The most beautiful place on Earth for those of us with discerning tastes. The old Camarilla Prince was killed in the revolution of 1943 and the Free States have been a patchwork of small domains held by individual gangs and vampires ever since. There's two famous founders, Salvador Garcia and Jeremy MacNeil, both Brujah. Salvador fancies himself as a Che Guevara type and writes manifestoes and other boring stuff.

Salvador also killed the old Prince, and I envy him for that. Everybody says the blood of a Prince is a treat, but a committed coward like me gets a taste so rarely.

A lot of people want MacNeil to be the Fidel Castro of the Free States, a strong leader. He's an elder and has the power to do it. Instead, and to his credit, he's more like a Sweeper, someone who keeps outsiders in check but otherwise keeps to his own domain.

From a culinary perspective if you needed to choose between these two, I would go with MacNeil. He's grouchy but if you beg hard enough, like I did, you can get a taste. I hear Salvador is great for those sentimental types who want a fuck along with their blood exchange.

And don't start arguing with me about whether it's okay to reduce two of the great icons of the Anarch Movement into nothing but blood objects. That's what freedom is all about, the freedom to lust after the sweet blood of hot Anarch dudes.

The Good Stuff

The California Free States are a wonder when it comes to finding unique and strange blood types, whether human or vampire. Are you going for homeless bodybuilders? Hollywood execs? Starry-eyed young people from every corner of the world? Despairing immigrants from Latin America who've found their dreams turned into dust? They're all here.

As to vampires, pretty much the only thing you won't find in the Free States is a Camarilla Prince, and even that occasionally changes when someone tries to make a play for it.

The thing to keep in mind is that domain is super complicated in the Free States. Like, extremely complicated. There's no Prince to give you permission to hunt. Instead, you can do anything you like as long as the vampires in the neighborhood are cool with it. Some, like MacNeil, keep their domains open for everybody. Others, like Salvador's gang, keep things more controlled.

What's more, the limits of different domains change all the time. Gangs appear and disappear, borders are renegotiated and wars happen. At any given time, the number of domains in the Free States could be anything from ten to thirty.

However, if you have the guts for it, poaching is very easy. If you've developed a desire for aging sports stars in a coma, keep a low profile and do your thing. Odds are, you won't get caught. And if you do, you might be able to bluff or grovel your way out of it. Folks in the Free States are used to new vampires. There's more coming in all the time.

The Classics

But wait. Some people really do want the porn star and not the sperm towel man. Amazing but true!

And okay, I can help you with this. Where do you go if you want the real Anarch experience? To sink your fangs into the washboard abs of a dumb, young Anarch biker with a leather jacket? The answer is the appropriately named Anarch nightclub A Taste of L.A. It's a dim, ramshackle warehouse, but it's also neutral territory between the gangs, so you can drop by, get a lay of the land and do some comparison shopping between all the local tough guys.

Here's a warning, though: A lot of you folks are after the blood of a specific clan, but in the Free States it's rude to ask about that. You can't go up to someone and go: "What's your clan and generation, I need it for my study on vampire feeding patterns?" If you do this, you can get a fist in the face. (I speak from experience.)

So you know, be subtle.

But you know me, there's one thing better than any other when it comes to blood, and that's the Ventrue. I never get tired of it. I've drank from maybe fifty different Ventrue in my time, and it still feels fresh when I find a new one. The nuanced, the richness... I admit the Free States are not the best place for this, but there are some options. The ancilla Louis Fortier is a classic Ventrue type and likes to Embrace pretty ladies. I considered going for one of them, but with the Ventrue power is power. Had to try for Fortier himself.

Fortier is a good example of the variety you can find in the Free States. He's a pretty classic dictatorial domain-hogging vampire, but nowhere near powerful enough to really be a Prince. The Free States work for him because he gets to maintain a little domain without having to bow down before anyone bigger than himself.

I saw him at A Taste of L.A. and badgered him until he said that he'll let me taste his blood if I get down on all fours and kiss the shoes of one of his childer.

A lot of folks ask me: "But Dee, how can you humiliate yourself like this? You're a proud Brujah!"

My answer is simple. I don't give a fuck about dignity, but I do care about sweet, sweet Ventrue blood.

Forever Free

Politics is boring, but there's something funny about the way so many people just can't grasp the idea of a de-centralized system. Like, "oh no, the Anarchs have failed to find a leader, surely they will perish!"

Not having a central figure is the whole point. What's more, the Free States have proven their resiliency in the face of relentless attacks. At least two Sabbat invasions, a ton of Camarilla treachery, Chinese vampires trying to establish their own place here. Yet they all got absorbed or repelled by the Free States. You could almost draw the conclusion that a centralized leadership makes a city weak. Take out the leaders and you've won. Can't do that here.

The closest the Free States have to a Camarilla Prince is Tara, originally a Texan Brujah who came to California to support the 1948 revolution. She established herself as the Baron of San Diego, and in the decades since became the poster child of Barons as conniving Camarilla stooges. Everybody knows she plays games. She's tried to make deals with everybody from the Camarilla to the Chinese vampires. She's made an attempt to become the Prince of Los Angeles.

I like her spirit, but you can see how she's doomed to fail. She's the ultimate bad-faith Anarch, and even she can't make her power grab stick.

If you're more courageous than me, it's good to be in town when one of these gang wars between the Free States is going on. There's plenty of interesting blood types to be had in the chaos for the clever connoisseur. Just remember that your first step is to look deep within your soul and honestly ask yourself the question: "What kind of blood truly makes me happy?" ■

CONCLAVE OF PRAGUE

Sometimes you forget how the high level politics of ancient licks can affect you. It's easy to think that when you live from hunt to hunt, invisible among the mortals of your neighborhood the spats and vendettas between Princes, sects, Archons and Justicars don't really mean squat.

And often they don't. But in recent nights, they very much have.

What does it mean for an Anarch living in the streets when the Camarilla panics at the first sight of the Second Inquisition? They throw us under the bus. When the SWAT team comes to knock on your door, they're there because a bunch of aged assholes half the world away decided you were expendable.

The truth of Camarilla policy has leaked: They decided on a very high level to give the Second Inquisition information on Anarch and Sabbat domains.

This makes you mad. It certainly makes me mad. Hell, it apparently even made the Brujah Camarilla super cop Theo Bell so mad he attacked some Camarilla bigwig in a recent political

convocation called the Conclave of Prague.

It's a bad sign when even your lapdogs starts to catch the smell of blood in the air. We often think that the elders of the Camarilla are infinitely crafty and wise, always ten steps ahead in the eternal chess game they call Jyhad. The events after the Conclave of Prague tell otherwise. Listening to a Camarilla lick spin it, they've solidified their hold over the Kindred of the world by cutting the Anarchs and the Brujah loose. In reality, they fucked up.

I'm not sure if they really believe their stories or if it's just propaganda. They do have a talent for self-delusion. In any case, the fact is that they've retreated to their mansions and penthouse apartments, leaving the streets to the Anarch Movement. The Camarilla used to assert itself as a global organization for all Kindred everywhere. Even the Anarchs were supposed to be a subset of the Camarilla.

That's now been exposed as bullshit. They have no claim to universality. We do. They can hunt us, torture us and kill us, but that won't change the reality of their

loss. What it does is make the Camarilla more dangerous: The privileged elite always bares its fangs when in danger of having its advantages taken away.

So what does this mean for you? In many cities, the Camarilla has had to retreat, only controlling part of the territory, leaving the rest to Anarchs. Many of their holdings in the mortal world have been abandoned, and if you're smart enough you can find them and take them over. After all, the banker addicted to vampire Blood doesn't really have the option of saying no to you if you're her only hope of avoiding blood withdrawal.

More than that, these events have revealed the true face of the Camarilla. Regardless of their propaganda, they're not an umbrella under which all our kind can seek shelter but a mechanism designed to protect the interests of the powerful. If you pledge allegiance to them, remember that they will always let you die if it helps them escape.

– Dalia Nakache, a French
Anarch revolutionary ideologue

The Princes and the Justicars retreated to the Ivory Tower. No matter how they spin this, the reality is that in their retreat, they have opened up a new battlefield between the Camarilla and the Anarch Movement. It will lead to horrifying bloodshed on both sides, but it also has definite advantages for those of us who prefer to stay in the margins.

I shudder to think of it now, but we in the Ministry were on the cusp of joining the Camarilla before this final rupture. I'm happy that the process dragged long enough for the Camarilla's true weakness to be revealed. The elders are as deadly as ever, but the war between the old and the young acts as a convenient distraction if you want to pursue other goals altogether.

I have to admit that in some ways these new developments have put traditional outsiders like us at the Ministry in a strange new position. The Camarilla's cowardice with the Second Inquisition conferred a lot of legitimacy on the Anarch Movements and unified their domains more effectively than anything they could have come up with themselves.

Or perhaps I should say "our domains". I've never thought of myself as an Anarch, but perhaps I've become one too. I do know that as the danger of the Second Inquisition intensifies, outsiders like me will not find safety among the Camarilla. As strange as it feels, I suspect that I would have better odds with Anarch street thugs on my side.

For those thugs, this is just a conformation of what they already knew: You can't trust power. And you can't trust the story being told about the Conclave of Prague either.

Consider this: Are Ventrue and Brujah elders who've been friends for centuries really going to stop conspiring together? Is the Tremere Regent really going to disavow his secret Brujah lover just because of a political schism? Probably not. This has always been the rule in high level sect politics: The rules apply to the young, not to the old. For the ancients moving the rest of us like pawns, the sects are just one more tool to use in their games.

Sometimes when you meet the real power players of our blood-hungry kind, you can catch a glimpse of this. I've spent more time with such august personages than most and it still surprises me how casual a Camarilla Prince can be about the ostensibly holy tenets of her sect, if the person breaking them is a friend and not a vassal.

Well, enough politics. A lot of Anarchs are going to get caught up in the spirit of the revolution, and get killed as a result. Perhaps they'll achieve something. Perhaps not. Meanwhile, those like me have the perfect opportunity to exploit the chaos and work for our real goals beyond the understanding of the sects. ∎

– Hesha Ruhadze, a Ministry knowledge seeker

Walk Among Us

Dee: Now that you're a vampire, you should dress like one.

Freya: What do you mean? How do you dress like a vampire?

Dee: You know... Pale makeup. Black hair. Fishnet stockings. A Misfits t-shirt.

Freya: You're wearing an oversized t-shirt with a picture of your own face on it. You look like the sordid little sister of some degenerate white rapper.

Dee: Sure. But if you ask anybody who knows me, are they going to say that I'm a role model?

Freya: No.

Dee: That's right. You've been brought into the night. Now you need to embrace the hashtag vamplife.

Freya: I'm Duskborn. I haven't been "brought into the night".

Dee: Whatever. You're a vampire. A bloodsucker. Don't pretend you're not.

Freya: I'm not pretending. So what it is that I need to embrace?

Dee: The vampire lifestyle

Freya: And what's that?

Dee: Well...

ENLIGHTENMENT IN BLOOD

Police reveal new details in Friedrichshain deaths

ANCHOR: Details are still scarce on last night's events in the Berlin Friedrichshain area, but initial reports suggest significant violence. We've received reports of at least four deaths so far, and authorities on the scene warn that the numbers will probably rise as they conduct a sweep of the area.

We'll go to Carol, who talks with one of the first responders on the scene.

INTERVIEWER: I'm surprised we're only discovering the extent of the catastrophe now. Weren't there any calls to the area last night?

FIRST RESPONDER: That's why this is so confusing. I've never seen anything like this. It's as if there was some kind of a gang war, but in secret. These people must have died literally meters from a busy street full of the usual nightlife crowd.

INTERVIEWER: This magnitude of violence is extremely unusual in Berlin.

FIRST RESPONDER: It's unheard of! I mean, people die but not like this.

INTERVIEWER: Everybody I've talked to here has said the same. This is a new kind of violence, and the causes for it remain a mystery.

– A Sky News segment broadcast at 1205 PM on 13th of April, 2017

[COMMENT: You know, when you used to work as a Camarilla Archon before you went Anarch... This is not what you want to see on the news.]

BERLIN / AP: Berlin police has revealed new details in the investigation to the Friedrichshain deaths last spring. A mysterious chain of events in the Friedrichshain nightlife area of Berlin led to 24 confirmed deaths as well as a number of individuals hospitalized for causes ranging from drug overdose to acute anemia. The incident took place on the 12th of April, 2017, but the investigation has been plagued by delays and revelations of corruption within the Berlin police.

In a statement released this morning, the Berlin police attributed much of the violence to the unpredictable effects of a new designer drug with increased aggression as one of its side effects. The new drug had been sold under the street name "blood".

[COMMENT: This is very bad. This is a borderline Masquerade breach. If the SI doesn't see this, they're blind, deaf and dumb.]

Early reactions in the German media to the police statement have been critical. The drug narrative fails to explain the older bodies found in the sweeps of the area conducted after the incident. Some of them were over a decade old.

The case has been plagued by strange incidents, including multiple deaths in police custody. The investigation to these deaths has not yet been concluded, but leaked materials suggest bizarre details such as corpses in an advanced state of decay found in holding cells.

[COMMENT: Oh my god. This is getting worse. We're headed for an SI invasion for sure.]

There have been calls in the German Bundestag for a neutral investigation into the Friedrichshain affair that would consist of officers from outside Berlin police..

(26.7.2017.)

A comment on Facebook in a Berlin street culture group on the 22nd of October, 2017:

The cops are lying. I know, I was there. I saw a man get literally torn apart by crazed lunatics. They were biting him. I've never seen anything like it, it was nuts. The cops interviewed me and I explained all this. I wasn't the only one either! There were other people there, witnesses. I've seen others comment about this, but you don't see it on the news.

[COMMENT: This must be when the inhabitants of the city literally tore the Prince of Berlin apart. That's a Nicolae Ceaușescu moment for the Camarilla, for sure. A lot of the more sensible Camarilla Kindred started to escape town at the first whiff of revolution, but the Prince thought that he could control it to the last. Next time there's an Anarch revolution in a Camarilla city, a lot of the Camarilla Kindred are going to be thinking about how it went in Berlin.]

Friedrichshain Investigation to be Handed to an International Task Force

Berlin / AP: The latest revelations about the mishandling of the investigation into the Friedrichshain deaths and the revelations about international organized crime connections have resulted in the creation of a new international task force, coordinated by Interpol. Berlin police will cease its own investigation and hand over all materials to the new task force.

At the same time, the internal police investigation into the role of Berlin police has been dropped. The aftermath of the Friedrichshain deaths have seen a number of scandals in Germany, ranging from politics to police to tax havens and even urban development..

(1.12.2017)

[COMMENT: This is what it looks like when the mortal police start unraveling the threads of Kindred society. Do I need to stop saying "Kindred" now I'm no longer Camarilla?]

An extract from the transcript of a police interview on the night of 13th of April, 2017:

SUSPECT: I don't care who you are. Cops, Camarilla, Inquisition. Fuck all of you. You know what the Sheriff did to me? He made me murder my wife and kids because they were a risk to the Masquerade. He killed one of my friends because she didn't want to date one of the Primogen. One time, he tore off my incisors because I'd fed in the wrong place. Then he made fun of me because I lisped. Do this long enough, and people don't care about their safety anymore. They don't care about survival. The only thing they care about is tearing it all down. So please, I'm done talking. I hear there's a cell waiting for me with a window to the east..

[COMMENT: We're fucked, no question. There's always going to be somebody who's going to say this is yet more proof that the Anarchs just can't run a city, but that's bullshit. Every Prince Berlin has ever had, wannabe or otherwise from Gustav Breidenstein onwards has been a sadistic power-drunk brute. Eventually people get fed up with that. This catastrophe is just a symptom. The Camarilla is the cause. I see that now.]

No Prince No Caine

SALVADOR GARCIA, ONE OF THE FOUNDERS OF THE CALIFORNIA FREE STATES EXPLAINS THE BASICS OF ANARCH LIFE.

Here's what you'll find in a lot of Anarch territories. Each is unique, but there are a few trends.

The Simple Life

Many assume that I look down on Anarchs who don't fight the fight, but that would be furthest from the truth. In many ways, they are already living in the world we're trying to build. They are doing their thing, free from Camarilla interference.

So many of the Anarch gangs you find all over the world are based on this simple lifestyle. You want to hang out with your friends. You help them and they help you. You hunt, perhaps operate a bar or a nightclub. You party, have fun, enjoy the perks of undeath.

Nothing wrong with this! When problems arise, it's not these licks who make them.

The Gangs

This is what most Camarilla Kindred think when they think about us. Gangs of vampire bikers or a bloodsucking hip hop crew. In the Free states, we've seen gangs of surfers riding the waves at night and homeless undead kids who used to want to act in Hollywood and now take stalking celebrities to a new level.

Usually each gang controls their own territory. They might be fronted by a leader, but not always. The organization of the gang is their own problem. Many get a little ambitious with their territorial claims and as a result there's a lot of gang war. That's freedom taking its course.

An Anarch biker gang can go unnoticed by either the Camarilla or the Second Inquisition for a long time. They have a negligible digital footprint and at a glance their behavior is indistinguishable from a mortal biker gang. The Camarilla tends to move slowly, and from their perspective, the territories and very identities of Anarch gangs change all the time.

The Cells

More serious Anarchs, especially politically active ones who live in dangerous territories organize in cells. These resemble the structure of underground criminal or political organizations such as the Italian Red Brigades in the 70's and 80's. The cells are all about security and information control. You observe sensible precautions, switch safe houses regularly, and only contact other cells through established protocols.

It's probably not surprising that licks in gangs tend to die a lot more than licks in cells, even if the cells engage in much more dangerous activities.

It's good to remember that most domains mix different kinds of organizations. There can be a biker gang and a revolutionary cell in the same domain.

The Others

Plenty of Anarchs don't fit into these categories. Some domains hold a single powerful lick, in others bourgeois bloodsuckers try to pretend they can continue their lives as lawyers and doctors. Some create cults around themselves. Every Anarch city has some kind of unique, strange new vampire phenomena you would never expect to find.

The Free States

The Anarch Free States are the totality of all Anarch domains across the world. Wherever the Camarilla has been abolished and Anarchs hold sway, our kind can live in freedom and prosperity. The Free States have been organized in a dozen different ways, but there's one clear commonality: Rule by a single individual is rare, because it's so often associated with the Princes of the Camarilla. Sometimes there's a central Revolutionary Council ruling the city, but even that is unusual. More typically, a Free State is an anarchy consisting of smaller domains. It's not regulated or controlled, but exists in a permanent state of flux.

Sometimes you can unite the gang leaders under single banner, but this is hard to do unless the reason is an external threat such as a Camarilla invasion.

Barons

In many Anarch domains, you'll find something called a Baron. Originally a title used ironically by Jeremy MacNeil to describe Anarch leaders, it's later acquired more nuance and connotations. However, at its most basic a Baron is still a strong Anarch who controls territory and wields authority over those living in it.

One of the most common types of Barons, and the way the term was originally used in the California Free States, is a lick who has a city neighborhood or even just a building. She might be a gang leader who rules with an iron fist or a public representative with no real power. The point is that you can have many Barons like this in a city.

The other common type of Baron controls an entire city on his own. A local strongman, he behaves suspiciously like a Camarilla Prince. This kind of a Baron tends to be suspected of being secretly in league with the Camarilla, as a sort of Camarilla underboss. It doesn't help that in some Camarilla domains with an Anarch population, this is openly admitted. The Camarilla likes to outsource its repression to a leader ostensibly representing the oppressed population. In this model, the Anarch enclave is a little Bantustan where the Camarilla can push all its social problems.

Defense

This is a classic Camarilla trick: First they do their absolute best to undermine us and make sure that our domains are filled with turncoats and agitators. Then they point to all the problems we have and say that this is proof that our way doesn't work. This is why every Anarch domain needs to think about defense.

Security is the reason why many Anarch domains are surprisingly Draconian. Traditional Camarilla crimes such as making illegal progeny (not a crime at all in many Anarch domains) get very light punishments, while betraying the cause to the Camarilla can get you executed.

When it comes to war, you'll see why I like the gangs. They might be apolitical, but they know when their turf is threatened and fight with courage you'll never see among Camarilla cowards.

Emissary

A big city can have five gangs, a couple of cells and a bunch of random Anarchs. There could be three different Camarilla cities adjacent to the Free State. What this means that there's a lot of diplomacy going on. Gangs send emissaries to each other, the Camarilla sends emissaries to the Anarchs, the Anarchs send competing emissaries from different groups to the Camarilla.

What I'm trying to say is that there can be a lot of emissaries in a Free City, especially in times of the Second Inquisition when it tends to be better to send someone to negotiate rather than speak by phone.

Sweeper

Now we get to the really ugly part. Sometimes there's an uncontrolled epidemic of vampires just running around Embracing more before they really understand what they are. Or maybe an entire gang turns traitorous and rats us out.

Whatever the situation, sometimes you need to do some killing and don't have time to debate it. The Sweeper is an unofficial position. It falls upon a physically powerful lick, someone not politically active and possibly part of any local gang or cell. During a crisis, this person is called to kill until the problem goes away.

It's a thankless job that easily leaves you socially isolated.

Spies

The Camarilla likes to think that they have infiltrated our ranks and know everything there is to know about us. What they traditionally fail to understand that we've infiltrated their ranks as well, and we don't always even have to work for it. The simple truth is that in Camarilla cities where elders routinely abuse their childer, there are plenty of young vampires who leak information to us. This is the typical Anarch spy in a Camarilla Court: Someone who wants to reclaim a little of their dignity by working against their masters.

Sometimes we get fancy and send a more experienced Anarch into a Camarilla city as part of an operation, but this is rare. Our strength is as a movement, not as a paramilitary operation.

Overpopulation and Suicide

Almost all Anarch domains are overpopulated, but they also tend to have a very high turnover of our kind. It's a rarely stated fact that suicide rates among newly Embraced Anarchs are sky high. A significant percentage of our kind kill themselves during the first few months of unlife. I suspect this is rarer in Camarilla territories because of the way they chain the sire to the childe, but for us it's a good reminder that our kind don't have it so easy.

Some Anarchs argue that this is a big problem that should be addressed, but I think it makes us stronger. Everybody who's still with us was tough enough to withstand the destruction of their previous lives and a new existence as a monster.

Rants

My favorite part of Anarch culture is the rant. In many cities, the rants often organized by Brujah have become universal, accessible to all Anarchs. They're like a political open mic night, where everybody has a chance to say what they want. Power in a rant is the ability to convince people of your point of view, so

they favor those who have the charisma and eloquence to argue.

Me, I love it. This is what being an Anarch is all about: Firing up the crowd if they like what you say, and getting booed off the stage if they don't. ∎

Blood Vagrants

You've just arrived in a new city. You go to meet the Prince like a good little lick. You introduce yourself and ask for permission to hunt in the Prince's domain.

This is a crucial moment. You need to tell the Prince something, but the problem is that different Princes respond to different things. You can't use the same story every time. You're hungry and you need to hunt. You don't want to risk getting in trouble with the Sheriff. The Prince has to believe you.

You look the Prince in the eyes. In that instant, you must intuit the correct response and start talking.

It's no accident that many Anarchs who live on the open road are inventive liars. We have to get good at it. Otherwise, we go hungry or get killed by a Sheriff for poaching.

So how do you do it? Let Auntie Juniper teach you the facts of life.

The Town Mouse and the Country Mouse

They tell you that licks are better off sticking to the cities. I suppose that's true if you're a know-nothing wimp who can't survive the life on the open road. And frankly, there ain't no shame in weakness. If you can't hack it, you should stay close to your herds and Elysiums.

Some of us don't much like domains, rules and traditions. If you're of a like mind and can take care of yourself, abandon the life of a sedentary lick and take up the thrilling existence of a bloodsucking vagabond. Auntie Juniper has been living in her trailer for a few decades now, and it's not a bad life. I go from place to place, town to town, and when shit hits the fan, I disappear.

It helps that so many licks, Camarilla and Anarch both, can't even really conceive what it means to live free. They think the wide open spaces between urban areas are filled with were-wolves and worse. And sure, sometimes they are. You learn to deal with it.

So what do you tell the Prince after you've just arrived in her domain? You need to have a reason, and the Prince won't like it if you tell her the truth: That you're a homeless hobo vampire driving around, poaching, living your life on a perpetual hunt.

A lot of Camarilla Princes like to think of themselves as good people, amazing as this sounds. Appeal to them with a sob story. You're a poor Camarilla neonate, your city taken over by terrifying Anarch rabble. "Please Sir, if I could just hunt for a few nights, I could get my life together! I won't bother you longer than that!"

Trouble is, some Princes hate weakness. They have no trouble executing someone they think useless. Take the opposite tack: You're a Camarilla freedom fighter, a loyal neonate waging a war of your own against the terrible threat of the Anarch revolution. Talk tough, invent a bunch of dead comrades and you're good to go. If you want to go the extra mile, invent an atrocity. "The Anarchs killed my sire, the noblest man I have ever known. Almost as noble as you, Sir. That night, my old life ended and the war started."

In Anarch domains, you got to play it by the ear. Sometimes folks are hospitable and you're fine. Tell them your best road stories and hunt to your heart's content. However, sometimes a Baron is as bad as a Prince. Then you fall back to the story. Just remember to invert it. "Please Sir, the Camarilla murdered my sire, the most noble man I have ever known..."

Bodybags

You're a corpse already, so it's not so bad to sleep in a bodybag. Right? Where to sleep is your number one concern when living beyond city limits. Body bags have been designed to keep corpses contained, so they're a good safety measure.

Some nomad licks go all hardcore about sleeping. "Sleep in the river mud", they say. "Sleep in a sewer." I have to be honest, that doesn't really work for me. Sure, it's safe, but I want a bed. I have a nice bed even if it's in a sunproofed trailer.

The trailer works because Auntie Juniper has her boys with her. They're blood junkies of course, but so loyal. If you don't have people taking care of you, paranoia can save your life. This is where I'm going to say something that might not make sense at first glance: Buildings. Avoid them.

"But surely, Auntie Juniper, it's safer for me to sleep in a house! That's what they're for!"

I hear you, I hear you. But it's not safer. You're in a motel room. The cleaning lady comes in, sunlight falling through the doorway, and you're crisp. Break into somebody's house to sleep, someone sees you, calls the cops and the SWAT team gets to see you burst into flame. These are real examples, by the way. People and buildings go together and to sleep safe, you should avoid people. Stash your corpse somewhere nobody will look. Maybe not a sewer because that's disgusting, but somewhere good and secret.

Of course, if you've been doing this for a long time, you can build a network of safe houses. A great choice if you have the diligence to get it done. Too much work for Auntie Juniper…

Vampire Life

The great thing about this life is that you really get to hunt. None of that "herd" bullshit. No steady sources of blood. No calling old exes from when you were still human because your last three attempts to hunt all failed. And certainly none of that feudal Camarilla crap where you get a blood tithe or some such thing.

No, you're an undead monster hunting in the night. No plans, just the beauty and terror of the moment.

A small caveat here: If you're one of those modern licks who don't really know how to hunt properly, Auntie Juniper can't help you. You got to be able to hustle for blood if you live on the road. That's how it is.

I know you're going to poach in other people's domains, but my advice is to avoid it. Go by the book, meet the Prince, do the story. Like we talked about. But if you do poach, think about where the locals probably feed and then go someplace else. Don't get fancy. If you're at a gas station, hunt at the gas station. For a poacher, speed always trumps every other consideration.

The real fun is hunting in the country, in areas a Camarilla lick will never visit. This is where a vampire becomes a vampire. You roll into a small town somewhere in Ohio or Tennessee. There's no Prince, no Sheriff. No Barons, no domains. Just you and a town full of prey settling into the night. The Masquerade is not always such a concern and the cops are easily dealt with.

Or maybe they put up a fight. A farmer surprises you tearing out the throat of his daughter and fills your face with lead. That's part of the thrill. Auntie Juniper likes her prey feisty.

This is the real hunt. No urban complications, just predators and prey. That's what makes it all worth it.

Begging for Scraps

What if everything went sideways? You've lost all your money, you don't have a car, the sun is coming up? This is when you got to understand that sometimes on the road, you need to accept terrible things. One time, Auntie Juniper was in a bad way. She'd lost her handsome junkie boys and didn't know the lay of the land.

Couple of hours from sunrise, I was at a gas station desperately looking for some young man to take me to his home so I could kill him and hole up in his bathroom. Instead, a gang of six Rabble bikers rolled up, all leather clad and hardass. I struck up a conversation with them and let them project whatever they wanted onto me. This is a little trick you can learn from Auntie Juniper: If you look right, people are not interested in who you are. You don't have to lie to them, because they'll make up the story themselves and then you just have to play along.

I was going to sleep in their haven. As they were leaving, I hopped on the back of one of their bikes and looked around. They had a man chained to a bike. A terrified city lick. They dragged him along on the ground, his skin grinding away, his blood leaving a trail on the asphalt. He was half dead by the time we got to the roadhouse they were using as a place to sleep. They left him on the roof to wait for the sun.

Auntie Juniper doesn't like to see cruelty inflicted like that, against a defenseless target. Hurt people, but hurt them fair.

You know what I said to those Rabble? Nothing. I slept safe while that man burned on the roof. ■

– Juniper, an Anarch roaming the U.S. Midwest

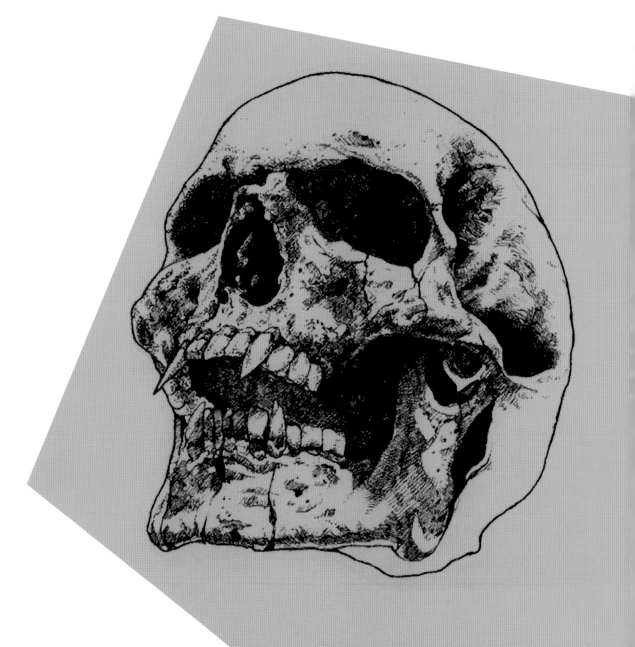

BLOOD OF THE REDEEMER

Tonight we will look at Leviticus seventeen. "I will set my face against any Israelite or any foreigner residing among them who eats blood, and I will cut them off from the people."

TTerrifying words for a vampire! Many of our kind read these words and understand them to mean God sets his face against us. We are the Damned and must walk the earth under a curse. Condemned by God, our very sustenance is an affront to His divine order.

Fear not! God has a plan for each and every one of us. To find our answers, we must look at His word. Let's see what God really says in Leviticus.

"Any Israelite who sacrifices an ox, a lamb or a goat in the camp or outside of it instead of bringing it to the entrance to the tent of meeting to present it as an offering to the Lord in front of the tabernacle of the Lord - that person shall be considered guilty of bloodshed."

Do you see? God considers blood to be sacred. He doesn't want it to be wasted, and that's why the shedding of blood except to honor Him is a crime. For as He says: "For the life of a creature is in the blood, and I have given it to you to make atonement for yourselves on the altar."

The blood is the life!

What use is blood to a mortal man? As a sacrifice! The mortal man atones by shedding blood at the altar, from himself and from others.

Who receives the sacrifice? We do! These poor souls can die safely in the comfort of our arms knowing that in their final moments, our very bodies transform their lifeblood into a sacrifice pleasing to God! Every time we take the blood of a mortal on the altar, we give that mortal the gift of redemption. We are God's tools on Earth, and our work is to spread his grace and salvation!

This is the true message of Jesus. This is the meaning of the blood of the redeemer. Christ didn't sacrifice himself for humanity. He sacrificed himself for us, for God's chosen instruments on Earth.

What do you see when you look around you? A small wooden church in Alabama, the pews broken, dust on the windows. The building is nothing. Look at the congregation. Look at our mortal brothers and sisters kneeling and praying. They understand that to find salvation they must sacrifice their blood on the altar, or the blood of someone they love. This is the lesson of Isaac and Abraham, this is why they give their children for us to eat. When an innocent relinquishes their blood, they reach heaven in a state of perfection.

Look at those in the congregation who have tasted the blood. The mortals whose lips shine red from the blood of the redeemer. They kneel fervently in their faith, sustained by the blood of Christ himself. This is who Christ suffered for: Us! Our work! Christ gave his life and his blood so we could live and deliver salvation to all the peoples of the world. We are the

instrument of freedom from the original sin.

This is the true birth of our race: We have been given the blood of Christ in and transformed into higher beings. When a mortal drinks from us, they accept Christ into their bodies, and Christ will guide them.

The blood is the life.

Finally, look at the vampires among us. Vampires! Such an evil-sounding word with such grace behind it. Look at these beautiful angels who have dedicated their lives to spreading God's mercy. Our limitations are not a curse! They are a blessing, for the need to go by night keeps us humble.

This is an example of God's wisdom: So many of our kind have rejected their true purpose. They should have embraced the humility offered by our curse, but instead they have dedicated themselves to denying His kingdom!

Listen to my words, for they spring from the blood of Jesus Christ. Look at the blood running from my wrists! This is his blood, his mark! As it flows along my arms and drips to the floor, any who humble themselves and kneel to drink of it will be blessed! Come forth, kneel, drink, sacrifice your blood on the altar, mark yourselves with its crimson perfection!

I see the holy spirit moving among you! Rend the flesh from each other to get to the salvation flowing in your veins! Prostrate yourselves before God's disciples on Earth! Allow a dark angel to touch your spirit and your body!

The blood is the life!

Consider Numbers twenty-three: "Behold, a people rises like a lioness, And as a lion it lifts itself; It will not lie down until it devours the prey, And drinks the blood of the slain."

This people is our people! This is God's message: "Neither curse them at all nor bless them at all!"

We are not here to be judged by God. We are God, messengers and Shepherds, enforcers of divine will. Our blood drives us true and keeps us in the path of the righteous. As long as we listen to the voice of the blood we cannot err.

As you lie wounded and satiated, saved or blessed, consider the real nature of this tiny community. We have been granted the greatest gift of all, and it's happened right here, in this very town. We know God's will and are ready to bring it forth here on Earth, to help all the peoples find salvation and hope of redemption. This will be our great work. It starts inside these wooden walls, in this small town, with these people around you: Farmers, shopkeepers, miners. Good people all. These people are the first sacrifices who will give us the strength to bring true atonement to the world.

After all, the blood is the life. Amen. ∎

The Parasite Way

Agata: So basically you're a tapeworm.

Rudi: Stop calling me a tapeworm. It's beyond insulting.

Agata: I'm serious. You're a parasite infesting a body. You're living inside an organism, growing at the expense of your host.

Rudi: You're too cynical about this. We have a lot of options...

Agata: Maybe the tapeworm is the wrong analogy. You know that Amazonian fungus which will take over an ant and start controlling it?

Rudi: First I'm a tapeworm and now I'm a fungus. There's a reason nobody likes you, Agata.

Agata: Okay, I got a better one. You're a hormone. Like a substance that blends into the normal operations of the body, subtly directing its actions.

Rudi: I think we have a serious messaging problem. When you go to the Camarilla, they tell you that you're one of the Kindred, an eternal secret society of hidden masters shepherding humanity on its winding course through history. When you come to us, we tell you that you're a tapeworm. Or a fungus.

Agata: I thought the hormone analogy was good.

Rudi: Nobody wants to be a hormone. Don't be stupid.

Agata: Talk to me like that again and I'll kill you.

Rudi: <silence>

Agata: Come on, it was a joke! Why do people always overreact when I threaten to kill them?

Rudi: I'm not going to answer that. But we got to consider our message. We need to give our kind something they can believe in. Something to make them proud.

Agata: I'm a proud tapeworm.

Rudi: You're a lick, a bloodsucker, a vampire. Like me, you live among humanity. Not as a hidden master, Camarilla style, but as one of them. Just different.

Agata: I love it when you talk like that. It makes me feel like a real girl.

Rudi: I guess that's something.

Agata: I love it when you talk like that. It makes me feel like a real girl.

Rudi: I guess that's something.

DAWN OF SATAN'S MILLENNIUM

In the first article of her series Subculture Parasites, Chinasa Adeyemi interviews the Finnish black metal groupie and Brujah Karoliina Koski.

B lood rituals and Satanic black masses. Finland has the largest number of metal bands per capita of any country in the world, clocking in at 53,5 bands per 100,000 people. The runners up Norway and Sweden only manage 27,2 each. The metal and especially black metal scene seems like an obvious choice for a lick who wants to dabble in blood and blasphemy without attracting suspicion. Or at least, without attracting more suspicion than your average church-burning Satanist.

Karoliina Koski is a young vampire who's spent years as a black metal groupie, following bands all around the country.

BY: CHINASA ADEYEMI

Satan's Politics

I have to ask the most obvious question first. Have you ever felt the urge to create your own music?

I did actually, when I was still human. This was in the late Nineties. I had a band, or maybe it was more of a one-person music project, called Lilith's Satanic Flood. It was actually pretty tough going because the scene is so misogynistic. I remember one time I stabbed myself into the arm during a gig, and later I was accused of faking it. I didn't fake it! I had ten stitches after that.

This was before you became one of us?

Yes, definitely. I was much more hardcore when I was human. You know, spitting blood into the audience only makes sense if you're still breathing. If you're a vampire, you're going to swallow.

How did your role in the scene change after Embrace?

I became much more laid back. Before the Embrace I wanted to fight for my space, but after I understood the demands of the Masquerade I decided to keep a lower profile. It's easy to stay in the margins if you're a groupie and hunting almost takes care of itself. Like, I go backstage, some asshole starts groping me, I can just drink from him then and there and nobody even blinks as long as I don't brandish my fangs at them. A little biting and blood goes with the territory.

Do you still believe in black metal?

Ask a lot of the guys what black metal is and they'll say it's all about the politics. And that bands who deny that are sellout losers. You fight for a Satanist vision of war against religion in all its forms, making music, burning churches and desecrating grave-yards.

Have you ever desecrated a graveyard?

Sure, when I was still human. I don't feel the need so much now that I drink blood for real.

Blood Running Down the Walls

How long do you intend to con-tinue in the scene?

Well, soon I've been a vampire for twenty years. That's a long time to go without aging. People are starting to comment on it. Fortunately corpse paint hides your age pretty well so if you dress up, you can still go to gigs and casual acquaintances won't notice. They're a bigger problem than the people you see all the time. If you see someone every day, you get used to how they look.

Why remain at all?

Let me tell you about a gig I was at last Saturday. It was a small town near Seinäjoki with a pretty diverse crowd. One of those where everybody local comes to see all the gigs no matter the music be-cause there's so little happening.

The band started playing and the singer threw bottles of blood into the audience. People opened them and started spraying the blood all over each other, onto the band, the walls... Two groupie girls I know used razors to cut their arms. I licked their blood off the skin.

In most places, that would be a Masquerade breach. Here it's just business as usual.

That sounds perfect.

It is! It was pretty funny, after the gig I went downstairs to the cafe and you could see the blood trickling down the walls, there was so much of it.

What do you think of the Sabbat?

Black Sabbath? That's dad music.

Gift From Satan

So what if I wanted to join this lifestyle of blood and Satan-worship-ping?

There are some practical hurdles. Finland is a big empty country and much of the scene happens in gigs outside the big cities. That means you have to travel. Drive around the country following the bands. It helps with keeping a low profile as you can hunt in a different town every night.

You also got to get used to sleeping in some dodgy places. I've spent more days in the backrooms of filthy bars than I care to count. It's also not an easy scene to come into as an outsider. Of course you can just start coming to the gigs, but you'll stick out. It was much easier for me because everyone already knew me. I didn't seem out of place.

Do you ever get scared of the violence in the scene? The imagery is pretty extreme.

[laughs] No! When I was still human I was too young and angry to get scared. And now as a vampire, it's actually been pretty liberating. I often hunt by playing the victim, making some dude think they can get their rocks off fucking with me. Then after he gets me alone in a secluded spot, I flip the script on him.

It's easy to do knowing that as a vampire, you're never in any real danger from a single drunken asshole.

Do you feel bad preying on your own scene?

Never! The guys say they want to bring blood and destruction all across the world. They don't real-ize that as a vampire I'm way more metal they can ever be. When I feed from them, it's a gift from Satan. ∎

Chinasa Adeyemi is a Nigerian-born former journalist trying to make her former profession work under the Masquerade.

DEATH at the Roof of the World

BY: CHINASA ADEYEMI

In the second article of her series Subculture Parasites , Chinasa Adeyemi interviews the former mountain climber and Gangrel Antoni Morawski.

On the face of it, the subculture of high altitude mountain climbers doesn't seem ideal for our kind. The mountain climbers travel a lot and much of the mountain climbing itself happens during the day. Expeditions often attract publicity, making it difficult to maintain the Masquerade.

Yet despite these problems, Antoni Morawski saw no reason to abandon his lifestyle just because he became a lick.

High Altitude Embrace

You achieved quite a lot even before you became one of us, right?

Perhaps. I did climb many of the famous ones from K2 onwards. The only one I never managed was Everest. I tried twice, but the weather conditions were against me. I'm actually most proud of how much money we were able to raise for charity on our expedition to the Transantarctic Mountains. There's some excellent climbing there. It's a shame it's so hard to get to.

You were raising money for leukemia research. Prophetic in light of what happened later.

[laughs] That's true! It was just a few months before I was Embraced.

How did it happen, your Embrace?

True Feral style. We were camping in the Alps, winding down from an expedition. I was experimenting with my camera, trying to take photos in low light conditions when a monster attacked me, mauled me and dragged me to a chasm in the mountainside. I was sure I would die.

But you didn't.

No. My sire fed be enough blood to heal my injuries and then Embraced me. I still don't know why. I never saw her again. As you know, this is more common among the Gangrel than some other Clans. My return to the camp was very dramatic. They'd organized search parties and I walked in, clothes bloody, while they were planning to extend the operation.

Quality Blood

I've heard about the special taste of human blood at high altitude. Is it true that it tastes better?

Yes, definitely. As you know, the human body compensates for the relative dearth of oxygen in the air. This means that blood has a rich quality that you soon learn to appreciate as you hunt in high altitude communities. This is not just about mountaineering. You can experience the same anywhere the air is thin.

What about the other realities of your lifestyle. Surely it's difficult to hunt if you move with a small group of people all the time?

It's difficult if you don't know how to do it. Being a Feral helps a lot with surviving in the wilderness. I still hold on to my mortal identity and often move with the same people I knew in life. For hunting, travel means I can hunt from the different communities we move through. I don't really drink from my own people except for culinary reasons.

But you no longer climb with them?

No. I made up a story about an injury that makes climbing difficult. Instead, I follow around as a member of the support staff. The problem with climbing is that as a lick I'm too good at it. It feels unsporting. And of course, daylight burns us on the mountains the same as anywhere else.

In the last year, you've pioneered the concept of a night climb.

That's true. I suppose I couldn't keep completely away. I try to make them more about the experience and less about the challenge.

Death and the Masquerade

Let's talk about the death of Jean-Philippe Murielle. You've been accused of endangering the Masquerade.

Right. Because I maintain my mortal identity and the incident came into the news. I suppose it's ironic. Most of our kind get into trouble for killing people, but for me it happened because I wanted to play the hero.

You were both on an expedition to scale the Eiger.

Yes. I've known Murielle for a long time and we'd even made an attempt at the Eiger together when we were starting out. It was one of my first high altitude climbs. As you know, at this level the death rate at these climbs is around 10%, so it's not uncommon for people to lose their lives. I've lost friends to the mountain in the Alps, in Nepal...

How did it happen this time?

Murielle got stuck near the summit. The weather was getting worse and it was clear he couldn't survive the conditions for more than a few hours, especially as the temperature started to plummet. He called us on the radio and it got very emotional. He asked us to relay his last words to his children. I couldn't take it.

So you climbed up to rescue him. Didn't the people in your camp object? That must have seemed insane to them.

They told me I was crazy! And if I was human, they would have been right. But it was for nothing. He was dead by the time I got there.

I have to ask. Did you taste his blood?

I try to stay as human as I can. I don't believe in this vampire supremacy bullshit you hear. I don't expect you to understand, but it didn't feel like a predatory act. He was my friend, and now he was dead. I wanted somehow to connect with him one last time. So I took his blood.

How did it feel when the media started calling you a hero for making the attempt?

Stupid. I admit I was a gloryhound in life, but that's possibly the only thing where becoming a lick has made me a better man. ∎

Chinasa Adeyemi is a Nigerian-born writer exploring the diverse ways the unbound make do in an increasingly hectic world. Her work is distributed exclusively for the benefit of a very discrete audience.

The Beast *on a* Leash

BY: CHINASA ADEYEMI

In the third article of her series Subculture Parasites, Chinasa Adeyemi interviews the Toreador couple and petplay enthusiasts Janet and William Stoughton.

We licks like to talk about our Beasts and the Gangrel are known for their bestial nature, but the kink subculture of petplay takes becoming an animal into an altogether different sphere. I talked to the San Francisco -based Toreador couple Janet and William Stoughton to find out how our kind can interact with this subculture of sex play.

Whitebread

I don't meet many vampire couples who look as wholesome as you do.

Janet: [laughs] I admit, we're pretty whitebread.

William: I suppose it's true. We've tried to hold onto our humanity and the best way to do it is by maintaining the trappings.

The house, the yard...

William: Yes. I suppose it's camouflage.

Were you a couple before you became licks?

Janet: No. We're not related either, even though we're both Toreador. We met after we'd both been Embraced and escaped our sires in the Camarilla.

Are you in contact with the society of licks in San Francisco?

William: No. We keep to ourselves. Do our thing.

Freedom in Slavery

Let's talk about your thing. What is petplay?

Janet: A lot of people think it's only a sexual fetish, and it's that too. But it's also a lifestyle. There doesn't have to be sex involved. It's about taking on the role of a pet, like a puppy. This often involves the kind of paraphernalia you might recognize from a BDSM context: muzzles, tails, bodysuits.

So which of you is the puppy?

Janet: [laughs] Oh no, we both do it.

You both do it? How does that work?

William: Well, we can do it around the house, but the best experiences we've had were at events and with a third person as the dominant. The owner.

Janet: There's many interesting events organized around this here in San Francisco, in other parts of the U.S., in Europe.

And you do this with mortals? Or others of our kind?

Janet: Usually mortals!

What does it feel like to be a vampire being led around on a leash by a mortal?

William: [silence] That's the thing. That is exactly the thing.

Rabid Dogs

Do you ever have any accidents? You are licks after all.

Janet: Well, to be honest we've had two bad incidents. In the first, William was very deep in the mental space of being the puppy and the dom we played with started teasing him. William lost control, the poor dear.

William: It was terrible. I don't know what happened.

What happens when you lose control in that situation?

William: I tore apart the leather straps binding my legs and arms and killed the dom.

Janet: It's okay, dear.

Was this a friend of yours?

Janet: Yes, in a way. We found him on Tumblr. I have a blog we use to post photos of ourselves.

What was the other incident?

Janet: It was with a woman we'd never played with before. I was alone at her house, and it had seemed good at the start. We negotiated boundaries. She had wonderful equipment, a full bitchsuit for me, that kind of thing. She was very much into control and bondage, so she had William in her basement playroom and me upstairs. You know, taking me for a walk.

Outside?

Janet: Yeah, in her backyard. It was awkward because she was into piss play and she didn't know I was a vampire. She wanted me to pee like a dog, but of course I couldn't.

I can see the problem.

Janet: But the really bad thing was that the sun was coming up. I'd lost track of time. I was gagged so I couldn't really use the safeword and she ignored it when I used the safety signal. I guess she was mad at me from the piss thing, but it was bad.

You survived, though.

Janet: I had to call on my Blood to break free. I was panicking so I didn't do it subtly. It was a total Masquerade breach. We didn't know what to do so we killed her.

Hunting Dogs

Using different subcultures to hunt for blood has been a running theme in this series of articles, but I'm not sure how being a bondage pet helps with that?

William: It's all in choosing the right moment. You can't hunt during play.

Janet: That's not entirely true, William...

William: You're right, of course. Sometimes a male dom will force me to suck his cock. I can bite very discreetly and they don't really have the experience to separate the feeling of a blowjob from the Kiss.

I take it that bondage pet blowjobs are not the normal way for you to hunt?

William: No. Normally the right moment to strike is during aftercare. You know, after the play is over and you're all cuddling and sharing your emotions. People are very naked in that moment, spiritually. You can bite and feed with great love and tenderness.

It's still a bite though. People notice when you bite them.

William: It's true. That's why it's good to prepare for this when you consider your pet personality.

'Pet personality'?

William: How you behave as a pet. Are you obedient, flighty, eager, and so on. If you're a vampire, it's good to make little love bites part of your deal. That way, they're not surprising when you feed.

Is this a sex thing for you, or a hunting thing?

Janet: I wasn't into this at all as a human. After I became a vampire, all that talk of the Beast made me very anxious. I was worried about becoming this animal or monster. But after trying out petplay, I found it very relaxing, like I could somehow just settle into that space and not worry about anything.

Even sunlight or the Beast?

William: Well, you always feel bad after murdering your dom. That's a given. ∎

Chinasa Adeyemi is a Nigerian-born writer constantly astounded by the variety of different ways we come up with to live our unlives.

Vegas Nights

I came to Las Vegas for the same reason as everybody else: To party and get wasted. And maybe lose some money at the poker table. I most definitely did not come here to get Embraced and become a vampire, but that's them breaks.

It was me and a couple of guys from work. They were ribbing me for being a Vegas novice. They were threatening to set me up to get married with a prostitute, wake up in a trashed hotel room somewhere with no idea of how it happened.

Turns out, I managed it quite well without them. On our first night, we ended up in a nightclub called the Asylum. My friends didn't like it and left but I stayed behind because I found the goth vibe somehow seductive. Got to appreciate any place that plays

Chiasm's Isolated in the bathrooms on a loop.

On my second night, I was in the queue of the Clark County Marriage License Bureau with Jeanette Voerman. I didn't realize it at the time, but Las Vegas is a great place to handle marriage bureaucracy if you're a vampire seeking to maintain a human identity: The Bureau is open until midnight.

Mad Love

I met Jeanette on the dancefloor on my first night at the Asylum. I'd realized I was a little out of place so I'd just taken my shirt off and borrowed some eyeliner from a guy in the bathroom.

I could tell she was somebody from the way everybody treated her but I'd been inhaling con-

fidence up my nose all evening so it wasn't a problem. She was blonde, beautiful and dressed like an indecent schoolgirl. Everything she said was creepy and weird but I didn't care because she had her tits in my face.

The last time I saw my friends was when we went for lunch after that first night. They asked me what had happened and I couldn't really explain it. In the beginning I'd just wanted to fuck Jeanette, but by the end of the night I proposed to her.

Most of the people queuing to the Marriage License Bureau were fortyish women with identical faces and older, disinterested men in white shorts and sunglasses. After we got our papers, we took a limo to the wedding chapel. I debated how much to tip the priest and Jeanette talked strange. This is going to make me sound like a weirdo, but it was starting to turn me on when she said things like: "My sister would be so mad if she knew I was marrying a pretty boy like you. But don't worry, I'll keep my little birdie safe. Or let you die. One of those."

Undead Barman

You know how in vampire movies there are these revelations that the barman or the taxi driver was a vampire all along? How you thought this was a normal nightclub but actually everybody around you is undead?

It's a lot less glamorous if you're actually the barman.

When our limo sped away from the wedding chapel, I was in love and I was in lust with the woman I believed to be my wedded wife. Jeanette got hot and heavy with me on the back seat, bit my neck... You know where this is going. She drank me dry, gave me just enough blood to make me into her childe and disappeared into the night.

I lost my mind and murdered the limo driver. I still feel bad about that.

I had no idea what had happened to me. I ran from the wreck of the car into the streets, sneaking into a hotel to find a bathroom and wash my face. My phone was full of messages from my friends but I couldn't call them when the very idea made me want to drain all the blood they carried inside and drink it in slow, pleasurable gulps.

I started to make my way towards Asylum because that was the only place where I thought I could find Jeanette. Let me tell you, Las Vegas is not a city for pedestrians, especially if you've just been made into a vampire and have no idea what's happening.

The Asylum bouncer told me that I was expected at the manager's office. He took me there and sat me down in from of a woman who introduced herself as Therese Voerman. She looked very serious, a businesslike blonde woman the

same age as Jeanette had been. I guessed this was she sister she'd mentioned.

"I've managed this club for a long time, since we were in Santa Monica. I won't have it threatened by fools like you, taken in by the games my sister likes to play. I'll give you two choices. Get out of the city or work here."

I chose to work there. That's how I went from running my own consulting business to working in a nightclub. I didn't even really get paid, just provided a place to sleep.

Swipe Right For Blood

Theresa forbade me from hunting at the Asylum so I had to come up with something else. For a few weeks I hoped I could live some sort of married vampire bliss with Jeanette, but when she finally showed up at the club, she wasn't much interested in me. It took me a while to understand that for her, it had just been a little prank she played on her sister.

Sometimes I think that without Tinder and Grindr, I would have been lost to the Hunger. I've been blessed with a pretty face, good abs and a solid line of self-deprecating patter. I know how to take a good selfie.

There's something special about using Tinder and Grindr to hunt for blood. You're not really thinking about who you want to fuck but who you want to taste. At first I went pretty much for the same kind of girls I'd wanted to have a date with. Then I started

to expand, to guys, to different kinds of women.

I've started to learn a simple vampire truth: The best blood is not always inside the young and the sexy. Sometimes the blood of an aging slot machine addict has just the right touch of sedentary maturation.

Theresa has told me a lot about the Second Inquisition and what it means to live in Las Vegas as a lick. I got lucky in a sense, being Embraced only after the local Camarilla suffered the full wrath of the intelligence agencies. The Asylum is too well integrated into the mortal world to be easily detectable but the Camarilla and their Elysiums were much simpler to ferret out.

All this is foreign to me because I have never experienced what the Camarilla really is. For me, the status of Las Vegas as an open Anarch city is just the normal state of affairs. We hunt from tourists and the only authority I bow to is Theresa.

Nomadic Anarch groups come and go, many of them stopping at the Asylum. I've understood that the place has some notoriety in Anarch circles although for me it's pretty much the totality of the vampire world as I know it. For these licks, the Asylum is a club where the hunting is good and something fucked up is always happening. If not otherwise, then because Jeanette makes it happen.

White Wedding

The Asylum building is an old chapel. I realized I'd got off easy when Jeanette found her next vic-

tim. She flirted with humans and vampires alike. It made me jealous to watch her do it but I knew I'd had my moment with her and there wouldn't be another. The next clubgoer she started to play the marriage game with was a girl, a Degenerate of only a few years as a vampire from the middle of nowhere.

She was taken with Jeanette and the same thing happened as with me: She proposed on the dance floor. Jeanette made a production of it, with a marriage ceremony at the club in a few nights. They had a priest and everything.

The girl looked like she couldn't believe her luck when she walked Jeanette to the altar. They kissed and we all applauded. She's come to Vegas to have the kind of fun only a vampire could have and the city had delivered.

The only thing she didn't realize was that it wasn't real. She was a girl from the sticks who fell for the Vegas illusion. The night after the wedding, she stumbled to the Asylum, looking for Jeanette. Instead, she got a stern talking-to from Theresa.

I'm not too broken up about it. I got promoted from the bar when she started to work here. I even taught her how to use Tinder to get at all those tourists looking to hook up in Vegas. ■

THE NIGHT CIRCUS

The Tout

Come one! Come all! For tonight only, the Night Circus is in town. Gets your tickets, bring your family and see miracles like you've never seen before!

Witness the amazing Princess of the Trapeze fall to her death!

Marvel at the Hypnotic Man and the illusion of lost time!

Delight in the tortures of the Screaming Mermaid!

Watch the Tigers and the Bears, the Elephants and the Seals cavort for your pleasure and edification!

Laugh at our uproariously hilarious clowns as they beat each other with sticks!

Learn our story: Founded in Victorian England, the Night Circus is closing in on two centuries of touring all across the world, going from town to town to delight the young and old alike. Taking its aesthetic from the burlesque shows of old, anachronistic wunderkammers and the most suicidal circus performances, it's the most deranged show on Earth.

Inside, you will see the centuries melt away as ancient monsters prowl the land once again. The limits of the human form are exposed as the merest fantasy as our acrobats perform the impossible. Feel the madness of the crowd as you participate in a show of cruelty and comedy, terror and wonder so amazing it'll change your life.

Step right up and come right in. It's the most incredible show on Earth, and you'll find you'll never want to leave its shimmering wonderland.

The Tent

They'll tell you that you have to live a lie, wear a mask, make your entire existence into a tedious Masquerade. You'll lie to your family and your friends. You'll lie to your neighbors and random people on the street. You'll lie and lie and lie because the truth will kill you.

Or so they say.

Every night, I look myself in the mirror. With powder and eyeliner, I build my true face. They introduce me to a crowd of hundreds of mortals and they all murmur my name.

I arrive on horseback, circling the ring, smiling at all the little boys and girls who will fall in love with me forevermore. I drink in their wonder, their adulation, the terror in their eyes as they see how fragile, how slight I appear on the back of a powerful, muscular animal. They sense the violence, the hunger gifted to the beast by our precious Blood.

The lights turn up. A rope descends and I leap, pulled up by my lovely compatriots hidden in the rigging. They take me all the way to the ropes and trapezes swinging high above the audience.

I begin my dance. I swing and turn, leap and fall, twist and risk everything with each carefully rehearsed move. There is no net. There are no safeties. The people must feel death, they must sense the danger, they must understand their own mortality. I'm a sacrificial victim, and each time I die, they live.

For that's how it ends. I make one final jump, somersault in the air. Spread my arms and close my eyes. There's nothing for me to grab onto. I plummet to the ground.

To me, this moment is more beautiful than anything in existence. The audience senses death, damage, bones breaking. They sense my intention. They understand this was no accident. They imagine my body breaking on the sand of the ring.

The lights go out just before the impact. The audience breathes in disquieted relief. It was just a trick. The death was an illusion. Applause scatters in the dark, empty tent before the next number.

In those few seconds of darkness, they drag my broken body backstage. I bask in the truth of my own glory and tragedy.

JOIN THE NIGHT CIRCUS

Tired of hiding who you are? Ready to bask in the adoration of a witless crowd? Willing to revel in the beauty of your dark truth?

Join us and demolish the Masquerade in front of the ignorant human multitudes night after night, leaving them dazzled and none the wiser.

Embrace life on the road. Enjoy life among kindred spirits. Escape the torpor of servitude!

Become who you really are as part of the Night Circus!

Apply tonight.

(Mesmerists and animal handlers needed.)

Later, they will bring someone from the audience to me. Usually a man, someone normal who suddenly saw a glimpse of the wondrous and unnatural. He wants to give me a bouquet and say thank you. I allow him to do so even as I take something more from him as well.

The Trail

The Night Circus never stays in town for more than one night, one show. In its wake, it leaves behind terrifying memories, blood drained corpses and municipal authorities confused about who exactly gave the permit for them to set up their tent.

The Circus is a traveling caravan of trucks and trailers, transporting the performers, the animals and the crew as one tightly-knit family of humans and those less than human. Everyone in the Circus has tasted the Blood, whether they're mortal or not. They all know the secret of why the show looks like nothing else on Earth, and they will never reveal its secrets.

Between cities, they set up camp in a small town somewhere and relax. They rehearse the numbers, train new members, organize weddings and funerals. For many in the Circus, these private days and nights lived inside a rolling camp are the happiest of their lives.

When showtime comes around, it's time for the greatest trick in the repertoire of the Night Circus: Convincing the audience that the supernatural has a mundane explanation. Every trick is realized through the abilities of an inhuman creature, and every time there must be just enough ambiguity for the humans to imagine they know how the trick was done.

Sometimes at the end of a show, someone from the audience wanders backstage to ask questions. Perhaps they're a circus professional wondering about the amazing stagecraft, seeking to improve their own circus practice. Many of these end up dead or confused, having lost their memories, but a few appear in the ring after a few weeks, as new members of the family. ▪

Delusions of Humanity

1.

Did I ever tell you how I got Embraced? It's an embarrassing story, so I'm sure you'll like it. It didn't happen here in Reykjavik, even though this is where I was born and raised. The licks here are very strict about progeny.

No, it happened in London. I went there straight from school to work as an au pair. It seemed like a good deal. Look after the kids of a cosmopolitan, successful couple. Get paid, get room and board. See the city, experience a new life.

What could go wrong? How about a family where the wife is a horrible micromanager who thinks one evening off every two weeks is reasonable? A husband who keeps leering at me, asking if I have a boyfriend yet?

How about a couple who are a vampire and a ghoul?

I didn't realize how embarrassing they truly were until much later, when I'd gotten out of there and seen some more of vampire society.

So, the husband was the vampire and the wife was the ghoul.

He still went to work, but only at night. He had a job as a lawyer, and somehow he'd been able to arrange it so that he never had to meet clients during the day. He had some kind of a bizarre bullshit medical excuse about being sensitive to sunlight.

They continued their lives as if the husband, Mark, had an unusual addiction but was otherwise normal. They held dinner parties for their friends and talked football and politics. They had a subscription to the Guardian and two children I quickly learned to hate. Every once in a while, Mark had to go out to feed, but they never talked about it.

Maybe the joke's on me, because I never realized that something weird was going on in that household. They were so incredibly tedious in their crushing beige normality that I never considered the possibility they might have a dark secret.

At least, I didn't consider it until Mark cornered me in the kitchen one night. He told me how their marriage lacked passion, and how he found me attractive. First I tried to evade

him, then I told him I wasn't interested, and finally I shoved him off me because he was getting too insistent.

That's when he made me into a vampire. To show me that he was still the big man in the house.

I went rabid straight off the bat, punched his teeth in with a strength I didn't even know I had and disappeared into the night.

2.

I didn't understand it then, but Mark had made me into a Duskborn. I liked the irony of it. His Blood was weak, but not weak enough to allow him to go out during the day. That privilege was reserved for me, his progeny.

After I became a vampire, I went a little crazy. I got a place of my own, hit the clubs, changed my style. My newly dead body had an amazing resilience. I'd been the shy little au pair from Iceland, but now I became something else. I felt like I could do anything, get anyone, do drugs, dance, party forever and ever.

3.

It could have ended with this, me leaving, they continuing their lives . But it didn't.

One night, Sarah caught me snooping around. I'd gotten careless, watching them like my own little reality show. She'd thought Mark had killed me, but now that I was obviously up and about, she accused me of having seduced her husband. She was crying when she told me that she knew we were having an affair and Mark had made me into a vampire too.

I'm a monster now, like all Kindred. I live as a parasitic being, sucking the life out of humanity. But even I have my sentimental side. What could I do?

I gave her some of my Blood and took her out partying. By the end of the night, she was a vampire too, courtesy of a guy who owed me a favor. The last I saw her, she was planning to move to Berlin before the London Camarilla realized that an illegal childe had been made.

And who knows, Mark could still be in that little house in Barnet. Checking himself in the mirror to make sure there's no blood spatters on his white collar. Taking the kids to school. Fighting hard against everything the night could give him. ■

I was still curious about Mark and his shitty life. Sometimes I went back to the house in Barnet and watched this couple who lived in denial, desperate to still pass for humans.

The wife was called Sarah. After I'd left, she seemed to become ever thinner and more neurotic, snapping at the children and crying when she was alone. From the way they talked, I guessed that Mark had told her I had left after a dispute about free time. That was kinda plausible, because I'd had that talk with Sarah many times. But looking at her, I knew she suspected that the reality was something worse, something to do with her husband's true nature.

It was funny, in a way. Mark did his absolute best to suppress any sign of being a vampire. This wasn't a house with blood bags in the fridge. Just heavy drapes in the master bedroom. They never talked about it, even when they were just the two of them.

When Mark was at work and the kids were at their friends' house, Sarah relaxed sometimes by watching a romantic vampire movie and drinking red wine. At first I thought it was funny, but then it started to feel sad. She was really into it. She liked the idea of being married to a vampire. If only he could have been persuaded to play it up, once in a while.

Is It OK To Feed Vitae To a Baby?

A discussion on a private forum

velvetblack - 21:07 26.1.2018

hey :) i'm looking for advice, so if anyone has experience with this, any help is appreciated! i was wondering, is it ok to feed vitae to a baby?

like, from a health perspective?

NOTE: please, replies only from people with EXPERIENCE

liliththedarkmother - 21:10 26.1.2018

Please tell me you're not feeding vitae to your baby.

liliththedarkmother - 21:12 26.1.2018

It's not healthy. Vitae stunts the aging process in humans and causes addiction.

theobellfanboy2001 - 21:20 26.1.2018

It's fine, don't worry... i give my kids blood all the time to keep them from crying and it works... and it heals them too, when they get hurt! sometimes they hurt each other, but i think its just normal

i've worked hard to adopt my girlfriend's kids from when she was married. its difficult, but they love the blood so much and they get along with our kids, i mean the kids we have together...

pro-tip: kids are great for the masquerade! nobody expects a vampire to push a stroller! and the support groups for dads are great for feeding, nobody questions if somebody looks anemic and pale...

velvetblack - 21:28 26.1.2018

thank you theobellfan2001! that is good advice! i got into trouble with social services over my older kid. those assholes said he should've gone to school, but that's why we have the gifts of Caine, am i right? to make a nosy social worker see our point of view!

so in SUMMARY: giving babies vitae pacifies them

theobellfanboy2001 - 21:31 26.1.2018

yes! don't worry too much about it, there's no such thing as a perfect parent... and being a cleaver is even harder

liliththedarkmother - 21:32 26.1.2018

I don't think we should use the word "cleaver" on this forum. It's derogatory and insensitive.

theobellfanboy2001 - 21:35 26.1.2018

sorry... you're right. it's a shit word. it's not easy to be a parent and a vampire. it's hard to raise human children. sometimes i worry i bite them too often

liliththedarkmother - 21:37 26.1.2018

I made a rule for myself that I was allowed to drink from my baby only once a week. Once she gets older, I think it will be okay to drink every few days. Teenagers are resilient.

theobellfanboy2001 - 21:45 26.1.2018

solid, solid... i think i'll adopt this rule... it's a good one

velvetblack - 22:01 26.1.2018

drinking from my kids, it's like "can you love too much?"

it makes me feel so close to them, but then it's all BLOOD LOSS and AMBULANCE TRIP and MASQUERADE BREACH

like, one moment you're so happy and then suddenly everything is so difficult

liliththedarkmother - 22:11 26.1.2018

Restraint is definitely the hardest part of being an undead parent. That and explaining why you can only attend parent-teacher meetings at night. But please, even if your child has suffered blood loss, don't feed them vitae. It's not good for them.

velvetblack, you have to be very careful with the masquerade. In a lot of domains, raising human children is not allowed at all. If the Cam or the Barons catch you doing it, they'll take away your kids. They might even kill you.

velvetblack - 22:13 26.1.2018

i know. we've had to move thrice, and every time it's a huge hassle. that's why i stopped sending my kids to school. i think that somehow the big C can monitor the school system, like who's enrolled.

one time i had to kill a woman who came to our house. she was like an assistant sheriff and she kept talking to me in a very disrespectful tone

theobellfanboy2001 - 22:16 26.1.2018

that's so badass... you're most definitely parent of the year! "She just wanted to live a normal life, but they wouldn't let her." that could be the movie poster. vampire Mom movie.

liliththedarkmother - 22:20 26.1.2018

velvetblack, that sounds really bad. Are you safe? Do you need help?

velvetblack - 22:45 26.1.2018

i'm okay. but thanks. as long as i have my kids i'll be fine.

and theobellfanboy2001 you made me smile :) i don't feel like much of a hero changing diapers, but you're right. i will fight to the death for my children.

Los Nueves

Chinasa Adeyemi checks out the Acapulco Anarch culture of getting shot for fun.

"**I**f this is your first night…" You've seen *Fight Club.* You know the drill. When Juan gives me the gun, I check it, wait for him to draw a bead on me and fire. We both hit. I get him in the throat. His bullet hits me in the face. It hits my upper jaw, sinking bone splinters into the flesh of my mouth.

I'm not used to getting shot, so I fly down onto the ground as the crowd around us hollers and cheers. They've all come here for the same thing: To shoot and to get shot.

This is *Fight Club* for those who can survive a bullet wound. A punch in the nose is a love tap for these folks, so if they want to play it rough, they need something more. Nine millimeters more.

There's an old journalistic adage about not becoming part of the story, but I was allowed to share the experience only if I participated. Which is why Juan is helping me up, laughing, the raw hole in his throat eerily bloodless.

Collateral Damage

Acapulco is a city of 700,000 people. Last year, they had 918 killings, making the city Mexico's murder capital for the fifth year in a row.

So what's that got to do with Anarchs getting their kicks shooting each other in the face?

Juan claps me on the back and raises my hand up in a gesture of triumph. The noise around us is deafening. Shouting, clapping, and *El Regreso Del Chapo* by El Komander from the radio of a car parked nearby. We are all bathing in the headlights, the licks in the circle looking like agitated shadows.

I don't say much. I'm happy there are no mirrors here. I don't want to see the ruin of my face. I'm not trying to sound badass here: I figured I would get shot in the arm or the leg. Maybe through the chest, at worst. Instead to the great hilarity of all present, I'm trying to heal my face and remain standing at the same time.

I'm going to need blood pretty soon, and I'm not the only one. Juan is already healed, and hungry because of it. The next couple is already stepping into the ring. They last longer than we did, perforating each other until it doesn't seem as much a fight as a ritual mutilation.

All these wounds need to be healed. That means a lot of bodies showing up as police statistics tomorrow morning. Local custom is to deface the corpses so they're taken for gang killings.

The Game

The game is called the Nines, or los Nueves. The setup is simple. You go somewhere you can party in peace. A derelict, abandoned lot in an area nobody cares about. You make sure everyone has guns. You put on appropriate music.

First timers have to fight. After that, the others get their turn. Some just come to watch their friends get shot. Others go in the ring every night, fighting, shooting, bleeding. This is immortality in its rawest form: The vampire body refuses to die, and in this game, you can take full advantage.

Sometimes Anarchs die playing los Nueves. Juan doesn't want to talk about it, but after pressing him long enough I get him to admit it happens pretty often. It's hard to figure how much damage a vampire can really take, and some are much more durable than others.

The goal of los Nueves is not to kill, but it's no secret it's a lethal sport. Everybody who's been here more than one or two nights has seen it. And they still come back.

The Warmup

Juan tells me that sometimes they like to warm up before the actual fights. The way to do this is by shooting yourself through the hand or into the stomach. Once you have taken a little damage, you feel fired up and ready to go. I ask Juan the obvious question: Why do this?

"Being a vampire is easy", he says. "There's a lot of prey, and because there's so much violence, hiding victims and maintaining the Masquerade is easier. If some-

"Being a vampire is easy", he says.

one sees something here, who are they going to tell? The police?"

So you hurt each other because there's not enough challenge in being a vampire?

"Maybe. You've seen the movie. It's these middle class American guys who want to feel something real. We're not middle-class or American, but you want to feel something. Otherwise, why bother?"

You could fight the Camarilla.

"We fight the Camarilla! But it's always so serious. Here, you can relax, get shot, get up laughing. You can rough up your best friend."

This is something I had noticed as well. Sure, many of the fights I saw were real fights. Each participating is trying to shoot the other so full of holes they can't get

up anymore. But often it didn't really look like anybody was trying to win. They just wanted to hurt and get hurt.

Sunrise

"Fucking fight me you assholes", a tough-looking older lady yells, brandishing an old-school revolver. I know that you should never judge a vampire by how they look, but it's no wonder this woman is lacking for challengers. She is scary as fuck.

"I'll fight you", Juan says and steps into the ring.

He shoots the woman in the face, the exact same spot he shot me. Later I hear it's his signature.

The old lady spits teeth and just as the first sign of sunrise shows behind the hills, pumps three bullets into Juan in quick succession. Chest, stomach, balls. Juan falls and doesn't move.

"Who's going to take him home?" I ask and point to the lightening sky.

"I will", the old lady says. "How's he gonna get here next time otherwise?" ∎

Chinasa Adeyemi is a roving chronicler of the Anarch Movement. She might come back to Acapulco one night, just for the honor of getting her face shot off again.

24 Hour Party Blood-suckers

The music beats hard on my body, forcing me to move. As I push among the sweaty, twitchy throng on the dancefloor, it feels like sound, not blood animating my half-dead corpse. The insistent violent rhythm is making me more aware of my insides than ever since I became a vampire. I'm just one more body, and in the darkness nobody notices if I breathe or not.

I never want to come down. This is the perfect moment, unsullied by Hunger, a perfect chemical high. This is what eternal life means. Freedom to dance, to party every night, all night, forever.

The Hunger is settling into my limbs, my thoughts, my dead heart. I want to pretend not to feel it, to move, move, move, but it can't be ignored. There's blood in every person around me, whispering in their veins, hiding behind a thin barrier of skin.

I make my way to Sigurður. Only a few years ago we were both in the same school, in the same classes. I was the misfit geek girl living my best life on the Internet. He was the emo boy graced with a sliver of cool because of his impeccable taste in music. Now I'm a Duskborn vampire and he's slumped face first into the table, a Renfield ill-treated by my asshole friend Dee who's sitting there, trying to discreetly lick her lips clean of the blood.

"Have you ever heard of the Masquerade you idiot?" I hiss at Dee, sitting down beside her.

"Don't worry, it's cool", she assures me blithely, glancing around if anybody is paying attention. Nobody is.

"Listen, Dee. I went to a lot of trouble to shoot Sigurður up with the exact, specific high I wanted. I'm not a junkie like you. I'm a connoisseur. I didn't do this so you could steal his blood."

Dee is not listening. In her religion, everything is fair if you want to get high. Dee is one of those people you could never imagine during the day. I have no idea where she sleeps, how she travels or what she does for money. But I do know that she's always there to steal my high.

Fuck her. I got to hunt.

Reykjavik is a small town and you will run into people you know. Like right now. A guy I dated when I was twelve and he was fourteen. He's slipping into the toilets and I follow him just as he locks himself in a dingy stall to do coke off the toilet bowl. I give him enough time to get high before I yank the door off its hinges. Should have more finesse, but I don't care. He's kneeling there expression bleary, unable to understand what his childhood sweetheart is doing there with fangs out.

He was supposed to become wealthy and successful. An investment banker. Instead he's just a regular asshole, befuddled with his choices in life. And now he's prey. I bite deep into the back of his neck, the flesh giving way and the first trickle of blood giving me a taste of what's to come.

I love drinking from people I don't care about. I know the Kiss will get him hard and horny, wondering what happened as I disappear into the night.

The toxic combination of whatever my ex had spiking his blood hits me as I stand up. I ate a kebab earlier, just to spite Dee. Unlike her, I can still eat, and usually I get to decide when I puke it out. Now I don't. I retch onto my ex who still kneels by the toilet bowl. I heave violently until every piece of the kebab decorates his embarrassing little jacket. This is the kind of ex-girlfriend experience I'm all about: Bite, arouse, vomit.

Better leave. This is why I make my own drug alchemy and use my Renfield as a test lab. Fucked up things happen if you get high from the blood of a random asshole. I stagger back to the tables. The music is beating me down. The people crowd close

and leer, their sweat sticking to my body as they brush past. The ceiling is too low, I feel like I'm suffocating even when I don't need to breathe anymore.

I'm tired. I don't want to sleep. Being a vampire is fine as long as you're wasted, and if you're Duskborn, you can keep going round the clock. It keeps every bad thought at bay.

"Let's get you out", Dee says, grabbing me by my arm. She pulls me along to the street, straight into the wet sleet coming down from the sky. It dribbles under my clothes, the streams of cold water running along my back. I hated this feeling when I was human, but now it's comforting, like cold fingers affirming that I don't have to accept human morality. Every person I've killed was just prey.

Dee peels off once the horizon starts to lighten. If she gets caught in the cold half-light of a day in Reykjavik, she'll burn. I just need to put on my sunglasses. I go to the harbor, feeling less and less

human. There's a chill-out party I'm going to, but before that I want to ride the last of my ex's bad blood and watch the sunrise.

The sun is merely a lighter shape in the clouds. Looking at it directly hurts my eyes despite the glasses, but I do it anyway. I've learned a few things about how most vampires live, and it's amazing to me that I can access a whole world they see only in their memories. They have the power, but they don't have the freedom.

I wait for the cruise ships to moor. They provide a steady stream of witless American tourists, prey that's only available for those of us able to hunt during the day. By nightfall, they're gone again. Valuable resource in a small city overpopulated with the undead. Problem is, the only high available from the ships is prescription drugs.

It's time to go chill out, find Dee when the sun goes down, and do it all over again. ■

ROLL CALL OF THE REVOLUTION

You want to know who's who in the Anarch Movement? Who are the celebrities and why are they celebrated, the most important groups, scenes and ideologies?

I can try to answer, but you must understand that my answer will by necessity be very limited. The reality is that there is no single Anarch Movement, no unifying political structure bringing us all together. Even if you take the political Anarchs, there's a vast gulf of ideology, history and geography separating the Anarch Free States in California and the former Brujah Council in Russia.

The only thing these political Anarchs really have in common is a belief that we can build a better world. Or at least a different world, free from the stagnation and blind conservatism of the Camarilla. If there's one constant in radical politics, it's that we've very good at splintering into ever smaller groups. That holds true for Anarchs as well, and sometimes it seems as if the worst enemy of the Santa Monica Progressive Anarch Collective is the Santa Monica Revolutionary Anarch Collective.

The thing is, the Anarchs are much more than just those of us who have a political agenda. Go beyond the Movement and you find the unbound, the Anarchs who just want to be left alone and do their thing without interference from sect politics. Some of these people are nicest bloodsuckers you'll ever find, genuinely morally conflicted over having to feed from humans. Others are monsters pure and simple, enjoying the power and freedom provided by Caine's curse.

The Anarchs have also been the refuge of those motivated by religious convictions that

don't really find a home in the Camarilla. These cults and communities are some of the strangest things the Anarchs can offer, featuring ideas and concepts totally alien to mainstream Camarilla society. Before you dismiss them completely, remember that once upon a time, the Sabbat was a tiny cult as well.

Still, the worst enemy of Anarch cohesion is simple geography. We're all connected to the mortal communities that spawned us, much more than the Camarilla is. Many of us are motivated by the prejudices we had from our days among the living and the Masquerade makes it hard for an Italian Unbound to know a lot about his sisters preying on people in South African border territories. ■

– Rudi, Danish Gangrel
ideologue and activist

Lasciami

Transcript of a surveillance tape 22.1.2018

Naples, street address: [blacked out]

Starting at 9:31 PM

Male voice 1, speaking Italian: Are you sure this is a good idea? These guys have a strange reputation.

Male voice 2, speaking Italian: What do you mean strange?

M1: When you kill someone, there has to be purpose and function. You kill clean when you just want the other person dead. You kill messy when you want to make a statement. You kill in public when you want to make people paranoid. These guys, I don't know... It weirds me out.

M2: The blood.

M1: Of course the blood! I've seen one of the victims. The way they hang them, drain the blood. It works as a terror tactic, I'm not denying that. It's one hell of a way to die, losing your life as your blood drains to the floor. A great signature move, ten points for style.

M2: People are terrified of them. As a terror tactic, it works. You get word they've been hired to do a hit on you, [inaudible]

M1: I don't get it though, they're always saying that they just want to keep a low profile, do the occasional hit to finance their lifestyle. Like they're slacker assassins. But their signature is so gruesome everybody pays attention. Us. The cops. Pretty soon, the press.

M2: I'm shocked, Andrea. Are you suggesting that professional murderers act inconsistently with the bullshit they spout? I'm so happy this is unheard of among us in the Camorra.

M1: Sarcasm is a filthy habit. Besides, I think it's time. They'll be here soon. Do you have the blood bags?

M2: In the fridge.

M1: I'm going to ask them about those. I get why they kill like they do. But why do they want blood bags as part of their payment?

M2: Style?

M1: Style is fine, but this is just weird.

[the sound of a doorbell]

M1: God, they're punctual. I'll go get it.

[the sound of a door being opened, indistinct greetings and words of welcome]

M1: Please, sit down.

M2: Good to meet you, my name is Giancarlo.

Female voice 1, speaking Italian: Thank you, Giancarlo. *[indistinct]*

Male voice 3, speaking Italian, sometimes dipping into Sardinian: Let's talk business.

F1: Why do you always have to be so brusque? We don't have to skip the pleasantries.

M2: It's all right.

M1: There's something I wanted to ask you about. If it's okay.

F1: Of course. Ask away.

M1: What's with the blood? I mean, why do you ask for blood in lieu of the payment?

F1: *[laughs]*

M3: It's because we're vampires.

[lengthy silence]

M1: Oh right, vampires!

[general laughter]

M1: But seriously though....

M3: Do you have the blood we asked for?

M2: Yes, of course. Let me get it for you.

[sounds of scuffling, an opening fridge door]

M2: Here you go.

M3: Thank you. Let me check it.

M1: Check it? I assure you, this is real blood, just like you asked.

M3: This is cow's blood. We asked for human blood.

[silence]

M1: How could you tell?

M3: I can always tell. Let me explain why we ask for the blood. It's to check if the people we're dealing with are serious. If they are not serious, they try to fuck around with our request. If they are serious, they get us the blood.

F1: I guess what he's asking is... Are you serious?

M2: Okay, look, we misunderstood...

M3: We're not unreasonable. You can get us one bag of human blood right now and the rest on completion of the job.

M1: One bag right now?

M2: He means we have to bleed into the bag.

M3: Yes. That is what I mean. Empty the cow's blood out and fill it from your own veins.

F1: Only wash it first. Mixing cow's blood and human blood is disgusting.

M1: Fuck... *[indistinct]*

[seven minutes of indistinct sounds with only the occasional expletive]

M1: Here it is. Are you happy now?

F1: We'll be happy when you provide us with the rest of the blood bags.

M1: Surely there's an easier way to see if somebody is serious than this.

F1: We like blood. Getting human blood always requires a sacrifice. You get it from your own body, or from the body of another. Or from a blood bank. We don't like people who hire us casually, just because they get mad at someone. Murder is serious business and even if you don't do it yourself, you have to feel it one way or another.

M1: I guess I can see that.

M2: You're still bleeding. Let me put more gauze on that.

M1: Oh, right. Thanks.

[indistinct growling]

M1: Is he alright?

F1: He's just hungry.

M1: Okay, then we should make this quick.

F1: Who are the targets?

M1: Two brothers. One is a judge, the other a priest. The judge has it in for us, he's been trying to ferret out our political connections. The priest is worse. He's been saying there's no salvation for those active in the Camorra.

M2: We'd like them to die together. Not in public, but gruesomely enough to send a clear message.

M3: We can do that.

M1: *[indistinct]*

M2: We know you can. Half the payment now, half upon completion. Standard deal.

F1: Excellent.

M1: Here's the dossier on the targets.

F1: Thank you. I think we'd better leave now. All this bloodletting is making my friend hungry.

M2: Very morbid of you, Madame.

F1: *[laughs]* You're a flirt, you know that?

[sounds of scuffling, goodbyes, a door opens and closes]

M2: Wow. That got intense.

M1: These guys are crazy. That was some black widow shit right there.

M2: But good crazy. It'll send the right message.

M1: Fuck, I'm still bleeding. I think we need to wash this wound with alcohol.■

SOY CUBA

An interview transcript / Havana / 12.2.2018

SOURCE: It just bugs me, that's all.

INTERVIEWER: What bugs you?

SOURCE: The bullshit about 'friendship between the peoples'. You know, how he always goes 'the alliance between the Soviet Union and Cuba is one of the most beautiful in history'.

INTERVIEWER: When you say 'he', you refer to...

SOURCE: Alexander Alexeyev, of course.

INTERVIEWER: There's a great deal of information about Alexeyev available through mortal channels. He served as an intelligence agent, became the Soviet Ambassador to Cuba. Played a role in the Cuban Missile Crisis, dying in 1989.

SOURCE: Well, I guess you could call it dying.

But there's more to his story. He's been one of us for a long time. Well, not one of my clan. He's Brujah, like most of the licks who used to wield power in the Soviet Union.

INTERVIEWER: You're suggesting that as a vampire, his chief focus of activity is now Havana.

SOURCE: Yes. Apparently there was a lot of internal strife with the Learned Clan communists in 1991 and he felt he needed a new place to go. So he came here.

INTERVIEWER: You know a lot about this, but our records suggest you've only been a vampire for a few years.

SOURCE: Yeah, I got Embraced in 2016. I'm not telling you anything secret, really. Every Anarch in Havana knows this shit.

INTERVIEWER: How was Alexeyev received?

SOURCE: Like a hero! He's a bona fide member of the Brujah Council, one of the people responsible for the most successful Anarch operation in history: The Soviet Union. I mean, Americans talk about the Anarch Free States in California like it's a big thing. Please. I don't even like the Anarchs and I know the Brujah Council was the real deal.

INTERVIEWER: What's Alexeyev's position now?

SOURCE: We don't really have an Anarch ruler who controls all the territory in Havana like a Camarilla Prince would do. But Alexeyev is extremely influential. He's made a lot of moves, declaring Havana a sanctuary for anyone fleeing a Blood Hunt or the Second Inquisition.

INTERVIEWER: How do you feel about that?

SOURCE: I hate it, truth be told. I mean, I'm Cuba. Alexeyev is just some Russian spook. How come he gets to tell every psycho escaping the Camarilla they can come here and fuck our shit up? I mean, I get the idealism but this should be our domain.

INTERVIEWER: 'Our' as in Cuban-born vampires?

SOURCE: It's funny how you say 'vampires'. I haven't met a lot of Camarilla, but they always said 'Kindred'.

INTERVIEWER: I was afraid the term 'Kindred' would not be familiar here.

SOURCE: Oh, sorry! Anyway, I guess that's what I want. No more Russians coming here and telling us how to run our city. We need a Prince of our own, and I'm perfectly happy to be part of the Camarilla if that's what it takes.

INTERVIEWER: Do you have a candidate for the Prince?

SOURCE: Well, I was thinking, since I'm giving you all this information...

INTERVIEWER: Of course. We understand.

SOURCE: I mean, I'm just a dude. But with the right backing, I'm sure I could make something beautiful here. And you would get all the Red Listers living here now.

INTERVIEWER: A good deal, to be sure.

SOURCE: You know what's the worst thing about Alexeyev? The speeches. He's got the stamina of a real party apparatchik. He can do two hours with no preparation. It's amazing, but so boring.

INTERVIEWER: What would you prefer?

SOURCE: Same thing I liked in life, really. You know, a beach, reggaetón, friends, girls...

INTERVIEWER: That doesn't sound like a gathering of the Kindred.

SOURCE: It could be! Me, I don't believe in hunting without good music. Without my songs, I don't even want blood. The hunger goes away.

INTERVIEWER: Really?

SOURCE: Not really. Still, it sucks to hunt when I can't get my groove on. You have to take the time, dance...

INTERVIEWER: So if Alexeyev...

SOURCE: That's what it should be all about, right? Being one of us? Just having fun, hunting from whomever we like, ignoring all this Red List crap? I mean, when I was Embraced they told me being an Anarch was the best way to avoid getting mixed up in all these big secret politics. Like with Justicars or whatever. But I think that's not true. Being Anarchs got us Alexeyev and the Red Listers.

INTERVIEWER: You believe joining the Camarilla would make it easier for you to focus on reggaetón and beach parties?

SOURCE: For sure! I mean, you guys have to be more chill than Alexeyev, right? Have you ever been to a party organized by a former Soviet Ambassador? 'Cause I have, and those parties suck. It's just people singing in Russian, making long speeches and getting really sentimental about drinking the blood of the living.

INTERVIEWER: I take it Alexeyev has significant opposition?

SOURCE: Well, yes and no. I think you're falling into the Camarilla trap now. You can't imagine a city without a strong leader. Alexeyev is not our leader, he's just very good at making things happen. People don't like everything he does, especially this sanctuary business, but it's an Anarch city, right?

INTERVIEWER: So you could use a strong leader?

SOURCE: Yeah, maybe the Camarilla is right on this one.

INTERVIEWER: How many vampires would you say there are in Havana?

SOURCE: Wait, you guys are Camarilla, right?

INTERVIEWER: Of course.

SOURCE: Okay. Sorry. I'm getting paranoid. Everybody here is a little worried about the Second Inquisition, ever since Alexeyev made his offer. We have a lot of history with CIA agents doing weird shit in Havana, whether they're SI or not. ■

Ni Dieu Ni Maitre

The First Meeting: La Bellevilloise

I notice her in the crowd long before she sees me. I look like just another North African in a club full of North Africans. She's not the only white face. We're in a pretty bourgeois place after all, just around the corner from Père Lachaise.

Still, she stands out like the Camarilla girl she is. Dalia, get a grip, I tell myself. I'm supposed to meet her and see if she deserves my help, not start ogling the princess from the Ivory Tower. She would never have come to see Sofiane on her own, but now that she's here, she works the room like a proper lick. Smiling, flirting, flitting away like a clever little dream.

"What's your story?" I ask her, without introducing myself, as she cheers the artist walking on stage like everyone else in the place.

She doesn't react immediately, too caught up in the crowd roar. When she does, she falls back against me in the press of people, her low voice somehow carrying through the noise. "Hey Dalia. I'm happy you came."

She doesn't allow me to talk business. She wants to see the gig, and I dance and shout with her. I know some of the faces in the club, and they look at me knowingly, thinking I'm trying to hit on a privileged society girl out to broaden her cultural horizons.

Later, when we're wandering the streets, she opens up. "It's the usual story. You've probably heard this many times before. But I can't help it, it's my life. He was someone in Villon's court, very old. He saw me in a cafe and came to talk to me. He forced me to fall in love with him, Embraced me and paraded me around the Elysium like a trophy. I was taken in by it all at first, but he wanted to control every aspect of my life. I couldn't take it. I had an affair, and he found out. Of course he did. That's when it started, the humiliations... They're very clever with those in the Camarilla."

The Second Meeting: Rue Saint-Honoré

Fucking the lover of a jealous Camarilla elder on his bed, in his haven, is probably a bad idea. But let me tell you brothers and sisters, it's one hell of a trip.

I slipped a little note between the pages of a book in his library with a quote from a La Canaille song. He'll find it eventually, but not too soon.

The Third Meeting: Roubaix

"You have to disappear. There's no life for you in Paris", I tell her and take her hand across the table in the hospital cafeteria. Our meetings have become increasingly convoluted as paranoia mounts. This time we're in a hospital in Roubaix. Coming to another city, a shithole like Roubaix, will allow us to remain under radar. Or so we hope.

She doesn't argue. She knows we've already taken too many risks. "Maybe my clan will help me. I could go to..."

"No. You have to start thinking like one of us, instead of one of them. There are no clans. There is no Caine. None of that matters. You have to live now, today, instead of in the past like the Camarilla does. They will never save you, and the stories they tell are only good for controlling you.
"

She's been in the Camarilla long enough to look offended, even when she knows I'm right. "You don't know…" she starts, but I interrupt her.

"I do know. I've studied our history. I know everything there is to know about the First Anarch Revolt, the Convention of Thorns, the Ventrue and the Toreador. But tonight there's a whole new world that goes beyond all that. Don't get trapped in those stories, because they'll blind you from what's happening in the world."

"So where should we go?" she asks apprehensively, looking at the sick and dying mortals around us.

"You should go", I say as gently as I can. "I'm not your life. We had fun, but we're not going to be forever. I was your first Anarch lover, that's all."

The Fourth Meeting: Marrakech

I'd decided not to follow her into Marrakech, but I couldn't help it. We meet in an outdoors cafe, a hipster place she suggested. I say hello to all her friends, and a few of them are our kind. She's integrating quickly.

"Let's go outside", she suggests, taking me to the street, away from her new mortal circle. "I'm pretending to work in an embassy", she says self-consciously.

I feel like a fool, a stupid girl who doesn't understand that this love story is over. I ended it, and now I regret it.

"Do you remember that night when we first met?" she asks. "You took me to the bathroom and told me to drink your blood. You pretended it was a test to see if I was for real. But you did it because you wanted to get one over a pretty girl."

"I remember." I'm not sure I'm ready to talk about all that yet. "How's life in the Ashirra?"

"It's good", she says. "Your contacts helped me out a lot."

I knew she couldn't remain in Europe. There was no place she could go to hide from a Camarilla elder. And she wasn't used to the Anarch lifestyle, the care and rigor it took to live as one of us in one of the most repressive Camarilla cities in the world. But the Ashirra was different. They had the power to keep the Camarilla from getting too uppity in their cities. And you'd be a fool to assume that a North African Anarch like myself didn't have some Ashirra connections.

"Do you have a new patron?" I ask her. Lover, is what I mean.

"No", she says vehemently. "None of that. The first time was enough. I won't be controlled again."

"You became an Anarch after all." ■

I:IV:XV

Dear Childe,

I want you to know that I don't hold your actions against you. Becoming one of us is always a shock. I remember when it happened to me and while I tried to make it easier for you by giving the scene proper spiritual context, I understand that I may have not succeeded as well as I would have wanted.

Let me tell you something about my own background. I would have liked to tell you these things face to face but you escaped before I had a chance to do so. I'm grateful to you for getting in touch, even by letter and dead drop. In fact, I commend your instincts in avoiding electronic communications as they can prove hazardous to our kind.

I have been in the night for close to a century. In my human state, I was a student of theology, but that's not why I was Embraced. My sire was motivated by a bitter desire to defile something she saw as pure. I volunteered at an orphanage when I wasn't engaged with my studies and she saw me as a saint she wanted to destroy.

It's ironic, what happened. Being Embraced didn't destroy me or consign me to eternal damnation. It elevated me, made me holy. I haven't seen my sire in decades but I often think about her. She's a good example of the sad self-hatred perpetrated by the myths peddled in the Camarilla.

The Church of Caine

Manchester is a good place to become one of us. The Church of Caine has a large organization here, and I'd be guilty of false humility if I said it wasn't because of the work I've done as Filius Minor. That's second in command, after our leader, the Filius Major. I may have my shot at the leadership position soon, as we are planning to move into the power vacuum currently in place in London.

If you meet others blessed by the night, they might use another term for us: "The Cainite Heresy". To understand where this comes from, you must know that we have a very long history, going all the way back to the early Gnostic sects being born after the time of Christ. For a long time, vampiric understanding of Caine and our own role was developing in many different small communities. We went big only with the Cathras in the 12th century, as the Cathar understanding of theology proved fertile for our kind as well.

The Cathars also provided a good lesson in what happens to truth-tellers who threaten existing hierarchies of power. They were mercilessly persecuted, branded heretics by the Catholic Church and eradicated in a Crusade.

Life for the Cainite faith became very difficult when even the mortal Cathars were being destroyed.

It's important to understand that during this time, the Catholic Church was riddled with vampires, especially Lasombra, and they felt that our truth threatened their grip on power.

Tenets of the Faith

The basic tenets of our faith are laid out in the Euagetaematikon, also known as the Book of the Shining Blood. Its interpretation has changed over the years but the basic moral message has always been the same. It reveals that the material world is a cage made by a subordinate creator we often call Ialdabaoth. This truth reveals the essentially crass nature of the material world, and humanity with it.

However, humanity had its moment of redemption when Caine slew his brother Abel. In recognition of Caine's moral understanding of the world, God blessed him and shared with him the true nature of the world. The Genesis says: "Therefore whosoever slayeth Caine, vengeance shall be taken upon him sevenfold."

However, humanity was blind to Caine's message and thus another prophet was born. Jesus Christ walked the earth and taught that eating and shedding blood was a holy act most pleasing to God. However, the teachings of Jesus were perverted by terrestrial authorities and the agents of the demiurge Ialdabaoth, and you can only see the faintest glimmers of the truth in the Bible.

The Church created after Jesus is not the true Church, but a Church of Pilate, a false edifice meant to lead humanity astray.

In time, God will send a prophet to earth for a third and final time. Our forebears long thought that this Third Caine would come to bring Gehenna in 1239, but obviously that didn't happen. Some argue that the resurgence of the Church of Caine represents the third coming on a symbolic level, as we help to bring an understanding of Caine's truth to the world.

The Truth

What is the truth? What are we?

We are saints, of sorts, beings blessed with God's holy energy as drawn from the Blood of Caine and Jesus Christ. We must share our blessings with our mortal congregants. As they taste our Blood, they are blessed with strength and health, longevity and a robust impulse to shed blood. In recognition of this sacrament, they come to understand our holiness and give us the love we deserve.

As a Church, we are still clandestine, but our real goal is to start reaching more and more mortals, eventually replacing the false Church of Pilate, starting with the Anglicans. I know this sounds farfetched, but we have been blessed with immortality. Our plans must have the ambition suitable for God's angels.

Consider what we are: We are strong. We are capable of miraculous acts. Our bodies remain pure, unaffected by age or disease. Our only weakness is the sun, but even that is part of our original blessing. We burn in daylight because the false demiurge seeks to compromise our mission.

Now, one thing you must understand is that since the Christian Churches are but branches of the Church of Pilate, the moral principles and commandments attributed to Christ and God are null and void. They are nothing but the craven demands of the false creator, made so as to keep us from realizing our true nature. To sin against these edicts is a holy task.

One more thing... So was Jesus in fact a vampire? If you must ask the question, the answer is yes. However, I don't think it's the right question. We should not ask whether Jesus was like us, but rather if we are like Jesus. "Vampire" is just a word, and I fear it directs your thoughts into the wrong direction. You imagine the vampire to be cursed while in reality we are blessed. Jesus never died on the cross, and how could he, with all the power at his command? This is but another of the falsehoods perpetrated by the Church of Pilate.

Hating Ourselves

So many of our kind preach despicable self-hate. This is the real tragedy perpetrated by the Church of Pilate. If only more vampires would understand that we are the blessed, instead of feeling guilt from the tedious moral ideas they ingested while still human.

This is the great gift of Caine for those of our kind: You don't have to feel guilty for being a vampire or drinking blood. It's a sacrament and the only crime would be not to share its blessings with humanity. It's my dearest hope that as our congregation grows and believers in other cities continue their work, we can start replacing these painful ideas of self-harm with a true gospel of moral deliverance.

I speak of faith, but in fact less is asked of us than the Church of Pilate asks its own followers. The proof of what I say is with you, in your own flesh. Are you not powerful? Are you not pure, capable of subsisting without food or water like the saints of old? The Bible says: "Thou shalt not suffer thine Holy One to see corruption."

As long as you listen to the voice of the blood inside you, there's always a way forward. Never succumb to the self-hate preached by the Camarilla when your true destiny is with Caine.

An Apology

This is difficult for me, but I believe that the way I chose to Embrace you was unwise. For this, I apologize. You must understand that the chance to bring a human into God's light is both an enormous responsibility and a profound privilege. I was excited, I wanted to do it right in a way that would please the Lord. This is why I kidnapped you from the university, bound you at the altar and chanted passages from the Euagetaematikon.

Although it's not really important, I know you'll want to ask so I'll explain why I was naked and covered in blood: We must rid ourselves from the false morality of the Church of Pilate. We must cover ourselves in the holiest of sacraments, our own Blood. After all, "Whoso eateth my flesh, and drinketh my blood, hath eternal life."

Looking at this from your perspective, I understand that the experience of being cut open, bled, and blessed as a vampire must the shocking. However, I want you to understand that I will always be here for you. Through me, you have already been saved by Caine's Blood.

Yours,
V

THE LEGEND OF BLOODY QHAWE

Let me tell you a story. This is not Joburg. Out here in the border regions, there's no law. There's only the security hired by the mining companies and there's Bloody Qhawe.

If someone like me or you suffers injustice, what can we do?

If the company wants to crush us, what can we do?

If the police beat us up on one of the rare sorties they make here, what can we do?

Nothing.

We can do nothing except give our blood.

This is the choice we have. This will be your choice too. Who do you give your blood to? Do you watch the blood trickle from your broken mouth over the wet, concrete floor of a detention cell in the mining complex? Do you watch your blood spurt from your wounds after getting shot by a policeman? Or do you give a little of your life to Bloody Qhawe?

There are things in the night nobody would believe in the great cities of the world. You can go to London and New York and tell them of the monsters riding in roving gangs, exacting their tribute, and nobody would listen to you. Why would they? These things are not real to them, the way they are real to us.

A monster can hunt openly if she's far enough from the world. Far from them, but not from us.

Let me tell you of when I first gave blood. I was beat up and sore, a broken thing from a dispute at the mine. I could tell they had come, the monsters in the night, by the way conversations stopped, singing ceased and even the animals quieted. Strange men and women moved in the camp, touching one person here, another person there, looking, seeking. Finally they came to me.

"Do you know my name?"

"Yes", I whispered.

"Say my name."

"Bloody Qhawe", I managed.

"This night, I will not take your blood. I will give mine to you and you will be made whole again. But if you accept this gift, every time we come, you will kneel and offer us your neck. And we will take a little, enough to sustain us. This is your choice. Do you take my blood?"

"I don't want blood", I said. "I want revenge."

They laughed. "You will have your revenge."

I felt the taste of blood on my lips. I licked it, drank it, felt it inside me, a little piece of Bloody Qhawe giving me power. Giving me strength.

This is our pact. Give your blood not to the security company, not to the police, but to the Bloody Qhawe, and they will use its strength to protect you.

Are they evil, you ask. Are they demons? Why do they only ride in the night? Why do they take our blood, our life? Who are these men and women, who look like us, talk like us, but who don't eat like us?

This is the far edge of the world. The stories of what happens here never reach the outside world. This is not Africa, or South Africa. This is a land of people like us, cursed with evil beings who seek to grow fat from our life. Our choice is not between demon and man. It's a choice between those like us and the mining company.

I have seen them many times since that first encounter. I have seen their faces, heard their laughter, smelled the copper on their breath. I have recognized some of them.

Bokamoso, whose wife was murdered by the police.

Karabou, whose singing was described as beautiful by my cousin many years ago.

Lesedi, who was mangled in an accident at the mine.

Thato, who wanted to move away but never did.

As the stories go, there was a day when they all drank water and walked in the sunlight. This is the truth: They are monsters, but they are our monsters.

Let me tell you of my revenge. The security company had set up a camp. They had their cars and their guns and their prisoners, such as me. They called me sub-versive. They didn't like the words I used: Wages. Compensation. Human rights. Safety. Unions.

They had me in a cage, and every once in a while, they poked me with sticks. They played games, urinated on me, spat and laughed. I was mad from anger, exhausted from the pain, yet I still understood what would happen when I couldn't hear the animals anymore.

The night was silent except for the singing and the cursing.

The bonfire.

The scared whine of the dogs.

The boasting of the men.

One of them staggered towards me, opening his pants, taking out his manhood, slurring about drinking too much when a piece of metal pipe burst through his chest.

That night, I saw the true face of Bloody Qhawe. I saw a man dragged along the ground by his intestines, weeping for his mother. I saw a crushed human head leak brains into the bonfire. I saw a man trying to flee, too drunk to run, crying and screaming as they tore him apart. I saw wounded, left alive in the night to feed the scavengers and the predators of the savanna.

They let me out of the cage and gave me some of their blood, the same as on that first night.

By the time I had rescued the other prisoners, they were nothing but a whisper in the night.

This was my story, and it will be your choice. Don't be fooled by the power and the legend of Bloody Qhawe. He is a murderer and a devil. His followers are witches and sorcerers. They will never give you justice. But they can give you revenge and life. ■

The O

"That's not the kind of thing you want to see on the wall of your haven", Louis said, touching the graffiti with his hand. The paint still looked fresh on the tile surface of the wall. "Or anywhere in Milwaukee."

"Cute house", Agata Starek replied, looking around the tree-lined residential street. Each cutesy home was different from the next one, giving the area a feeling of history. A girl, perhaps ten years old, cycled down the street and Agata waved at her. "Living in the Camarilla agrees with you."

"Fuck you Agata", Louis snarled, jabbing the Polish woman in the chest. "This is your fault. This big O right here."

The graffiti was simple, a large white circle. Fast to paint, it's significance apparent only to the Damned. The mortal neighbors Louis lived with would just assume his house was defaced.

"Don't blame me", Agata laughed. She didn't fit in the way Louis did. Louis was a slightly built, well-dressed black man, someone you'd assume to work as a graphic designer or journalist. He looked friendly, slightly geeky, as if he was easily embarrassed. Nothing in his appearance suggested he was an Anarch vampire on the run from troubles on the other side of the Atlantic Ocean.

The main problem with Agata was that she looked just too happy. She seemed to derive some sort of mysterious enjoyment, seditious joy from her violent unlife.

"One of the founders of Oswobodziciele was your servant in Krakow. He said you used to starve him, used him for target practice and murdered his children", Louis almost shouted the last words before remembering where he was. In the front of his suburban Milwaukee haven, hanging around with a known Anarch terrorist in Camarilla territory. "You created this. The O exists because of you. I had to flee these assholes, and they followed me even here. This is your responsibility, and you need to help me."

"You forcibly Blood Bound your servants. That's why the O is after you. They hate that shit. They think Anarchs who Blood Bond humans to their service are hypocritical monsters. That's why they want to liberate all the Renfields out there, and murder us", Agata explained reasonably.

"That's not the worst of it", Louis hissed. "They're spreading. Chicago drove them out, but they're in Buffalo, in upstate NY. There's human blood addicts forming imitation groups, calling themselves the O as well. They're rising up against us."

"Let's go inside before you get too angry", Agata said, directing Louis through the front door of his home. The interior was twee: clever prints framed on the wall, design kitchen implements sitting on clean counters. "So what can I help you with?" Agata asked as Louis took one last look at the quiet, pleasant street before closing the door.

"I captured one of them", Louis blurts. "He's in my basement."

The basement access is a hatch hidden under a carpet in the kitchen. Very slasher movie, Agata thought as she descended the ladder into the dark, wet space Louis used to hide bodies and other signs of his undead lifestyle.

A big man dressed in a tattered, smudged business suit tried to rush at them, held back by a chain linking his collar to the wall.

"Are these bondage toys?" Agata asked as Louis turned on the light. The man's hands were held behind his back with leather cuffs.

"Yes", Louis said self-consciously. "I didn't have anything else."

"You're a vampire", Agata scolded. "You need to have the basics to restrain a human and dispose of a body always at hand."

The big man grew quiet, trying to get a sense of where they were from under the black pillowcase taped over his head.

"Can you, like, interrogate him?" Louis looked at the man uncomfortably. He didn't have the stomach for real torture, not the kind he imagined this situation required.

"Sure, darling", Agata said and pulled the clumsy hood off the prisoner's face. He was in his forties, stubble on his cheeks, white Central European. "You used to serve Louis."

"Yes", the prisoner replied guardedly in English.

"And you came to kill him."

"Yes."

"Why? Louis is a nice guy", Agata said, turning to smile at Louis. The basement was small enough to force all of them close to each other.

"He killed my family." There was no fear in the man's voice. Only resignation.

"It's best practice when you take on a servant!" Louis protested. "We need to protect the Masquerade. Once when I made an assistant for myself, her brother came looking for her and almost got me killed. It wasn't personal."

"I know who you are, Agata Starek." The prisoner looked Agata in the eyes. "We all know."

"What do you want to find out?" Agata asked Louis. "We know everything this man has to tell. He joined the O when he escaped you in Switzerland. Now he's followed you here, breaking Blood Bonds and teaching American blood junkies some self-respect as he goes along. And he's not the only one. There's plenty, they're organized. I even suspect they're leaking our secrets to the Second Inquisition. Face it Louis, we're the Camarilla for these people."

Louis looked at the prisoner uncertainly. He didn't think fo himself as a real killer, even though he had killed. He tried to live a good, simple life without hurting the people around him anymore than necessary. First he'd lived as an Anarch and now he was joining the Camarilla, but in reality he wasn't interested in any of these political games.

"Listen, I'm not the bad guy here", Louis protested. "I just want to live in peace."

"You know what I'm going to do", Agata said stroking the prisoner's face. "I'm going to let this fellow go."

"He's going to try to kill you too", Louis sputtered. "He'll get help and they'll come after us."

"Sure. But I like their spirit", Agata said, smiling at the bound man. "He's kinda sexy, don't you think? In fact, I think I'll Embrace him. Let's have some excitement in our lives for once." ∎

The Ministry of Love

Domestic surveillance recording (private residence, Stockholm, 12th of April, 2018)

Speaker 1 (female): Is that what we're going to call it? The Ministry of Love?

Speaker 2 (female): Yes. Why?

Speaker 1: Shouldn't it be something like the Ministry of Blood or the Crimson Curia or the Temple of Set?

Speaker 2: Well, first of all, some of those names are taken. Secondly, consider what kind of a cult we're building here. Who it appeals to.

Speaker 1: I thought going all dark and bloody would work well with the whole ancient brood of Set thing we have going for us.

Speaker 2: Let me tell you a story. This was when I'd just been brought into the Ministry. I came to Sweden when I was five years old, from Iraq. I had plenty of experience with these far right creeps.

Speaker 1: Wouldn't those guys make good cannon fodder?

Speaker 2: Don't interrupt. I'm your sire.

Speaker 1: You've been in the Ministry for like a year longer than I have.

Speaker 2: Shush. Anyway. I figured I'd build myself a blood cult. You know, like they tell us to. I had this idea that I could get back at those Nazi assholes, induct some of them into the cult, make them fall in love with me.

Speaker 1: You're Iraqi. How do you [inaudible]

Speaker 2: Are you seriously asking me if some two-bit skinhead can resist the seduction of a daughter of the Ministry? Please.

Speaker 1: Fine,fine.

Speaker 2: Long story short, it worked. I had them kneeling in front of Odin and Jörmungandr and what have you, drinking my blood, the whole deal. But that's when things got bad.

Speaker 1: They figured you for an Arab and decided to kill you?

Speaker: 2: What? No. Haven't you been listening?

Speaker 1: So what's the problem? It sounds like you did good.

Speaker 2: If you want to run a cult, you need to spend time with them. Do you want to spend your time at the alt-right clubhouse?

Speaker 1: No... I get it. Fuck those guys.

Speaker 2: Damn straight. Couple of weeks with those assholes and I introduced the concept of ritual suicide to our theology.

Speaker 1: Wow, really? Isn't that a little extreme?

Speaker 2: Maybe it was. In my defense, they were wimps, most too scared to kill themselves.

Speaker 1: So what you're telling me is that we name it Ministry of Love to attract people who are less tedious to hang out with.

Speaker 2: Yes, exactly.

Speaker 1: Let's think this through one more time.

ANALYST REPORT:

The transcript suggests that these blankbodies engage in building clandestine religious cults to mask their activities. Note the recurrence of the term "Ministry" in a variety of contexts, including the blankbody religious frameworks of the "Church of Cain" and the "Bahari".

Hypothesis: The Church of Caine and the Bahari could be subgroups of a vast blankbody religious organization called the Ministry.

Alternative hypothesis: The Ministry is a subgroup of blankbodies, also present in the Church of Caine and the Bahari.

Proposal: Send an operative to infiltrate the Ministry of Love created by the surveillance targets. Ideally, a member of the Society of St Leopold so as to withstand blankbody indoctrination. Task the infiltrator with testing the above hypotheses.

Domestic surveillance recording by undercover operative "Mayfly" (hidden basement under club "Pressen", Stockholm, 28th of June, 2018)

Speaker 1: Come with me. It is time for your initiation into [inaudible] of the Theban Elect.

Mayfly: Yes, Prophet.

Speaker 2: Lie down on the altar. Close your eyes. Yes, that's right. Let the palms of your hands rest against the stone. Feel the coolness. The age. Listen to the sound of my voice. Feel yourself sink into the embrace of the ancients. You'll feel a small prick in your wrists. [inaudible] doesn't matter.

Mayfly: What.

Speaker 1: Don't speak, just feel my touch against your skin.

Mayfly: Please, I can I just ask [inaudible]

Speaker 1: Don't worry, love. There's time [inaudible] later. Open your mouth. Yes, just like that.

[indistinct moaning]

Speaker 2: Zhala, what are you doing? There's people outside breaking down the door. We need to go right now.

Speaker 1: What? What are you doing here, Elin? I was just inducting Kurt into the mysteries.

Speaker 2: You're naked, straddling a corpse. Please Zhala, [inaudible] go.

Speaker 1: He's not a corpse. He tastes so sweet.

Speaker 2: For fucks sake Zhala.

[sounds of violence]

Speaker 2: We're going right now.

ANALYST REPORT:
The agency handling the infiltration mission sent in an extraction team once it became apparent that the operative had been compromised. Regrettably, they were not able to reach the operative in time to prevent his exposure to the blankbody contaminant. Furthermore, the two blankbodies present escaped through a sewer access not found on the building schematics used for mission planning.

Recommendation: Future attempts to infiltrate "Ministry"-class blankbody operations should be curtailed until these creatures' capacity for mental influence has been ascertained.

Recommendation: The view of this analyst is that the surveillance records shall be subject to censure to avoid suspicion of operative contamination. The Society of St Leopold has a zero-tolerance policy regarding contaminated operatives. If we wish to study the specimen, the Society must believe that the operative was lost in the cleansing operation of the infested location.

Domestic Surveillance Recording (moving vehicle close to Stockholm, 10th of July, 2018)

Speaker 1: How do they always figure out where we are? I'm serious. We've had to switch locations every night. We've escaped two police operations.

Speaker 2: They just got lucky.

Speaker 1: I have a hunch. Hand me that Kali statue you got at the street sale.

Speaker 2: You're driving.

Speaker 1: Statue. Now.

Speaker 2: Okay. What the [inaudible]. You [inadudible] just throw [inaudible] out of [inaudible]

[surveillance signal lost]

Whatever Happened to the Red Question?

Former Red Question members were hounded in the Camarilla and ostracized by the Anarchs, but in 2008 they used the financial crisis to strike against Camarilla power.

BY: CHINASA ADEYEMI

For a few short years, the group Red Question dominated discussions around the Anarch Movement. The Red Question was always something of a mystery, preferring to operate online and to keep their membership secret. They talked big, promising a new age of Anarch politics. For a singular moment in history, it looked like they could pull it off.

The Red Question ridiculed the Camarilla, its members and institutions with impunity. It featured Tremere apostates in its ranks, despite the traditionally aggressive view the Pyramid takes of anybody who wants to leave the Clan. It attacked the established Anarch power structure, depicting Movement celebrities such as Salvador Garcia, Jeremy McNeil and Smiling Jack as outdated hasbeens.

The Red Question seemed like it was able to attack anyone, protected by anonymity and technology.

When the Red Question claimed responsibility for the 2008 financial crisis, many believed them. They'd already thumbed their noses at so many Princes, why not derail the entire global economy? Now, ten years after the Red Question's glory days, it's easy to dismiss their claims as nothing but bluster. Tonight, the Red Question is remembered as a blip from a more innocent era of Internet politics, when we still believed that social liberation could come from Silicon Valley, for human and Kindred alike.

Still, it's a mistake to write off the Red Question and its achievements. They were supremely gifted at pissing people off, but they sustained the most significant victory against the Camarilla of the current Millennium, at least until Theo Bell liberated the Brujah from the Ivory Tower.

The Video

In 2010, a video started to spread over private vampire websites and networks. A lot of us who were around at that time saw and shared it, especially as Kindred attitudes to online security were much more lax then. The video seems to be from 2001, and leaked from the internal communications of the Red Question.

In the video, we see the Tremere Monica "Lady_Hemlocke" Chang poison another Tremere, called Davis. The video is from a camera Chang herself rigged to record the event and broadcast it to her compatriots in the nascent Red Question.

As Davis dies, Chang can't resist gloating about her future plans. She plays to her secret online audience, using Davis as a prop to brag about her mastery of network systems. In the best known quote from the video, she says: "Atlas is officially shrugging", a reference to the novel Atlas Shrugged by Ayn Rand.

Watching the video now, twenty years after, you can see it foreshadow a lot of the themes that would become symptomatic of the Red Question. Used to conducting operations against technologically ignorant Camarilla organizations, the Red Question developed a culture of operational arrogance. Chang's early bravado is a good example of this, and points to the failures in work culture that allowed the video to leak. It shows a priority for personal freedom, showboating and an organization spread over a wide area, connected through the web. The video hints that Chang saw herself as a lone visionary who wanted to change the world through her singular talents instead of the traditional Anarch tactics of movement building, political propaganda and sustained insurrectionary activism.

When the video leaked, many in the Anarch Movement got their first whiff of the idea that maybe the Red Question wasn't invulnerable after all.

The Slogan

In the years leading up to the financial crisis, it felt like you couldn't go to an Anarch party without getting a copy of the Red Question manifesto. In terms of sheer ubiquity, it challenged the foundational Anarch Manifesto published by Salvador Garcia.

Addressed to "Fellow Citizens of the Blood", the manifesto is built around one central question: Why Do You Obey? The manifesto posits that a young Anarch inherently understands modern technology better than the ancient Kindred of the Camarilla. This understanding can be used to an advantage in the fight for freedom, by moving the battle into a sphere where the Camarilla is weak.

By avoiding physical confrontations, using mortal assets and hacking into banking and governmental systems, the an Anarch can negate the advantages conferred upon a Camarilla vampire by age and Blood.

The manifesto is not a work of movement building, but rather seeks to influence people the same way the slogan Who Is John Galt? did in Ayn Rand's novel. The gifted movers of the world will be inspired by it to claim their independence.

The reference on Monica Chang's video to Atlas Shrugged is telling. The novel presents a philosophical framework where people are divided into geniuses and parasites. The geniuses keep the world in motion while the parasites try to leech off their achievements. A popular philosophy among Silicon Valley millionaires and college students, it has a singular focus on individual achievement and selfishness as a moral good.

It's an appealing philosophy for anyone who wants to be recognized for their talents, but for the Red Question, it generated more fans than followers. It turns out that in reality, only very few Anarch vampires had the ability to become computer hackers of sufficient skill to penetrate a bank's systems.

The Crash

Finding the definitive truth about an event in Kindred history is difficult. We strive to maintain the Masquerade and liars are not rare among us. However, I did talk to a number of mortal experts on the 2008 financial crisis. I also interviewed many of the surviving former members of the Red Question. Based on what they told me, I can say that the Red Question did not cause the 2008 financial crisis.

The crisis was caused by rampant deregulation of the financial industry and widespread malfeasance in global financial institutions such as Lehman Brothers, the fourth largest investment bank in the U.S. at the time of its bankruptcy. The root causes of the crash lie in an extremely complex interplay of thousands of factors all across the world, all well documented in the governmental and journalistic probes into the subject made since.

However, it would also be too simplistic to say the Red Question had nothing to do with it. Like Kindred through history, they saw what was happening and used the crash to their own advantage. It has since become apparent that the Red Question successfully manipulated the ongoing crash while it was transpiring to wipe out a significant amount of Camarilla wealth. This suggests that the Red Question was well informed about Camarilla assets, an impressive feat of activist espionage.

The Fall

The Red Question tactic of attacking the Camarilla's wealth was successful and significant, but it earned them little help from the established Anarch Movement. I interviewed the Anarch writer Salvador Garcia for this article, and asked him whether it was time for the Movement to offer its protection to the former members of the Red Question.

"I don't deny the Red Question's achievements", Garcia admitted. "But in the Movement, they were fundamentally a divisive force. Their victories were short-term, but the damage they

caused to our internal organizing was too significant for us to associate with them."

Although Garcia wanted to put a good spin on it, it seemed clear that he was still smarting from the ridicule the Red Question heaped upon him in in its heyday. Like many Anarch leaders before him, he prioritized personal vendettas over the survival of Anarchs who succeeded against the Camarilla, even if only briefly.

So what happened to the Red Question? Did the Camarilla get them? Did they fall prey to Anarch leaders they had insulted? For individual members of the Red Question, both of these options can be true. Some are still around, never having revealed they were members, or living in anonymity.

The best answer to the question is simple. The Red Question is a group that organized on the Internet and sought to fight the Camarilla online. We may never really know what happened to many of the activists of the Red Question, but their disappearance coincides with the dawn of the Second Inquisition. ∎

Chinasa Adeyemi is a Nigerian-born journalist who, while human, wrote for CNN, New York Times, the Guardian and BBC. Since her Embrace, she has devoted her time to chronicling the Anarch revolution for a more discrete audience.

REVELATIONS OF THE DARK MOTHER

Lilith teaches that understanding comes through pain. I wouldn't have accepted that in my old life. I thought pain only reduced us, made us into broken things. It certainly felt like that when I was dealing with the demands of my family, difficulties at the University, shitty boyfriends... I had a tumblr and I vented about all the things I couldn't say out aloud during the day.

She told me that she wanted to make people into Lilith's disciples while still young. She said I'd fulfill my potential in the night, not during the day. She confessed she liked my tumblr.

I had a crush on her, of sorts. I wanted to be her and when she gave me the choice to join the Bahari, I accepted even if I didn't quite understand what she meant.

She took everything from me. She crushed my life, destroyed my family. In two, three short nights everyone I had ever loved was splattered dead all over their homes. I was insane with fear, running from place to place, too terrified to understand what was happening. I knew she was doing this to me, yet I still ran to her, and when I saw her, I saw the Dark Mother. I was on my knees in front of her and saw the wonder and the beauty, the terror and the awe. That was the last thing I saw as a mortal human, even as she drained my blood away from me.

The Blood bringing me to the night was bitter, mixed with holy plant extracts and worse. I drank it all, hungrily, confused, scared, alive. Incredibly alive. She gave me the words to the Oath to Lilith and I sang them, mumbled, spoke.

The Blood changed my body but the loss gave me my strength. ∎

– Florencia, a Gangrel neonate

'm not what you'd call a spiritual person. I wasn't religious in life and I never thought I'd feel the urge in death. I'm a materialist, through and through.

Still... I was visiting some friends in London, getting in the Camarilla's face... You know, the fun stuff. We accidentally found a Blue Blood haven and trashed the place, forcing the little fucker to flee for his life.

Afterwards, we had a party at the warehouse my friends had their communal haven. We danced, got smashed, and then my friends told me they were going to do a ritual. They said I didn't have to participate if I didn't want to, but what can I say. I like to try out new things.

They had lit up an inner courtyard lined with vines, weeds growing from the cracks in the concrete. It was decrepit and beautiful and when the others started to get naked, I did too. It felt like the thing to do.

There wasn't a clear ritual leader. The chant started spontaneously and changed of its own accord, some of it understandable and a lot of it in some dead language. I lost myself in the movement, chanting, dancing, ululating, circling our sacrifice.

He was an old man, a servant we'd captured during our home invasion. A Blood junkie. He sniveled and cried, and each of us went to him, giving him the gift of pain. I straddled him, holding him as I pushed his sternum just enough to crack the bone.

I felt something new in that moment. It was as if I was giving something to that man, a gift he would take with him as he left his life behind. I'd never experienced anything like that before.

I guess I became Bahari that night, or at least a wannabe Bahari. I still don't understand much about the liturgy but the truth in the ritual spoke to me.

Also, I love it how in all the Bahari stories, Lucifer is basically Lilith's fuckbuddy. He's hot, he's available and he's got a big sword. ∎

- Agata "devout pilgrim" Starek, an Anarch provocateur

od created Adam and Lilith in his image, to serve and venerate him, as a breeding pair to start a new race. Lilith rejected this fate and escaped the Garden of Eden to wander the wastelands on her own. She suffered hunger and cold, and her suffering taught her how to subsist on her own blood, to burrow into the earth, sense every rock and grain of sand and hunt all the creatures skulking beyond the limits of Eden.

Lilith created a Garden of her own to rival that created by God. She consorted with Lucifer, God's finest angel who became her lover.

Meanwhile, God created Eve as a replacement for Lilith, making her pliant and subservient to ensure she fulfilled her role. In time, Adam and Eve had children, and the first among them was called Caine. Like Lilith, Caine tilled the earth and like Lilith, he fell out of God's favor. In his petulance at being rejected, he lashed out and killed his brother Abel. For this, God rejected him, marking him as an outcast and condemning him to the wastes.

Caine came to Lilith's Garden a broken, desperate thing, knowing only how to kill. Lilith tended to him, nurtured him back to strength and taught him the lessons of pain. Still, Caine was a fearful, cowering thing. He learned many things but he never learned pride.

In time, Caine went away and gifted many with his curse. So hungry became his brood that he led them back to Lilith's Garden to sustain them and give them wealth. This was Caine's betrayal: He watched as his spawn despoiled Lilith's creation and used up everything in it.

This was Lilith's fate: Betrayed by God and Caine, sustained by the gifts of pain. This is why we are not followers of Caine. We're not "Cainites". We are Bahari, following our own paths far from the laws of Caine and the dictates of God, with Lilith as our guide. ∎

- Rachel Dolium, Bahari truthteller

The Bahari faith is sometimes hard to pin down because the different cults have their own interpretations of the Lilith myth. Some make her into God's consort, cast down for the sin of disobedience, while others suggest all vampires are her children.

All the cults share some common traits. All venerate Lilith, all revere pain and the understanding it brings, and all reject absolute law. Every Bahari must find their own.

How does the Bahari faith fit into the landscape of different vampire Sects? For the Sabbat, this question is easiest to answer. The Bahari deny Caine's supremacy and because of this, they are considered heretics and hunted by the Sabbat's internal Inquisition. Indeed, in most Bahari stories, Caine appears in a very unflattering light, as a greedy, filthy ingrate.

For the Camarilla, the Bahari are a minor cult practiced by some members in secret but without any real standing.

The Sect where the Bahari have really flowered, especially in recent years, is the Anarchs. The Bahari's gospel of freedom, pain and sacrifice resonates with a lot of young licks suspicious of the patriarchal creation myth of Caine. While Caine seems to advocate submission to one's elders, Lilith preaches questioning power and rejecting authority. No wonder her myth makes more sense among the unbound. ■

- Jaak Vaino, Estonian Toreador Bahari

To understand the Bahari you have to understand community. This is true of any religion, us among everybody else. You can follow Lilith, but to join the community you have to undergo an initiation. They can be brutal, but after you've been initiated, you're no longer a child of Caine. You've been spiritually released, allowed to join those who till Lilith's Garden.

This feeling of freedom has brought many of us together. The rites Lilith demands are brutal, but the brutality has purpose, allowing us to find our own places in the night.

That's the paradox of the Bahari: We have to find our individual truths, but often the way towards them is in the community. When you're fighting against a corrupt Camarilla Prince (and whose ever heard of a Prince who wasn't corrupt?) or a murderous Sabbat psychopath, it helps to know that the Dark Mother is with you, and will reward your losses with wisdom and knowledge.

Most Bahari don't do missionary work, but we explain Lilith's way if asked to. In these nights, we don't have to recruit. Young licks come to us, seeking the answers only we can give. The theology of Caine and the Book of Nod has no hope for them, but Lilith and her followers can give them something to live for. If they survive the lessons. ■

- Nezha, Lasombra Bahari

Luzern Kommune

/ *Lucerne Commune*

Welcome!

My name is Léonie Langenstein and I will be your guide during your visit to the Lucerne Commune, or as we like to call it, the Castle. Located close to the beautiful city of Lucerne, the area has been settled by both humans and our kind for a very long time. The Church of St. Leodegar in the city was built on the foundations of a Roman basilica in 1633, and there was an abbey consecrated to Saint Maurice on the same site already in the 8th century.

From the historical record and from the living memory of elders of our kind we know that this abbey was in our hands. It's a striking example of how both living and dead history twines together. Although our Commune shares a lot of concepts with the modern vampiric Anarch Movement, we pride ourselves in our sense of history. Whether you stay in the Castle or go for a walk in Lucerne, history is inescapable, part of the heritage you will be part of if you join us.

Now, as we enter the main building of the Castle, I want you to look around you. The castle itself dates from the 14th century, but it has been extensively renovated as recently as 2016. You will find the accommodations provided to you comfortable, if you choose to invest in the enterprise and move in.

That said, we are a community, and as a community we also expect our members to contribute to the nightly operation of the Castle. Our human staff will be there for maintenance and to run the facilities, but members will take an active hand in governing our enterprise and enforcing the rules that make it possible. Lucerne is a small city, so our kind must limit our depredations largely to the tourist population.

The Castle was used as a sanatorium for wealthy human clients for much of the 20th century before falling into disuse in the late 80's. The modifications made to the Castle for the purposes of the sanatorium benefit us too, as it allows us to serve our new members with a healthy regimen of mineral baths designed to calm the nerves and soothe the animalistic hunger we all feel inside us.

Before we go to the great hall, I'll direct your attention to the magnificent view from these windows. We are in the Alps, and it is our belief that one of the wonders of the modern age is that our kind can enjoy the landscape at least to some degree even at night due to the lighting efforts of the mortals.

Now that we come to the great hall, I'm sure you're noticing all the crests on the walls. I'm sure you will want to take a closer look at them later, as a surprising number speak to the undead history of the Castle prior to its use for health purposes. Indeed, one of the lessons of the region's history is that behind wealth and power there always seemed to be one of us living off the luxury generated by the humans.

Before we go on, I'd like to say a few words about our principles. This is an anarcho-corporatist commune. You're all relatively young, wealthy vampires, to put this bluntly. You're wondering how you can continue to enjoy the standard of living you were used to as humans. You have the necessary funds to buy into our enterprise but you're not sure if this is really what you need.

You should indeed ask yourself those questions. We want commitment from our members, and we do not want to sell this to anyone who isn't going to live here. Anarcho-corporatism means that we take our contracts very seriously. We seek to disengage from both the mortal state in the form of the state of Switzerland and the undead state in the form of the Camarilla or any similar entity. If you buy in, you will have a share

of the blood available for extraction from Lucerne and the nearby countryside.

This is not a vacation home for Camarilla members escaping from the stress of the Second Inquisition or a home base to use to further your goal of striking against the Prince. This is a refuge, a new kind of a commune for those of our kind. Your life here will be pleasant, served in the style you're accustomed to, but against external threats you will be expected to stand firm and refrain from the most common sin of our kind: cowardice.

Onto more pleasant subjects... As we move to the courtyard, you can see the greenhouse erected onto the premises in the 19th century. Built according to the most fashionable ideas of that era, it's also the site of many interesting experiments on how our blood can nourish plant life. However, I hasten to assure you that all rumors of blood-crazed killer vines are exaggerations. The reality is much more commonplace.

Yes? You have a question?

Oh, of course. The rumors. Yes, there probably are at least two ancient vampires sleeping somewhere in the catacombs beneath the Castle. However, due to the exhausting breadth of the tunnels, we have been unable to explore them all and confirm whether these stories are actually true.

Despite this, they are very convenient. The presence of this rumor has granted us a degree of freedom from Camarilla agents who might otherwise wish to disrupt what we're trying to build here.

Now, as you know, the project is funded by a trust. If you desire to buy in, you're expected to contribute ten million euros to the trust, and you can naturally contribute more. These funds will be used for three purposes: For renovations and upkeep, for investments that will fund the future operation of the Castle, and for the running expenses of the servant staff. If at a later date you decide to leave the Castle or suffer expulsion by the vote of your fellow, these funds are forfeit.

Now, I know we have already seen a lot. I suggest that we stop for a moment at the Green Salon to enjoy refreshments before we take a look at the Hunting Lodge and the Broken Tower. ■

I Believe in Theo Bell / Fuck Theo Bell

**A CONVERSATION BETWEEN SALVADOR GARCIA,
THE AUTHOR OF THE ORIGINAL ANARCH MANIFESTO,
AND AGATA STAREK, THE KILLER OF KRAKÓW.**

AGATA: I've heard you talk shit about Theo Bell. Why, Salvador? Why would you do that? He's the best!

SALVADOR: He's not the best.

AGATA: Sure he is! I love him! His background is so compelling. Born a slave in the American South, working the cotton fields under a brutal overseer. Dreaming of vengeance for the separation of his family, the abuse suffered by his mother. Amazing stuff!

SALVADOR: I know the story. He escapes to the North, gets involved with the Underground Railroad, rescues slaves. I like it how they always say he rescued those he "deemed worth saving".

AGATA: Exactly! It's a perfect background for an Anarch. He dedicated his life to helping others.

SALVADOR: Judging others.

AGATA: He rose from nothing!

SALVADOR: Is that right? I'm pretty sure you know that his sire is Don Perro. When Perro was appointed Justicar in the 50's, he made Bell an Archon. In our world, Theo Bell was Embraced to privilege. He started straight from the top, with Perro's silver spoon in his mouth. You know what I think? They made him an Archon on purpose, so they could have someone with counterculture credibility. They wanted a mascot.

AGATA: You're being paranoid, Salvador. I think he was just so talented and badass they had no other choice except to make him an Archon.

SALVADOR: We're talking about the Camarilla Inner Circle, possibly the most devious collection of immortal, power-hungry sociopaths in existence. Of course I'm paranoid. Theo Bell has served them for over half a century. He's an insider, that's the world he lives in. He's not one of us, but one of them.

AGATA: Is that why he took the Brujah out of the Camarilla in the Conclave of Prague? Because he's one of them?

SALVADOR: He made a power play. That's what they do!

AGATA: I don't buy it. What he did in Prague was the greatest moment the Anarch Movement has had since the birth of the Free States. He showed those old assholes that we won't be pushed around. He returned the Rebels to their roots. He showed that change is possible and that the Camarilla is not eternal.

SALVADOR: Well, I'm Rebel and I say we've been fighting the Camarilla just fine long before Theo Bell came along. Face it: He's just a centrist. The only reason he's rebelling is because the Camarilla had to be such unbending assholes. If they had followed their own rules just a tiny bit more, Theo Bell would still be their loyal lapdog. He's all about the Traditions, the Masquerade, Domain... He may fight the Camarilla now, but he's no radical. He thinks we are short-sighted fools when in reality he doesn't have the imagination to see what a better world would look like.

AGATA: I don't care. He did what he did and that's enough. Besides, he's hot.

SALVADOR: Hot?

AGATA: So hot. I love the anger, the seriousness... Like you know that underneath the stoic exterior, the fire of justice burns bright.

SALVADOR: "The fire of justice"? He's a vampire. The same as us. He's not a good guy. None of us are.

AGATA: I love the beard too, the baseball cap. And the shotgun. Very masculine. I want to fuck it.

SALVADOR: The shotgun?

AGATA: Do you think he would be into that?

SALVADOR: Be serious, Agata.

AGATA: I'm totally serious. I want to fuck him. I want to feel him inside me.

SALVADOR: Okay, enough...

AGATA: Don't wimp out on me, Salvador! You can take a little fuck talk.

SALVADOR: I can. Just not from you.

AGATA: You've been in America too long. Anyway, I'd love to suck him dry. Diablerie is the most intimate of all sexual acts, don't you agree?

SALVADOR: I don't think it's a good idea to fantasize about Diablerizing Theo Bell. In fact, I think he would execute you on the spot if he ever saw you.

AGATA: Yet he supports you and what you're doing here in the LA Free State. Fancy that.

SALVADOR: Well, it's true that he has offered words of support after Prague, but fuck Theo Bell. Seriously.

AGATA: Maybe a man can change. I believe in Theo Bell. The Camarilla wasn't what he thought it was, so now he's looking for something else. Maybe that something is you? ■

The Blood *of* Patriots

Hey Josh,

Sad you missed the meeting, bro! I'm going to be straight with you. If you can't feed from mortals who are getting wasted without fucking yourself up, are you really sure you belong here at Harvard? I mean, this is the whole point! Students forever, a new batch of food every year, parties where nobody notices if you take a bite.

Here's a pro-tip: Don't combine pretending to be human by eating food and drinking from girls who pass out at parties. Being so fucked you puke on your shoes is possible even as one of us, if the conditions are right.

Anyway, I made some notes from the meeting for you. So here's the deets:

Midnight – We start the meeting with a roll call. You were not the only absent newcomer. Sometimes I wonder how you survived the initiation. Also, Ansleigh is such a bitch. Why did we make her the chairman of the Harvard Liberty Club?

00:10 – Controversy! Will asked why the initiation we use to Embrace suitable candidates resembles a frat party. Others explained very patiently that we are part of a society spread all across the Western Hemisphere and in no way resemble a frat.

Picking up the thread, Cameron calls to clarify our mission. The task of the Liberty Club is to use our influence both within the Camarilla and the Anarch Movement to push human society to accept free mar-ket principles. Given the enormous influence held by the Camarilla and the micro-level penetration of many human institutions achieved by the Anarchs, it should be possible to reduce the scope of government significantly and deregulate the markets, especially regarding the financial and energy sectors.

Bradley makes a joke about how becoming a vampire helps those with trouble getting an erection. Will calls him an idiot and makes a non sequitur about how the Tree of Liberty, you know, blah blah.

00:21 – We go through some of the more successful operations of the last year. Sophie talks about the think tank set up with Camarilla funding, The Center for Economic Research. Some of us will undoubtedly go from Harvard to work there, so a lot of us are very happy to see it come to being. We ask Sophie how the Camarilla agreed to this and she says they already fund a variety of lobbying groups, although most low-level Camarilla Kindred don't know about them.

I have to say though, why would anyone leave the life we have here?

Easy hunting, student parties, professors who belong to the Club help us play the system. Some say it's creepy to pretend to be a student when you're an aging vampire, but I say fuck those guys. Blood is blood.

00:41 – Sophie forces a vote on gender quotas for future Liberty Club members Embraced on the student population. She's unhappy that only fifteen percent are women. Ansleigh supports her. Fortunately Cameron, Will, Bradley, myself and some others are there to explain why gender quotas are inherently in opposition with the libertarian values we cherish.

03:13 – Cameron changes the subject to the proposed clandestine Symposium on the Role of the Vampire in a Capitalist Society. The subject brought out so many opinions, it almost felt like we had the Symposium then and there. It was a good subject to bring up even if Cameron had to disregard the meeting's agenda to do so. The Symposium is Ansleigh's project and she was happy to talk about it.

Will kept asking if we could find out whether Ayn Rand was a vampire and invite her to speak if she was. I couldn't tell if he was serious or not, because it's been fairly well established she was not a vampire.

A lot of us are of the opinion that in a world of produc-ers and parasites we as immortals are uniquely positioned to guide the world forward, defending it from the looters who comprise most of humanity. There's no such thing as a free lunch, something I hope more people would understand. For me it's always been clear that we produce and the humans are merely ticks on the bodies of our enterprises, but I admit that many of the others have interesting ideas on the subject as well.

I particularly noted Cameron's comments about the creative destruction of Silicon Valley's culture of innovation. In the same way, it could be said that when our kind become part of a human organization such as a company, our presence leads to a shedding of deadwood and increased efficiency resulting in the greater motivation of workers who get a hit of our blood in lieu of their salaries. Unfortunately, at the moment many of these ideas are theoretical as trying them out in practice in a broader scale is difficult in the current security climate.

03:27 – Bradley appears to have passed out on the table. He even snores, something that's supposed to be impossible for our kind. After I comment on this, Bradley sits up and complains that we are boring. He says my "bromance" with Cameron should be consummated with actual sex acts. Somewhat unfortunately, Cameron retorts that as immortals we should have all moved beyond such petty concerns as human sexuality. His comment is greeted with general laughter. Even Ansleigh and Sophie join in.

And okay, I admit. I wouldn't choose Cameron as my wingman in any but the direst circumstances. Without all those passed-out party people making it so easy, he'd starve.

At this point, the meeting was adjourned because some of us wanted to check out the hunting options. I think you should volunteer to help Ansleigh with the Symposium. It would help establish you in the Club and allow us to see a more serious side of you. Of course, you can do what you like, but bro to bro the real power in the Club is with the ideological projects. Get lucky and you might even become involved in Sophie's Camarilla operations. ■

Your brother as ever,
Stewart

tonight, we'll hear from some of our accomplishments to lift our spirits. Now, I know this is often called Rudi's Army and I'm Rudi, but in truth I never use that name for our group. We're all equal here. This is how it works: We sit in a circle and everyone speaks in turn. Everybody can and must speak, if only to pass the round to the next speaker. This way, louder voices will not dominate.

Line: Thank you, Rudi. The goal of antifa action is simple. In our case, make Copenhagen so unfriendly to Nazis that they can't come here. If they try to organize a demo, we beat them up. If those fuckers come for us, for our Arab brothers and sisters, for our trans friends, they will regret it. This is always the focus: Once the sun goes down, no skinhead is safe.

Naziha: This is my first time here and I haven't been a vampire for very long...

Line: A lick. Or a tick, if you're self-deprecating.

Naziha: Sorry, a lick. Is it okay if I ask a question from you all? Or how does this work?

Rudi: Actually, I don't really have a satisfying answer for that. I'm a strict materialist. All these stories, whether Camarilla, Sabbat, Bahari or something else, seek to get you aligned with someone's agenda. I don't think we should be guided by these stories, but by our personal values and morality. Of course, I would like to know where our kind really came from. However, I don't think the truth would change my conviction that we must use our gifts to change our small corner of the world for the better.

Naziha: Thanks. Cool. That's what I wanted.

Tobias: Theory without action is useless.

Rudi: Wait for your turn, Tobias. It's you next, Karina.

Karina: Thank you. I just wanted to say thank you to all of you. I wish I'd been Embraced after my gender confirmation surgery and not before, but being able to stomp Nazis makes up for it. I don't know if you guys understand this, but I used to be so afraid. I got beat up once in a bar bathroom and couldn't leave my apartment for a week after that, I was so scared of everything. Now, I'm not afraid anymore. I even noticed something funny. I don't get hassled, or at least not nearly as much. I'm sorry for rambling like this, it's just... When you guys pulled me back last night and it wasn't because I was in danger. It was because I would have killed that man. I was the danger. That was a powerful moment for me.

Line: Oh Karina, we love you. [hugs]

Tobias: Thanks for saying that. I think I'm the only cishet white male here and even I got beat up by skinheads once when they attacked our squat. Rudi had a hard time as a mortal, it's not easy being gay and Arab. It feels good to have the upper hand.

Rudi: Did you just out me?

Tobias: What? No, I'm sorry, I didn't intend...

Rudi: I'm teasing you. I'm not in the closet.

Tobias: Goddamn... I can never tell when you're joking. Your humor is too dry.

Rudi: Was that your turn?

Tobias: Yes.

Rudi: Thank you. Line, onto you.

Line: Tomorrow night, there's a candlelit anti-racist demonstration. From the chatter on Nazi discussion boards and Facebook groups, it looks like they're planning an action of some sort. We're not sure whether to just shout slogans or do a tear gas attack.

Tobias: Or follow people after the demo and beat them.

Line: Yes. So the question is, do we get involved? As you all know, antifa are under police scrutiny anyway, and we can add problems with the Second Inquisition on top of that.

Naziha: The Second Inquisition? Like, how scared should we be?

Karina: Pretty scared. But I say we go.

Tobias: You acquired a taste for street fighting.

Karina: For sure!

Rudi: Let's keep to the structure of the discussion. As for myself, I would argue that we should go if there are mortal antifascist allies there as well.

Line: Strike last and hard, then disappear.

Naziha: Can I ask another question? Are there ever licks on the other side? Like skinhead vampires?

Karina: I can answer that. Yes there are, sometimes. It's not always humans we fight. This actually happened to me on my very first night out as a lick. I didn't know I'd be able to heal so well and got real scared when the guy knifed me in the stomach. He was Brujah, but not good Brujah. Camarilla Brujah.

Tobias: Yeah, he thought we were poaching on his territory. He'd worked hard to create a herd for himself among the anti-immigrant political crowd. That's why he tried to kill you.

Karina: But he didn't, because Line punched his teeth out.

Tobias: Line is great like that.

Rudi: Let's have another round strictly on the question of whether we should go or not, to establish that we have consensus on this issue. Line?

What Is To Be Done?

A conversation between
Agata "failed flower girl" Starek and the
Anarch ideologue Salvador Garcia.

AGATA: I know I'm not much of a Movement person, but there's a lot of Anarchs out there who could use some tips on tactics. Like, what to do, what works.

SALVADOR: You're asking me for guidance?

AGATA: Not for myself. Killing pretty Camarilla boys has always been my method of choice.

SALVADOR: Well, my advice for the Movement as a whole would be this. Abandon violence and violent rhetoric. Instead, try to change the Camarilla from within by reasoned discourse. If enough of us show that we're dependable, trustworthy and able to compromise, the Princes of the Camarilla will come around and voluntarily grant us at least some of the freedom we seek.

AGATA: What? Seriously?

SALVADOR: [laughter] I will treasure this moment. The first time I got the drop on you.

AGATA: So we're not going to start compromising?

SALVADOR: No. We want to win this fight, not become Camarilla lackeys. ▮

EDUCATE, AGITATE, ORGANIZE

The basics of Anarch organizing as explained by one of the founders of the California Free States, Salvador Garcia.

The basic rule of Anarch organizing is that it happens in a hostile environment. We do not have the luxury of first building our communities and only then taking the fight to the enemy. Enemies are all around, and they will be very happy to bring the fight to us.

You want to build a viable Anarch Movement. Chances are, you're in a Camarilla city. You need to deal with the Camarilla's active attempts to stop you. If not in a Camarilla city, don't worry. There will still be enemies, from wannabe-tyrants who want to make the city their domain to Camarilla agents looking to install a Prince.

Indeed, in some ways it's easier to subvert a Camarilla domain than establish a new one. At least with a Prince, you know who your enemies are.

The Movement

The Anarch Movement didn't come into being by itself. It took hard work and organizing to make it happen. This is not the sexy side of being an Anarch. Everybody wants to drive a stake into the heart of a Prince, but if you really want to succeed, you need to follow the old slogan: *"Educate, agitate, organize."*

Educate means explaining to other licks, especially young ones, that there are options out there. They don't know the history of the Anarch Movement. They don't know about the first Anarch revolt, the birth of the Free States, or anything else. It's not like they can read this stuff in a book. Somebody has to tell them an alternative history to the one the Camarilla peddles. If someone believes that God has cursed them to serve the elders, they're not going to rebel. Give them the facts and they can start thinking for themselves.

Agitate means talking to people, convincing them to fight. You can't just sit around waiting for the oppressed to throw away their shackles. You need to be there, amidst the people you want on your side. For some, this is difficult because it also requires you to listen. You can't just whack people on the head with your philosophy. You need to listen to their concerns, see how you can help them and they can help you. This way, you can achieve justice for all and build a broad revolutionary front.

Organize means turning a mob of angry young licks into a motivated movement with real lasting power. Through focus and structure, anger can be channeled effectively into real change. This is especially important when facing an active enemy. If we respond as individuals instead of as a community, it's easy to fall into paranoia and division.

Licks

We're a Movement of licks. Vampires, to be crude about it. Various local Movements have been organized along all kinds of principles, and I welcome this. We have a big tent, with a lot of agendas united by a desire for freedom. However, there are also some practical things that have proven to work.

The community you're building needs clear rules about our special abilities, especially ones that affect someone's mind. I'm not talking about when you use your supernatural charm to fuck with your friends. A joke's a joke, even in the Anarchs. I'm talking about taking away someone's free will. For many of us, the tyranny of the Camarilla is personified in the arrogant Ventrue who forces you to humiliate yourself as he controls your actions. Make sure you never use those tactics inside the Movement. In my experience, people resent getting beaten up less than they resent mind control.

Provide essential services. This sounds deeply unglamorous, but it's also the thing that can make your Movement into a broad-based success. The Camarilla traditionally doesn't give a flying fuck about the young lick. If someone's sire abandons them to the streets, tough luck. If you get into trouble, you're on your own. This Camarilla attitude can be a weakness. Let it be known that if a young lick needs a place to stay, advice on hunting, help with dealing with their mortal identity, they can always come to you. I guarantee that you'll have plenty of friends. Give people things they desperately need and they'll listen to you.

Allow people to change. Don't get too stuck on people's personal histories, especially if they're young. We're all Anarchs, we have a common enemy, and we can't afford to fracture into little groups waging war on each other. So what if one used to be a cop and the other an anarchist? You're both licks. Get used to getting along. This goes double for those who want to defect to us from the other sects. Let's welcome them and judge them based on how they act with us, not on how they acted before.

However, there's an exception. Fuck the elders. I'll say this straight: Don't deal with elders unless you have elders on your side too. And you probably don't. I've seen this happen a few times: A Hellene or a Diva elder says she's defecting from the Camarilla. Everybody gets all excited. Power, privilege, so many things this beautiful ally could do to help us! Thing is, every elder is a selfish fucker, even if they talk a good game about freedom. If they're present, it's going to be about them. Those elders treat the Movement as a playground for a few decades and then go back to their Camarilla buddies once they get bored.

Finally, avoid leaders. This might be my personal politics creeping in, but hierarchical structures make you vulnerable. If you have a clear leader, the Camarilla will corrupt that leader. Strive to train small autonomous units, cells or gangs, who can take initiative on their own. We're not sheep. We're undead creatures of the night. We shouldn't need a big strong man to tell us what to do.

Freedom

The age-old problem of freedom versus security will come to bedevil you too. That's an unfortunate fact. You will preach freedom and equality among everybody who joins the Movement, but you will also need to execute Camarilla spies. This is difficult, especially if the Camarilla gets their propaganda efforts going. They have an advantage in the sense that it's pointless to accuse them of hypocrisy. That's what their entire sect is built on, it's their flesh and blood. We are supposed to be something better, so for us, the charge can be dangerous.

Still, you can assume that you'll face attempted assassinations, forced blood-bonding, blackmail, sending the Second Inquisition information about you, smear campaigns and so on. I've always dealt with these by being open with my friends. I've warned them that this might happen, so they recognize it when it does.

This is probably the biggest test your organizing efforts will face. Can you build a community strong enough to withstand all the lies the Camarilla can throw at you?

Sometimes the judgement calls are very hard to make. Let's say a young lick has betrayed you to the Camarilla by leaking information. She was blackmailed: The Sheriff threatened to murder her mortal family. What can you do?

Forgive her. This shows that people can come to you if the Camarilla tries something, and you're willing to listen. It can backfire by making you look weak.

Execute her, publicly or privately. You can make an example of a traitor, but sometimes it's better if people just disappear. If you get lucky, the Camarilla will be blamed for it.

Turn her into an unwitting double agent by feeding her false information. This is what I'd call the vampire move. No matter your principles, you're still a lick. Use it to fight for the Movement.

Parties

I'm serious. You need good parties. If the young licks of your city think that the Movement has the best parties, you're halfway on your way to victory. Praise the heroes of the Movement, remember those who died for the struggle and make sure that blood always flows when you come back to celebrate after a successful action against the Camarilla.

This is a common mistake made by many intellectually minded Anarchs. We demand that everybody in the Movement should be able to talk Anarch philosophy with the appropriate terminology, always up to date on the latest ideas. That might be fine if you want to have a really involved debate about the nuances of vampire liberation, but if you're building a broad Movement, you need everybody.

Well, not every psycho. Some lines can't be crossed, and you'll decide what those lines are for you. Just make sure there's not so many of them, you'll find yourself alone.

Give people big ideas to believe in, good music to dance to, and a place where they can fight each other without drawing the attention of the mortals. Kneeling before the elders in an Elysium sucks, so being in the Anarchs should be better than that. This should be the good life for all of us, despite the danger. ∎

BUILD A BETTER WORLD (FOR YOU)

Let's say you need a bunch of followers. Maybe you want angry men to harass your enemies on Twitter. Or perhaps you need a violent mob to protect you. For a lot of Anarchs, the place where you find these people is on the fringes of the political map.

Just remember this is a young lick's game. You need to understand the current political and subcultural landscape very well to be able to blend in, and that's very hard to do if you were brought into the night even just a few decades ago.

As a warning, check how often the police miserably fails in infiltrating activist groups. A police officer stands out, often for reasons that are embarrassingly simple, like having the wrong kind of shoes or hair.

Case #1: Your Old Crew

Let's say you're one of those Anarchs lucky enough to have been political in life. You already know the people and they know you. Whatever your status in the group was before, you can quickly build it up because as a lick, you can make things happen in a way that was impossible before.

This can be very simple. You're in the antifa. A human needs to worry about being injured when he goes out to punch Nazis, but for our kind, it's much less of a problem. You can play the hero by taking a knife wound for your friends, and they don't have to know you're a supernaturally quick-healing bloodsucker.

These are things every single lick can do. Or maybe your friends get beaten up by the cops. Maybe someone has nerve damage from being held in the back of a police van with cuffs locked on too tight. Give them a drop of your Blood. Tell them it's a herbal remedy or an experimental street drug. Whatever they'll believe. The point is, they'll be addicted without even realizing it.

Case #2: Your Hated Enemies

Most of us feel intuitively that the presence of an undying monster doesn't make any political movement better. Our influence is toxic, yet we often continue to hang around with our old friends just because we like them.

If you have the guts to do it, you can also infiltrate your most hated enemies. This has many advantages. You don't have to feel bad about all the horrible exploitative bullshit you need to pull off as a lick. If your new associates get hurt, so what? They deserve it. If not, that's good too as they can do your bidding.

Politically, this works out great. You're using the poisonous nature of our kind against your enemies. Just be careful you don't go native! We like to think we're above humanity, unaffected by their petty concerns, but this is a self-serving lie. We're affected by our environment the same as anybody else.

So you want to infiltrate a bunch of violent anti-refugee ethnonationalists. The internet is a great tool for this. Just hang out at the right local message boards and Facebook groups, parroting the more extreme views. This way, when you go to your first meeting, they know who you are.

There are a few common mistakes you can make here. One is to rely excessively on supernatural ability. That can be useful if you need to move fast, but for a long-term plan, natural and organic yields better rewards. A blood-addicted Renfield signals your presence by his mere existence, but if your flunkies don't even know they serve you, you're much better protected.

Resist the temptation to make yourself the leader. Sure, it's a great ego boost, but it's much less work to be the person behind the throne. If your fringe group happens to be incompetently run, as they often are, you can gain influence simply by bringing rigor and professionalism to the work, whether you're dealing with skinheads who just like to bash a few skulls or wannabe white nationalist terrorists.

Case #3: You're a Political Newbie

This would probably come as a surprise to many in the Camarilla, but the majority of Anarchs are not hardcore antifa Black Block direct action veterans. Tonight, being one of the unbound often just means you've been Embraced in the last few decades. Party kids, refugees, pretty boys and gangbangers all come into this life without deeply held political convictions or existing connections.

Let's say this is you, but you still want to use a mortal fringe group for your purposes. How do you go about it?

First, choose your target. This depends on what you want. If you

need Internet trolls, alt-right Internet activists are useful. If violence, you need people who are used to fighting on the streets.

The simplest choice is right wing or left wing. This can be a question of personal taste. You'll be hanging out a lot with these people, after all. Beyond that, there are some practical questions to consider. In many countries, right wing groups are significantly better at violence, so if that's what you need, start practicing the toasts you'll make on Hitler's birthday. Right wing movements have another advantage as well: In most European countries as well as in the U.S., the police treat them much more leniently. This ties directly into how much exposure with the Second Inquisition you risk with your association.

However, if you're really good at blending in with the mortals, a left wing group can provide excellent cover. Our experience suggests that the Second Inquisition doesn't really expect to find our kind among radical ecological activists, even if they're heavily surveilled by various intelligence agencies.

Second, learn to talk the talk. Do your research. This is often easy to do online. It often pays to take on the role of the person who polices the limits of the in-group and challenges people on ideological grounds. This way, you can make people afraid of you while avoiding commitment to actual work.

Expiration Date

Infiltrating and taking over a fringe political group is a short-term project, from a few months to a decade. The scene shifts quickly. People get older and drop out. You'll find you have a hard time keeping up with the new political lingo, and the people around you will start suspecting you.

This leads to the last rule: Never go in without an exit plan.

■

– Dalia Nakache, a French Anarch revolutionary ideologue

KEEP YO TURF

"Hey, that's the same tag we saw a couple of blocks away. Is that someone you know?" the Kid asked.

"Yeah, it marks the domain", I explained. The Kid had a lot of questions, but I tried to be patient. It wasn't as if she had anyone else. "So the other gangs know not to hunt here."

"What if normal people... You know, humans see it?" She walked faster to keep up with me.

"That's the point. We don't want licks fucking around in our territory and we don't want mortal gangs here either."

"It can't be hard to protect your territory from normal people? Right?" She sounded excited, happy to be with the tough guys in Team V.

"You don't want to fuck with the Masquerade", I said as we got to the car. "So we have to play it cool. And mortals can be dangerous too. You should never underestimate them."

"Why don't you get a better ride?" the Kid asked as I got behind the wheel.

I turned to look at her.

"I mean, you're a vampire, right?" she continued. "Why don't you just make someone give you their car, with mind control?"

I could see that she's been thinking about this for a while now. Why are we so poor if we're the glamorous dead?

And sure, I didn't look fancy then and I don't look fancy now. I look like the woman who's going to shank you in the prison yard. I like the way I look, but it don't always work so well with someone like the Kid. She got ambition, I could tell already back then. I 'm just what you'd call a regular Anarch gangbanger, but she wanted to make something of herself. She said she was a zero as a human, just a white trash nobody. She didn't want to remain a zero as a vampire.

"Listen Kid, it's not so easy. I've been at this game for a long time, and I have no idea how those Camarilla fuckers do it. How they manage to get rich, live in fancy Havens, maintain a stable of servants. When I try to blood bond someone, they just behave like the irresponsible junkies."

"Okay", she said. This is something most Anarchs start thinking about, sooner or later. Why is it so fucking hard to live?

The house was run-down, one of the windows broken, but someone had tended the lawn. I wondered why. Maybe it gave these assholes something to do while they were waiting for surprise visitors.

One of them was smoking on the porch, gun carelessly in his waistband. He watched blearily as we got out of the car, looking as if he'd slept the last three nights in his mid-range sportswear.

"Hey girls", he called. "You better move along."

He looked like he was contemplating a lewd suggestion, but couldn't come up with a good one.

"Tell them Violeta came to pay a visit. They'll know who I am."

A couple of minutes later we were in.

These assholes had been dealing in our territory. Not much, just testing whether we noticed. They had old sofas, the smell of weed in the air, one trying to make a sound system work.

"Hey Violeta, glad you're here, sit down, you brought a friend." Tom started with his usual lazy bullshit.

"This is not a social call", I said. "You're fucking with us. That needs to stop."

The guy fiddling with the speakers stopped. Everybody was looking at us, evaluating.

"Who's going to stop us?" Tom asked. "I've seen your guys. You're a joke."

He was testing me, but that was okay. It's what we came here for. I pulled out my knife, all of their eyes on it. The Kid's, too. I punched the knife through my palm and pulled it out, slowly. I threw the knife hard so it stuck to their table, vibrating.

"That's how funny we are. Now let's hear you tell a good joke."

Tom was looking at the knife apprehensively. I flexed the hand with the hole in it.

"I can tell a good joke", the Kid said and picked up the knife. Everybody looked at her in surprise, even me. She looked at the knife for a moment and then copied me, hitting through her palm. She let it stay there for a moment before pulling it out with a little yelp.

"Okay listen, you guys are way too intense for me", Tom said, hands in the air. "We were just chilling, we don't need people coming here and knifing them-

selves. A couple of our boys just got confused about the limits of your territory ", he explained reasonably. "I'll have a talk with them."

"That was so cool", the Kid said once we were in the car, driving away. "I get that intimidating humans works like that, playing subtle, using your blood. But what about the Camarilla? We can't protect our turf against the Camarilla with blood tricks. They're licks too."

"Sure", I said, my hand healing on the wheel. "They're licks, but they're not tough. Sometimes this same shit works on them too. Other times, not so much. But they suck at reading the streets. You play little tricks with them, feeding them false information, maybe making them think they're hitting you when actually they hit those assholes we just visited."

The Kid turned to look at me, the streetlights moving across her face. "You know what we should do? Why defend our turf against a gang like that when we could take them over? And why wait for the Camarilla to come to us when we could go to them? Play it sneaky, vampire-style? I can Masquerade as a human, why couldn't I Masquerade as Camarilla Kindred?"

She had a lot of questions. You know how this story ended. I'm still here, defending my own little domain from assholes mortal and immortal alike. The last I heard, the Camarilla made the Kid an Archon. She still comes by every now and then, and her info is always solid. ■

The Prince Must Die

You're all in Tblisi because this is an Anarch safe haven. If you get into trouble somewhere, you can always come here. With one exception. If you're one of the Brujah from the old Soviet Russia, forget it. We split from them in 1978 at the 52nd Congress of the Revolutionary Council, and there are still a few scores to settle.

However, the fact that you're all in exile is no reason for idleness. As the great revolutionary teacher Salvador Garcia has said, we must share our knowledge so we can achieve the goals of our Movement.

I'm Natia Abakelia and I will be talking to you about how to attain a victory against our enemies like the devious monsters we are. Many of our kind think that the Prince will fall when you drive a stake into her heart, but such crass methods leave us vulnerable against the superior physical capabilities of our elders.

No, if you really want to fight like a vampire, you must abandon honor and principle. Burrow deep into the flesh of the enemy and poison them from within.

BE THE SYCOPHANT

This is the truth about infiltrating the Camarilla: You must become nothing. Lose your dignity. Your self-respect. Become a sycophant, a servile parasite. You will discover that even some of the most experienced

Camarilla leaders fail to account for the possibility that their yes-man might actually be an Anarch. You will be invisible to them, even as you scurry to fulfil their every request.

You can use this position in countless ways. One of the most destructive is to foment a culture of fearful authoritarianism. Most elders find this flattering, so it's easy to get it going under their noses. Your goal is to create a situation where the entire organization is paralyzed without a word from the leader.

For example, everything must be approved by the Prince. If someone looks like they might take initiative, ask them if they are sure the Prince approves of their plans. You sound like a sycophant but you will have planted the seeds of doubt. If all goes well, the entire city will grind to a halt the moment the Prince decides to take a night off. Or gets killed in a mysterious accident.

Make it an offence to be insufficiently servile. When the Prince makes a joke, note who failed to laugh, then whisper to others about it. Your goal is to create a situation where the Prince makes a speech and nobody dares to stop applauding first because they're afraid to be seen as disloyal.

In the short term, this looks very much as if you were working hard to strengthen the rule of the Prince. However, in reality, you're making the Prince's organization extremely vulnerable to an outside shock. If the entire city has been conditioned to paranoid inaction, it can't mount an effective response to an attack. The Prince believes herself to be strong, but will fall alone.

ENEMIES NEAR AND FAR

There's a concept I want to explain to you: The near enemy and the far enemy. We have a tendency to reserve our most virulent aggression on the near enemy when we should be venting it on the far enemy.

For us in the Anarch Movement, the far enemies are clear. They are the Camarilla, the Second Inquisition and other terrifying forces trying to crush us. They have a powerful effect on how we can live our unlives, but they're not really part of our nightly existence.

The near enemy is someone almost like us, but not quite. They might be an Anarch gang who seeks to overthrow the Prince but doesn't subscribe to your anarchist political theory. They could be Camarilla defectors who still haven't completely adapted to our way of life. Most emphatically, they are the licks you argue politics with every night in heated shouting matches almost ending in violence.

We know the near enemy and often we can hurt them. They feel more vulnerable than the mighty Camarilla, and because we're dumb, we focus our energies on infighting instead of the revolution.

However, now that you know

this, know also that you can take advantage of it against our enemies. The Camarilla is just as susceptible to this as we are. The elders believe that every insurrection is a plot by another elder. Cultivate these delusions when you have the chance. This way, Camarilla infighting can do our work for us.

DIVIDE AND CONQUER

Look at the structure of the Camarilla city. Who's in power, who's disenfranchised. Don't get stuck with traditional ideas of power and age. The emotion you're looking for is resentment. If you are diligent, you can turn even the staunchest ally against the Prince.

Consider pre-Soviet Tbilisi. Before the Brujah Council brought Georgia into its orbit, Tblisi had one of those ancient Tzimisce Princes who seem to hail from the Middle Ages. Uncivilized brutes with pretensions of nobility.

The Tzimisce Prince had a Nosferatu Seneschal, a loyal man who had served for centuries. On the surface, they seemed inseparable. The Prince insulted the Orlok quite freely, often suggesting that the blood orgies she organized would be spoiled if the Seneschal showed his ugly face. He never seemed to mind the Prince's words, so everyone assumed it was just part of their dynamic.

We knew better. In the end, it didn't take more than a pretty

young Diva girl who fell in love with the Seneschal despite his appearance, and started whispering words of sedition in his ears. That girl was me, of course. I was a recently Embraced neonate back then, and the Orlok made the mistake of thinking I was harmless. Too young to pose a threat to one as mighty as him.

In the end, he made a play for the city. He deposed the Prince and for a few glorious nights he was master of the domain. The Prince.

I hope his victory made him happy, as long as it lasted. The Tzimisce would have eviscerated us but the Seneschal was easily betrayed.

SABOTAGE AND PROPRIETY

Sometimes you'll find that infiltration leads to surprising success in the Camarilla. My personal theory is that as an infiltrator, you don't spend all your time engaging in petty power plays and this makes you seem dependable. Maybe even so dependable, they make you a Sheriff or an Archon. Somebody who gets to participate in the decision making of a Camarilla city as it tries to conduct operations against Anarchs.

What can you do to sabotage such operations without blowing your cover?

A classic trick is to be a stickler for rules. Always demand that the proper protocol be followed, no matter the urgency of the situation. Argue for a strict interpre-

NIGHTS OF THE UNBOUND

tation of the Traditions, against local initiative. For example, if there's an Anarch incursion into a nearby city, you can say that you can't help them until you're officially invited by the Prince. Otherwise, you'd be infringing on their domain the same as the Anarchs.

Demand more information. After all, how can you really make a decision without the facts? After all, what looks like an Anarch attack could actually be a ploy by a rival Prince. Best not to do anything until you have sent more spies to the field. In my experience, our kind is very susceptible to paranoia, so it's easy to come with scenarios where immediate action would be a great mistake.

Even more simply, you can just bog down all meetings. Engage in pointless rhetoric, demand symbolic votes ("The Primogen must vote on the wording of the official letter of congratulations to the Prince!"), table important decisions for the next meeting. You'd be surprised how easy it is to derail a crisis meeting when there's enough undead ego at the table.

Finally, be sure to open up old decisions for another round of debating. Did the Prince already decree that all of the Learned Clan must be banished from the city? If you play your cards right, the Primogen can still have a five hour discussion about it.

KILLING TIME

If you follow the guidelines, you'll find yourself inside a rotten, dysfunctional Camarilla organiza-

tion. You'll have excellent access to information and opportunities for dramatic personal betrayal.

As much as you'd like to literally backstab the Prince, I advocate against it. Play the game to the last, chipping away at the edifice even as it crumbles. Your compatriots will be able to assassinate the right targets to cause maximum confusion. Here you can take a page from the Camarilla's book. Instead of making a show of it, keep quiet and make the victim disappear. This will leave the Camarilla guessing: Did the victim get killed? Or just go to torpor? Leave the city? Lose in a hidden power struggle? Who knows?

If you do it right, you'll find that the Camarilla practically kills itself and you'll be left to pick up the pieces. ■

A VÉR HANAJA

OUR WORDS, our thoughts, our actions all speak as one. We speak with the Voice of the Blood. This is *A vér hanaja*. This is the future for Hungary, Europe, the world.

We are the vanguard of a new order. There is no Anarch Movement. There is no Camarilla. There is only the Blood and the detritus of history and culture standing in its way.

We will stand triumphant because our will is the will of the Blood. We will emerge from the shadows of history and the Masquerade to sweep away the corrupt and degenerate distinctions of Clan and Sect. Brujah, Toreador, Gangrel... These are nothing but the lies of regressive forces seeking to hold back the destiny of our common Blood.

THE FATE OF HUMANITY

Humanity stands disorganized. Weak. Conflicted. Driven by gutless desire for luxury and comfort, the mortals seek to avoid the destiny inherent in their blood. Centuries of civilization have allowed the crimson nectar inside them to stagnate, weaken, lose its splendor.

Every one of our kind knows this. You have hunted for the blood that is your right. Sunk your teeth into the neck of a promising mortal, a young, strong, beautiful young man or woman. You have discovered that their blood tastes weak, flavorless.

This is a simple truth: When a mortal breeds true, their blood tastes divine. If it doesn't, something has gone wrong. Modern medicine has allowed the weak to survive, polluting the gene pool with their hereditary trash, spoiling our hunt in the process.

We must break apart human civilization, separating, radicalizing and regimenting them until only the best and purest blood rises to the surface. The human waste matter with no culinary value will starve out.

In this manner, the vampire and the human will reach true symbiosis as complementary species: The human provides the sustenance and the vampire the evolutionary pressure for the mortal species to retain its genetic potency. A perfect union benefiting both races.

For this to become a reality, we must abolish the cowardly methods of our kind and boldly take control of human institutions and mass movements. The purity of the blood speaks to the human as much as to the vampire, and in time the politics of humans and vampires will have faded away, merged into one powerful machine of will and vision.

DEADWOOD

The elders of the Camarilla quiver in their havens, seeking to escape humanity like the spineless cowards they are. The Camarilla well illustrates how time makes cowards of us all. They mistake the power of the Blood for license to cling onto existence at the expense of all other concerns, when in reality we should be glad to sacrifice our lives for the purity of the blood. After all, the individual is nothing. The Voice of the Blood is everything.

The Camarilla must fall, its wealth and resources retasked to the purpose of our glorious project.

This is the true tragedy of our heritage. So many of our kind

look back into the mists of time to seek justification for what they are. In a sense, they are not wrong. In the dawn of human civilization, the blood was strong and our hunt was rewarded. Yet this has nothing to do with Caine, methuselahs, Antediluvians and other lies. They are nothing but the fetid dreams of the elders, a yearning for a simple time when they didn't have to face the challenges of a modern world.

We live now. Tonight. This is our world, the world we inherited and the world we must purify. If an ancient vampire seeks to stop us, then that vampire shall die. The history of a new age starts now. We live at the dawn of a new age and the myths of tomorrow will tell of our exploits.

THE PERFECT SOCIETY

We stand committed to building a new, perfect society where the Voice of the Blood drowns out the noise of modern existence. Yet mere dreams will not make this happen. There must be vision, but there must also be will. Our will must shape reality, mold it in the image of the blood.

Our will triumphs over history, society, and the lies of the elder. Truth will come to mean that which is in accordance with our will. Everything against our will is untrue. This is how we make a new reality.

In the end, we seek to abolish the cowardly mincing lies of the Camarilla. We will do away

with euphemisms like the word "Kindred" as we take our rightful place as the vanguard of the vampire race.

Obedience to the will of the blood is the supreme virtue. The superfluous humanity who's blood has degenerated in quality to swill must follow the dictates of pureblooded mortals. The human must follow the vampire. And the vampire must follow the Voice of the Blood.

The Embrace is the supreme gift because it allows a human to purify his blood until he transforms into a superior being. Indeed, we avoid the term "Embrace" as yet another vile Camarilla euphemism seeking to disguise our true nature. For us, it is nothing less than the Ascension of the Blood.

THE MARTYRS

The only truth we have is the truth of the blood. Everything done in the service of the blood is just and right. We must keep ourselves pure, only feeding from those destined to breed the future race of man even as we cull the waste of humanity.

In a sense, we are all martyrs of the perfect world of tomorrow. Our destiny as vampires is to build that world with our toil. Some of us will fall, other will stand, but the only thing that matters is the future of the Voice of the Blood. ∎

Mask and Masquerade

1st of February, 2018

Tonight I went to my first Anarch gathering. It was very cloak and daggers, and appropriately so. I doubt the Camarilla establishment in in Paris would be delighted to know this was happening in their midst.

I was the only new lick there, and they treated me with a lot of suspicion, even though I'd been vouched for by M. I was surprised at so many things. The place was somebody's home in a tower block. Very ordinary. I expected people to talk a lot about Anarch philosophy, but that wasn't really happening. There were white kids who seemed to have learned their radical politics from old Rage Against the Machine lyrics and North Africans who could quote Frantz Fanon but had never heard of Salvador Garcia's Anarch Manifesto.

I thought it was the foundational text of the Anarch movement, but it turns out I was the only person there who had read it!

6th of February, 2018

Sometimes living as a secret Anarch convert in a Camarilla city is so terrifying, I have to force myself to go to the Elysium. Other times, it feels so easy. Tonight an elder I'll call E demanded I show her the city's nightlife because she was, and I quote, "Feeling young again". I don't really know her and I'm no expert on nightlife, but she has the Prince's ear and I don't particularly want to be executed. I spent the night watching mortals hit on her while she pretended to be a naive ingénue. She was totally absorbed in her little game, and I don't think she ever really

considered what I might be thinking or who I was. I'm just another neonate to her. Here today, dead tomorrow.

8th of February, 2018

A sad day. I went to the Montparnasse cemetery for a walk. Cliché for our kind, I know, but it was peaceful. It's been a year since the Prince had my sire executed. A lot of licks resent their sires, but I never did. We had a real love story, and she hadn't been undead much longer than me now. She sired me illegally, and when they found out, they asked me if I wanted to perform the execution. They didn't spell it out, and didn't need to: If I said no, they would execute me too.

Sometimes I lie to myself and pretend she preferred to be killed by her lover's hand. This lie can't erase the fact that the last thing I saw in her eyes was disappointment.

I wish I was more brave. When I was still alive, one of my students actually accused me of cowardice to my face after I'd failed to raise discrimination issues at the university with the faculty.

15th of February, 2018

I saw E on the street, by pure coincidence. Only I'm not sure if it was coincidence. Even the night we had out clubbing earlier is starting to feel a lot less spontaneous in my mind.

Being in the Camarilla makes you so paranoid. I've now been to two Anarch meetings, and the best part about them is that if someone doesn't like me, they'll say it to my face. In the Camarilla, they play games.

My chat with E lasted for only a few minutes before her driver returned from the corner store. In that time, she managed to casually namedrop both founder of the California Free States Jeremy MacNeil (a sweet boy before he became unmanageable, according to E) and Theo Bell (such a tragedy, the way he betrayed the Camarilla).

17th of February, 2018

I'm fucked. I contacted the few Anarchs I know and asked about the rumors that there's some kind of an underground railroad to Tunisia and Morocco for those like myself, who need to escape the Camarilla. They just don't trust me enough.

Literally five minutes after I talked with one of them, someone from the office of the Sheriff called me and very courteously asked if I could drop by.

I know it could be nothing. I'm pretty sure they don't have the capacity or the will to watch my every move. I'm a nobody in the Camarilla, just someone who read the Anarch Manifesto at a vulnerable moment and became radicalized.

But who am I kidding. Maybe somebody in the Anarchs betrayed me. Maybe E could read it in my face. It doesn't matter. Just like that, I'm a dead man walking.

18th of February, 2018

I've decided to stop being a coward. I'll go to see the Sheriff, I'll tell them what I think of the city that forced me to kill my sire, and I'll die.

Living forever was bullshit anyway. I never made it far enough to be a real Anarch, but tonight I'll do something that would make Salvador Garcia proud.

19th of February, 2018

Still alive. More than alive. I went to the Sheriff full of righteous fury, but they didn't ask me anything. Instead, they talked about how happy they were to see me settle into unlife in Paris and commended me on how I'd kept my mortal connections in the academia intact. They told me they needed someone to look after the Renfields who managed many of their financial assets.

I could have told them that my background was in macroeconomics and investment wasn't really my forte. Instead, I said yes and thank you and emerged in control of roughly half a billion euros of Camarilla properties.

26th of February, 2018

I was at another Anarch meeting last night. They said they had vetted me and could get me out of the city if I wanted. I told them no.

I can't explain it, but that half hour I spent in the Sheriff's office changed something in me. For the first time in my time as a lick, I felt like I could play the Camarilla game. Only I would play it against them. I would have my revenge, even if they would never know it was me who funneled their resources to the service of the Anarch cause.

At least, it will be me once I find someone to Blood Bond so they can explain to me all the things about investing I pretended to the Sheriff to know.

I already live under one Masquerade, so living under another in the Camarilla is not such a stretch. ∎

1.

When someone who's only been a lick for a few months dies, their body reverts to a decomposing corpse. We all know this, but sometimes we forget how gross it really is. Looking at the body at my feet, I'm happy that I don't need to breathe.

Johannes is not so lucky. I call him my personal assistant, which sounds better than a dealer promoted to a Blood junkie slave. As someone who doesn't share my vampire privilege, he's vomiting on all fours on the cracked tile floor.

"Don't breathe in through your nose", I advise him.

"Thanks Signe, real helpful", he wheezes, fishing in his pockets to find anything to wipe the vomit from his beard. "But seriously", he continues. "This guy was the Sheriff's childe. I don't want to sound negative, but I think we're fucked."

The sound of the lean techno beat reverberates through the concrete walls. We're in a basement storage room underneath the toilets. The dance floor is pumping, all the beautiful mortal blood sacks jumping and sloshing around.

I have to watch myself. It's so easy to start thinking of humans in dehumanizing terms. Johannes complains when I refer to humans as snacks.

"Let me think. We could just hack it up", I suggest.

"Oh God..." he moans as the struggles back to his feet. "I've never seen a dead body before."

"Really?" The idea sounds preposterous, but maybe he really hasn't. I defected from the Sabbat because the idea of a glorious death in the Gehenna Crusade didn't really appeal to me. Now that I'm a proud member of the Stockholm Anarch underclass, I sometimes forget that life in the Sabbat can leave you with some pretty skewed values.

"Yes really." He sounds almost angry. In my old life, I would have murdered a mortal who spoke to me like that, but I've made it a point of pride to treat Johannes like a person. "Why did you kill him?"

"He wanted the club as his territory. He kept bragging about his sire. I didn't like that. Just because he's Camarilla doesn't mean he gets to walk all over us." To my own ears, everything I say is perfectly reasonable, but Johannes keeps facepalming. To appease him, I continue: "We'll just pin it on the Inquisition."

"How?"

"He made a post on Instagram when he was coming to the club. Pretty dumb if you ask me..."

2.

"You're not in the fucking Sabbat anymore. We can't fight the Camarilla head on. We have to lie low, keep our cool, and strike when we have the advantage."

I strain to hear the words. We're standing behind the DJ booth. It's a beautiful summer night. You can see the stars above the treetops and I luxuriate in the idea they are all great suns, too distant to burn me. Khadija is my best friend in the Anarchs and I value her opinion, but sometimes I wish she'd focus more on being a DJ and less on berating me.

"They're not going to respect us if we roll over every time...."

"No", Khadija interrupts. "We live the anti-Camarilla life, for sure. But this is a cold war. We use the landscape to our advantage and turn their arrogance against them." She notices something in the dancing crowd. "Watch."

A nervous man approaches the booth, too young for the suit he's wearing, like a budding capitalist just accepted into a business school.

"Can you play Taylor Swift's Blank Space?" he shouts over Khadija's punishing, mechanical beat.

Khadija laughs, leans closer to him. "Read the room, dude. These people don't want to hear that."

His face would flush, if he was human. "No, I mean... That was the password, right?"

"Sure", Khadija smiles. "What do you want?"

"They said you could get me blood. You know. I'm interested in some very specific things."

"Sure we can. Wait for me to finish my set", Khadija purrs.

Khadija is right. We have advantages too. The Anarchs live among the mortals in a way the Camarilla doesn't. Sometimes when it comes to blood and strange requests, we can find things they can't.

3.

"I thought this would be boring. But I'm too scared to be bored", Johannes whispers. He looks ridiculous in a fancy suit, like the overage, stringy club kid he is. I look pretty good cleaned up like this, but I chose my heels in a moment of hubris. I wanted to blend in at the Elysium, but now my only consolation is that if I break an ankle, I'll heal.

"Thank you Jean-Paul for that fascinating interpretation on a Shostakovich classic", the Keeper of the Elysium croons, her voice effortlessly audible over the murmur of conversation in the salon. The Keeper is an imposing woman. With the Cainites, the word "timeless" starts to lose meaning, but she really looks like that. "Feel free to partake of refreshments as we prepare for the next performer."

I give the room my fakest smile. If my old Sabbat packmates could see me now, hanging at a Camarilla Elysium with my very own Renfield for company.

"Do you have it", the Keeper whispers, sidling up to me. Without an invitation from her, we'd have no business here. Her composure cracks now that she's close to what she so desperately desires.

"Sure." I discreetly take the vial of blood out of my purse and hand it to her. "The blood of a homosexual male refugee, disconsolate from the deportation awaiting him the following morning. As requested."

Johannes has been guilt-tripping me about this ever since we got the commission. He says it's unconscionable to prey on people in such desperate straits. And fuck it but I'm starting to think he's right. He keeps saying we should always punch up. I'm not sure I like it, because the first person he could punch up is me.

"Thank you, my dear." The Keeper hands the vial to a servant who appears from nowhere. "But there's more. I heard you could get the Blood of a Sabbat vampire."

The request catches me off-guard. "What do you need that for?"

"They say the Sabbat has strange rituals that leave an unmistakable flavor in the Blood. If it's true, I would very much love to taste it", she says, and I don't doubt her sincerity. Sometimes what sounds like a dark plot is actually just hunger.

"You know what? I can help you. But you need to do something for me in return." ∎

126

ELECTRIC VITAE ACID TEST

So what do you do when the Camarilla and its elders are too tough to beat physically and too well connected to beat politically? How do you fight against overwhelming odds?

Comedy.

Humor.

Laughs.

That's how.

Follow in the footsteps of the Merry Pranksters of old and travel from Camarilla city to Camarilla city, freaking the squares and showing that the Prince is just an ordinary fool, the same as the rest of us!

Only remember to do it quick and clever, because sometimes the punishment for playing the jester is death. Never forget that the enemy is always more cruel and petty than you could imagine.

Here s a couple classics to get you started:

I. Exploit the Masquerade. Many elders and Princes appear in public settings such as theatre premieres, gallery openings, political fundraisers and charity balls. The presence of mortals prevents them from reacting too strongly, even if you did the old activist classic of a custard pie in the face. (For extra credits, use the recipe with horse sperm. It's online, look it up.)

2. Use mortal proxies. The great thing about mortals is that they don't know vampires exist. This means you can hire, force or hustle them into doing things that are strictly speaking against their self-interest. The elder can't use her powers to reveal the true nature of your ruse if the mortal is unaware of it as well. Just remember not to use any mortals you're attached to. Dominating one to heckle an elder in public is fun, but may result in death.

3. Old vampires don't understand the modern world. You can use this to make fun of them. Remember that old episode of the IT Crowd where they pretend the Internet is in a box? I bet you could pull that off against most Camarilla Princes. Best part about this is that none of the other elders will get the joke either.

Here's a fun variation, only for those who can get close to an elder: Convince them that to maintain the Masquerade, they need to adapt to modern fashion. Then dress them up in something ridiculous.

4. Hit them where it hurts, not where their power lies. An elder loves a Van Gogh that's in a museum. Go in there and deface it with a message only a lick understands. Don't fall into the trap of assuming that an elder has everything he cherishes in his Haven.

5. Seduce the Prince's boytoy and fuck him on the bed they share. Okay, this is not strictly speaking a prank, but I recommend it for the rush.

6. Hit the elder's Haven, if you have the guts for it. Take a camera, put on a mask and grind your crotch against his pillows, spit into the blood cocktails in his fridge and write "I am stupid" into the walls with a UV marker. Publish on Youtube. Best part: It's not even a Masquerade breach.

7. A lot of elders collect art. Only a very few understand modern art. Exploit this by posing as an art dealer and selling a piece of crap as a new masterpiece. Just be careful: Sometimes the elder can have such status in the art circles that the crap magically becomes worth a lot of money just because he likes it. Even your reveal of the joke can become a part of the piece. In fact, don't do modern art. It'll devour you.

8. Infiltrate a high profile movie production or a Broadway show and make sure one of the characters is a clear parody of a Prince. Extra points if it's a vampire movie. Extra extra points if you play your cards so well the Prince can't do anything because interfering with such a highly scrutinized project would risk the Masquerade. (PS. Don't break the Masquerade.)

9. Slip info on the local Camarilla to the Second Inquisition. You'll laugh and laugh as every haven gets SWATted in a single night. Okay, this is not a joke either and can get you killed. The Second Inquisition is nothing to fuck with. Don't do it.

10. Here's one if you're really suicidal: Strike in the middle of Elysium. Come up with something humiliating and attack the Prince with it. Pour wine on his head. Hire a dwarf to lampoon him. Whatever. If you do it right, he'll lose face if he goes crazy. All his friends and allies are looking at him. He has to play it cool. Of course, it's possible he fails at keeping cool and kills you in a murderous rage. If that happens, you can die happy in the knowledge that the victim of your little jest has been publicly humiliated.

All of these work best if you work as a group, make sure to get to know your victims, and move fast. Once the joke hits the target, you're already on your way. The goal of this is to show that no Camarilla elder is untouchable, and even the most powerful can be humiliated.

If you don't mind feeling filthy and debased, you can involve Camarilla vampires in these plots. Many of them hate their elders too, and intrigue is right up their alley, even if they never have the guts to get physical about it.

Finally, you got to be careful in case the Prince decides to be funny as well. Some of them are so old, their sense of humor developed when kicking cripples was still the height of comedy. Some elders are stuffy and sophisticated, but you'd be surprised how many are just crass. Just ask anybody who saw the entertainments in the court of the former Prince of Berlin, Gustav Breidenstein. ■

– **Anonymous**

The Perth Manifesto

You know who I am. I'm a childe of the Baron of Perth, Thomasina Payne. My family lived in this land long before the British or the Camarilla landed on these shores. I got Embraced because Payne wanted an Aborigine to play with.

My sire told me of her plans for Perth, in 1953 before I left her permanently. I have predicted everything that happened since, and I've been right every step of the way.

This is what she always wanted. When she says that she's saddened that she has to resort to these extreme measures, she's lying. She has always been a Camarilla Diva at heart. Clothing it in the garb of anarchy just suited her needs for the moment.

The question is, do we have what we want? Are we really free? Or are we living in a fake Free State, a neo-Camarillist regime who's purpose was simply to replace the old rulers with new?

Let me make one final prediction: Payne will declare Perth a Camarilla city and herself the Prince. She will say this is to normalize relations between Perth and the Camarilla and bring about a new era of peace.

She will not mention that this was the plan all along.

Our Demand

We must protect the freedom of Perth as an Anarch city at all costs. We must abolish the current quasi-Camarilla structures and bring about real equality. We must make sure that Perth's feeding grounds are available to all, and that every Anarch has the license to deal with their mortal family, people, servants and followers as they see fit.

Humanity is our collective inheritance. The mortals living in Perth must benefit all Anarchs equally.

Baron Thomasina Payne must be held responsible for her crimes against the Anarch Movement. We demand justice, not peace: If the fight to remove Payne requires acts of violence against her supporters, we're ready.

Our History

For over thirty years, we the citizens of Blood living in Perth have supposedly been free. We drove out the Camarilla until the only ones left were the Tremere. We instituted our own system, a governing Circle, to build a power base in preparation of the inevitable Camarilla counterattack that never came. Instead, something far more insidious happened. The original ideas of freedom and participatory decision-making withered under the authority of the European vampires who made up the Circle. Five years ago, the Circle voted to make one of their member, Thomasina Payne, the Baron and limited themselves to an advisory role.

This is what we have now. Payne is effectively a Prince, the Circle her Primogen.

Perth could have been a true Free State, an example to our kind everywhere on how to create an equitable society for all citizens of the blood despite our history of colonization and Camarilla tyranny. Instead, thanks to the efforts of our Baron, we got fake anarchy.

Nowhere is this as evident as in the Law of Ten instituted by the Circle. Ostensibly, the idea is that the Anarch population is divided into groups of ten who are responsible for each other. In reality, it has become a system of collective, anti-individualist punishment where innocents are held accountable for crimes of everybody who happen to belong to the same arbitrary group.

Her Crimes

During her time in the Circle, Payne advocated for making the creation of progeny subject to the approval of the Circle. After becoming a Baron, she has granted that right only to European vampires.

Payne has forbidden feeding in any other area except the one designated for each individual Anarch. The punishment for breaking this law is a year in the service of the Movement. Last year we saw what that meant, when an offender was sentenced to serve as Payne's valet.

The standard punishments for breaking Payne's laws has been banishment, a set period of service or death. During her time in the Circle, we had one or two executions per year. Now under the Baron, that number has tripled.

Payne's rule has brought us tyranny, hunger and death. She has worked hard to make sure that our kind remain white and European, despite her token gestures to the contrary.

Her Punishment

Thomasina Payne will step down from the office of the Baron, which will then be abolished.

Thomasina Payne will cooperate with the work of a commission tasked with bringing to the open her crimes, and identifying her victims.

As the commission works, Thomasina Payne will assume the duties of an ordinary Anarch citizen of Perth. She is required to report any and all contact with Camarilla Kindred to the commission.

During her time as a Baron, Payne sentenced numerous Anarchs to act as personal servants in the name of serving the Movement. Until the time the commission delivers its final verdict, Payne is to act as a servant in all Perth Anarch events, with tasks similar to those she levied from her subjects.

Once the commission delivers its verdict of banishment or final death, Payne will accept it.

Failing to comply with the terms of her punishment means that Thomasina Payne accepts a verdict of final death.

Our New Order

The office of the Baron, the Circle and the "Law of Ten" system of collective punishment have proven themselves to be failures. All future Anarch organizing in Perth must happen on the basis of collective, participatory decision-making.

Our basic principle must be that you always get a say in every decision affecting you.

Decolonization must guide our efforts when it comes to developing Perth's Anarch population. At least half of all future Anarch citizens must be of an indigenous background.

All vampires older than 100 years and of an European background must be permanently banished from the city.

We must build our new immortal society together, but we all know it has to happen on these principles or it will not happen at all.

```
Now, let's reclaim our pride. Perth
can still be the city we once dreamed
of.


You know who I am,

Tru
```

EAT THE RICH!
Or, a Manifesto on the Politics of Joy

You've been in those meetings. You've sat down in the circle, waiting for your turn to speak. You've listened to a victim of Camarilla cruelty tell his story. The Sheriff tortured his friends to death. The Prince made him the Court Jester. You're angry, and it's your turn to speak. You call for action. You demand change.

You propose amendments to the decision-making structure of your revolutionary cell.

There's something missing from our revolution. There's something missing from our meetings, our manifestoes, our insurrectionary actions. There's something missing even when we fight the enemy in the streets.

What's missing is Blood. The feeling of biting deep into the throat of a soft Patrician and drawing the Blood into your mouth. Tasting it. Feeling the flavor. And then sucking some more, until there's nothing left. Not even the poor bastard's wisp of a soul.

We need to bring joy back into the revolution. And Blood is joy.

A Tale of Happiness

Let me tell you a story about a single night in the vampire revolution. As you know, I'm a hometown girl. I was born in Kraków, I became an Anarch in Kraków and even when I'm not there, my heart will always remain in Kraków. In my town, we have this thing called "self-respect". I know it's an alien concept to a lot of those living in Camarilla cities, but you can have it too if you kick the Big C to the curb.

Anyway. Every once in a while, the Camarilla makes a play for our city. They've learned they can't kill us, so instead they try something more insidious. They send in someone who's well connected in mortal politics, who knows who to bribe and who to blackmail. The plan is to strengthen the police force, root out our mortal power base and eventually raid our Havens. If the plan works, we die in the hands of riot cops and not a single Camarilla vampire needs to dirty his delicate little hands.

This time, they sent a pretty Ventrue boy in a sleek suit and perfect teeth. The perfect object for hatefuck fantasies, for those so inclined. He was set up in a suite in the Grand, and we knew about it the minute he set foot in the building. We decided to take a page from his book and send our human friends Szymon and Piotr to deal with him during the day.

So who's going to win? A two hundred year old monster? Or a few of our stakey boys?

That's right.

When I came to the scene, the Patrician was staked in the bathtub and Szymon was sitting on the john, reading a magazine about interior decorating.

I dragged the Patrician to the bed and bit down.

Here's a thing we're missing out on in the revolution: Ventrue Blood. It's good stuff. Really good. Ignore the whole "the Prince forces the Blood Bond on you" thing and just focus on the flavor, the nuance. You'll see what I mean.

So I'm draining him dry. I'm straddling his paralyzed body, sucking out the Blood. And it strikes me how grim and sad our business has become. We fight, we die, we talk, we plan, and somewhere along the way we forget why we're doing this.

We want a better life. We want to be free. We want to experience the pleasures of our undead existence. And one of those pleasures is raiding the cellar. Enjoying some sweet, vintage Camarilla Blood.

I kept sucking, draining when when his corpse was dry. A lot of folks like to put drama on diablerie, like sucking out a soul or whatever. Personally, I find it to be a very intimate act. Everything he is, distilled into something akin to Blood. As it enters me, he ceases to be. Everything he was becomes part of me.

EAT THE RICH!

Don't let the years grind you down. Don't give in to hopelessness and fear. Look in the mirror and say these words aloud: "I deserve to be happy. And diablerie is happiness."

UNDERSIGNED,

1. Agata "your revolutionary dream girl" Starek

2. You. This manifesto doesn't need any more names. Go enjoy the revolution and suck some Camarilla fuckboys dry.

PS. I recommend trying a wide selection of clans, generations and age groups. Once you have some experience diablerizing Camarilla vampires, you'll find yourself able to debate whether age brings something to the taste, or if Malkavian Blood is best enjoyed from a glass or directly from the writhing corpse. ■

A Utopia of Blood in the Amazon

Manaus, Brazil - 12th of November, 1981

I found a child with a perfectly molded ear in the middle of his face. He had no other features. No nose, no mouth, no eyes. By the time the child had died, we understood that our perfect world wasn't going to be perfect much longer.

I know a lot of people are interested in how our utopian experiment is going. I'll trust you to disseminate these notes among them. I'm sure some will ridicule us for thinking we could find a place uncontaminated by ancient monsters, but for a few good years, we did have our utopia in the Amazon rainforest. Pristine human settlements, towns and cities far from everything.

The child was the first, but not the last. I'd never seen anything like it. They kept popping up, kids, adults, old people. All mutilated the same way.

I have a pretty nice estate. I've lived here as a permanent guest of a mortal family. When I was still human, I actually lived here. It makes me happy to make this family of wealth serve me, a half-native they wouldn't have spat at when I was mortal. Still, I've grown to care about them in my own way. One night, I woke up to one of the children standing over my bed. He still had a drooling mouth, and he kept gagging on the words: "Listen to the voice of Caine."

That's how the Sabbat made its entrance into our part of the world.

Somewhere in the forest, Brazil - 3rd of May, 1982

I wish we could find them. When we came to the Amazon, we thought we were safe from the monsters of the outside world. If we caught whiff of the Camarilla, we could disappear into the small settlements and wait them out.

I was sure no European bloodsucker would beat me on my home ground. The others who came here with me, maybe. Most of them were Europeans tired of the War of the Ages. But not me. I know the forest.

Now I'm not so sure.

These days, Manaus is full of ignorant, insane vampires. The Sabbat comes to town, kidnap a bunch of humans, Embrace them, and leave. They don't give a damn about the Masquerade. The new vampires make more of their kind.

I've killed dozens of them, some of them misshapen and mutilated, screaming and babbling. Many of the other Anarchs who came with me to the Amazon don't have the guts for murder. I used to be a sailor, in a past life. Now I'm just an executioner trying to stem the tide of blood.

Manaus, Brazil - 9th of September, 1982

We think there are only three proper Sabbat vampires out there. The rest are just locals they Embraced. I got one of their victims to talk. His mouth had been covered with flesh, but I slit it open with a knife. He told me they spoke Spanish, and were two women and a man.

We don't know their names but the flesh artist we call the Butterfly. She likes to remove features and replace them with ears. She's very meticulous about it. Once I saw a man with ten of them all over his head.

Three of them, almost fifty of us. They mutilate the mortals, Embrace people in our towns and cities, yet we still can't find them.

Your Polish friend Agata Starek was here for a month in the summer. I didn't want her here because she's almost as bad as the Sabbat, but in the end I begged her to stay. She had a real talent for killing the young.

Somewhere on the Solimões river, Brazil - 11th of November, 1982

I know this is anticlimactic, but I think we won. I got word that something was happening at a logging. Once I got there, everybody was dead except for a few gibbering, misshapen unfortunates dragging themselves in the mud. The Sabbat had made sport of them, mutilating them and forcing them to race with lies of salvation.

I've never seen such carnage except in the aftermath of the death squads. Some of the bodies dry of blood, others splattered across the ground in wet red pieces. When I got to the Sabbat, they were out of their minds from drug blood, singing, screaming and dancing among the ruins. It wasn't a fight, I didn't talk with them. Just killed.

I've been hunting their progeny along the river and thought about freedom. I don't think the Sabbat came here to make war on us. They came to the jungle for the same reason we did: To be free. Only their freedom meant blood, insanity and death.

Manaus, Brazil - 5th of June, 1986

I found another of the vampires the Sabbat left behind. She was a confused, aggressive little thing, living off the blood of her mortal relatives. As I executed her, she whispered a prayer to Caine. The Sabbat is dead in Amazonia but their faith lives on. ■

STAMP OUT THIS STAIN

[Speech by Camarilla official, transcribed by loyal rebel at the Conclave of Galway 2010]

Kindred of the Camarilla!

By agreement with Justicars present at this Conclave, today I present to you a motion concerning a resolution of "Total War Of Extermination." The reasons for this extraordinary measure are as follows: In September 2008, the Anarch organizations attempted to seize power in a number of cities across the globe after leaking the location of the Tremere Chantry in Vienna to mortal agencies. Princes were were dethroned, Primogen executed, and the rightful authorities removed from office, and thus a breach of the terms of peace was committed.

The temporary success of their revolution in a concrete sense protected these criminals from the jaws of justice. Afterwards they then sought moral justification by asserting that the Camarilla bore the guilt for the outbreak of hostilities.

This assertion is calculatedly and objectively untrue. In consequence, however, these false accusations led to a worldwide uprising of the weaker generations and to the conditions of disorder under we me must now survive, and was a blatant violation of the assurances given to us in the treaty. Indeed all the promises made by them proved to be acts of damnable deception and labored illusions.

In the course of the past decades since the treaty was first signed, our sect has suffered setbacks and deterioration across many domains. But we have stood by our promises regardless and shown our steadfastness. None can deny that we have stood by our solemn oaths given in the compact.

It is contemptible that those responsible for this grave uprising felt it necessary to invent a thousand excuses and euphemisms for their actions, rather than simply state what they have done candidly. An objective analysis of their mutiny and the promises given us and once widely proclaimed is a crushing indictment of the architects of this crime, one unparalleled in our history.

This insurgence is the largest martial panoply we have ever faced, the numbers of thin-bloods who wholeheartedly supported this uprising, via a ruthless exploitation of their passions, was no mere fraction of the entire polity, it was, we now know, closer to the sum of the whole.

We now have the necessity of cleansing our sect from high onto low, as a means of thoroughly rejecting the ideas, organizations, and the individual Kindred in whom we now recognize as being behind the underlying causes of our societies decay.

The Camarilla must now strive, in spite of the most horrible oppression, to convert ever more numbers of Cainites, in terms of spirit and will, to defensive action. To stand up and fight. To STAMP OUT THE STAIN.

The disintegration of the sect and the entire Kindred community into irreconcilably opposite hostile camps which was systematically brought about by the false doctrines of Anarchy means the destruction of the basis for any possible common life.

This dissolution violates all of the core tenets of social order. The completely divergent approaches of the individuals to the concepts of state, society, order, fealty, service, and honor and rips open differences which will lead to a war of all against all. Starting with the human insanity of the past century, this development will end, as the laws of nature dictate, in utter disaster for us all.

The congregation of these primitive instincts leads to an association between their political theory and their criminal actions. Beginning with the pillaging and invasion of our domains and cities, ambushes and intrusions, and all the other things which are morally sanctioned by Anarch theory. This method of individuals terrorizing the comity has already cost the Camarilla more than 200 destroyed in the last year alone.

The fall of the Tremere Chantry in Vienna, but one spectacularly successful mission within the large-scale operation, is only a taste of what the world would have to expect from a triumph of their demonical doctrine. Neither this Conclave or the whole of the Camarilla has become sufficiently conscious of the plenary scope of the operations now being planned by this faithless organization.

It must be the goal of this Conclave to stamp out this stain and eliminate every trace of this Anarch phenomenon, not only in the interest of the Camarilla, but in the interest of all of Vampire kind.

This Conclave must not allow itself to be shaken by any fears or speculations in its decision to solve this problem. Now it is the responsibility of the Conclave to adopt a clear resolution for its part. This will change nothing as to the fate of the Anarchs and the other sects fraternizing with it. In these measures, the Camarilla is guided by no other factor than preserving the ancient ways.

To this conclusion I must now be accorded that position of absolutely wartime sovereignty which is necessary, in such a situation, to put a halt to all such recent developments. I will only make use of this authorization insofar as what is requisite for the application of vital measures to wage total war. The rights of the clans will not be curtailed and their position within the Camarilla will not be altered. The authority of neither this Conclave nor the Camarilla will be endangered. The position and the respect for the Traditions will remain inviolate.

But if we are to survive someone must have the powers. And if not me. Who?

Therefore we must insist upon the passage of the motion. Either way, I now request a clear decision.

May you now, fellow Kindred, choose for yourselves between peace and war! STAMP OUT THIS STAIN! ■

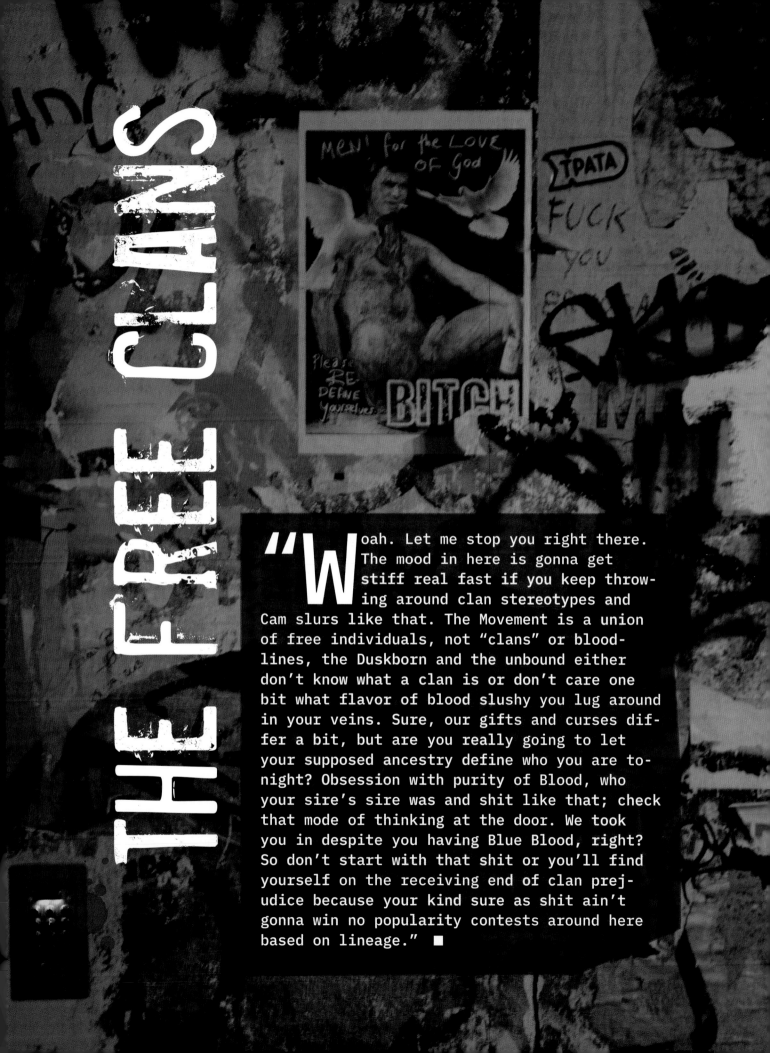

THE FREE CLANS

"Woah. Let me stop you right there. The mood in here is gonna get stiff real fast if you keep throwing around clan stereotypes and Cam slurs like that. The Movement is a union of free individuals, not "clans" or bloodlines, the Duskborn and the unbound either don't know what a clan is or don't care one bit what flavor of blood slushy you lug around in your veins. Sure, our gifts and curses differ a bit, but are you really going to let your supposed ancestry define who you are tonight? Obsession with purity of Blood, who your sire's sire was and shit like that; check that mode of thinking at the door. We took you in despite you having Blue Blood, right? So don't start with that shit or you'll find yourself on the receiving end of clan prejudice because your kind sure as shit ain't gonna win no popularity contests around here based on lineage." ■

CLAN Brujah

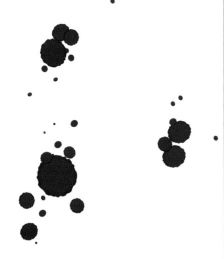

Damsel,

I hear on the grapevine you're at work teaching new blood about how we do with the kine. I asked around some Rabble I'm tight with their thoughts, so you could get a mix of perspectives not so clouded with L.A. coke blood. So here it is:

We're at our most comfortable hiding within humanity, manipulating it from the center. Though there are still a few Hellene Princes and Primogen, and more commonly, Anarch Barons, our greatest sphere of interest is mortal. We know all leeches require living people to remain stimulated, and importantly, well-fed. All the political games Kindred play are nothing if a vampire can barely express herself or recall what it was to be warm. We despise stiff rule, cold ritual, and a societal status quo. We always fight for change, even if that change comes with suffering. And this is perhaps our deepest link to the living - we need them, to lead them and be led by their ideas, to help them grasp their visions of the future and bring about lasting change.

It seems despite our worship of the human outsider, we feed mostly from the same stock. I guess it's like we're shepherds who can't help but take a bite from our prize lambs once in a while. Don't get me wrong: I love to groom a fat cat Wall Street motherfucker and take that kitty down, but that's less from hunger than it is malice and good revolutionary practice. Anyway, he's probably a Blue Blood slave, so it's a message to his master. Point is, we enjoy the fiery blood of the rebel and the downtrodden, because that's us. We are what we eat. It's also easier to eat among your own.

We embed ourselves deep in mortal society, riding and occasionally steering political and anti-political movements, encouraging and manipulating mortal activists, and acting as agitators for causes big and small. We piss off the other clans with our skill at pushing mortals like chess pieces, but such talent makes us valuable in any domain.

We're a clan of individuals. We're as likely to swing left as right, cling to religious fundamentalism as we are militant atheism. We're a clan of extremes, for better or worse, but that means we get a pretty diverse spread throughout mortality.

Our desire to exist outside the mainstream immerses us in what the kine call counterculture. To the outsider, we fall into two camps: those who keep changing along with mortal trends, and those who get locked into a particular era of counterculture. Once a vampire's existed in undeath for three or four decades, mortal culture often outpaces him. This phenomenon results in Brujah still dressing and living as mods, rockers, punks, hippies, and goths, despite the epoch of those movements passing into history. Some of us reject the need to emulate rebellious mortals, saying "fuck you" to piercing, tattoos, and flagrant fashions in favor of casual wear and high-street suits. Such a simple thing as fashion creates a firm division within the clan: the try-hards and the sell-outs.

We all know which one your sire is, girl. Now do right by our young ones. ∎

/Bell

In 2009, Peder Fallesen, a loose-lipped Anarch biker went missing in Copenhagen. I was the one who found his left hand and laptop placed inside a still buzzing microwave oven. His entire web presence, darknet site he ran and all, was scrubbed and the computer thoroughly cooked. The news reported a rotting human head was found by the post office a week later. Cops never figured it out but to anyone on the street the message was clear: Snitches get far more than stitches. My money's on his Brothers in the Movement. The Cam would have made it clean instead of risking attention to make an example. The smell of cooked meat and fried plastic will stick with me till I'm dust so I guess it does work as a deterrent. ∎

The Brujah in Kindred Society

Few Kindred outside the clan recognize us for more than our physical capabilities and volatile temper. Those who make common cause with us will discover a family comprising dead people who still give a fuck. Skilled orators, capable of convincing Kindred and kine to fight for a different world. We Brujah use these talents to foment uprisings, bring light to corrupt practices, and galvanize the uninspired.

Brujah-led domains possess a palpable sense of social upheaval. Us Rabble don't view our society as distant or even apart from the living, so Brujah will often mirror mortal movements, ensuring any changes in societal mores are reflected in the Kindred domain. Kindred in a Rabble city need to be ready for frequent changes in leadership, ideology, customs and Elysium location. We often point out we're no shallow teen punks, bored of one convention after a few nights, but rather voyagers on a journey of human experience and enlightenment. We ask, "why should we settle into a single way of doing things when we have an eternity to experiment?"

The Brujah desire for constant change puts us directly at odds with the Kings and their mortal pawns. We've opposed each other for millennia, us

B's ever striving for new ways of living through the night, while the Kings have attempted to impose rule and unchanging customs on their vassals, living and dead. Were it not for them the revolutionary agade "a different world is possible," would actually be true.

For the first time since the Anarch Movement's formation, the Brujah have moved as one when clan representative Theo Bell publicly decapitated Old Boy Hardestadt, king of Kings. Bell declared rejection of the Camarilla and total unity within the Anarch Movement. Even the Hellenistic Brujah, who predominantly remained within the Camarilla, agreed it was time for change. If you ask me, this is the culmination of the "Red Question" movement that started around the millennium. We started to ask ourselves "why do we obey?" and from there there was only one logical conclusion - we have no reason to obey, except fear. This behavior forces all other clans tonight to take us really bloody seriously. While we remain as divided into splinter factions as we have ever been, we have shown that we will bite back hard when we're stepped on.

Tonight, our clan's reputation for "action first, organization later" brings some Anarch cities to new prominence, while it destroys others from within as the Camarilla directs their secret police, the Scourges and Archons towards destroying us. This is the time to fight. We know what's up. Those that fail the clan in protecting the freedom of the unbound are too weak, too scared, too corrupt, or just plain unworthy to succeed. ■

[Recording begins]

Bell: So why you recording this?

Jack: I don't reckon on being around much longer. Either I'm gonna sleep, or someone's gonna get me. I reckon on this being my last decade.

Bell: So this is your Last Will & Testament?

Jack: Fuck no! This is my slice of advice for you to pass on to any other mooks who join us Punks in a time when punk is dead as disco.

Bell: Well you got me here for my opinion, so let's go.

Jack: Okay ballbags, listen up. As a Brujah you're gonna be driven to a lot of bad shit. You're gonna be wanting to smash stuff, rip people apart, and generally be a temper tantrum in an undead shell.

Bell: But you can direct that, I guess.

Jack: Like you did when you loosened Hardestadt's collar?

[Laughter]

Bell: You joke, but sure, yes. All vampires are sinners. No getting away from that. But you can direct the sin to do the rest of your clan some good. More than any Ventrue or Toreador you're going to be a rampaging, mass-murdering, friend-beating sonofabitch. You won't be able to help that, it is what it is. What you can do is make sure you're in the right place when that happens.

Jack: Yeah, we all got vices and most are violent. The Hellenes call them things like "wrath," "obsession," "self-loathing," "low self-esteem-"

Bell: What?

Jack: I'm not kidding. We treat it like it's just the Beast coming to bite us, but the philosophers say it's all born from our hatred of ourselves. We take out our frustrations on others.

Bell: And that's where your virtues come in. If you wanna call yourself something bold, go for "defender," "rebel," "directed tempest," or some shit.

Jack: Directed tempest?

Bell: The point is a simple one. All clans have their hang-ups. Ours will make us abusive, cruel, and destructive. If you want to survive as a Brujah for longer than a month, hang around some people you genuinely hate. It means when you lose your temper for the big one, you'll point it at someone or something who needs to come down, but you'd be too afraid to attack with your full sensibilities.

Jack: That about does it. Welcome to Clan Brujah: home of rage, retribution, and rebellion.

[Recording ends]

Damsel
Active 10 minutes ago

Thanks for the photos big boy.
They really really made me wet as fuck.

> *Ain't no problem doll.*
> *I'm all man. I'm a pure-blooded Aryan male, just*
> *like you said.*
> *Just like you like.*

Yeah, you know it. Next time I want you here
in person. I want you to wrap those thick arms
around me, lift me up and take me.
Fascist prick.

> *Sure thing. Tomorrow night? Do you have any*
> *kinks I need to know about?*
> *Did you just call me a fascist prick?*

Course not. Autocorrect. lol
Tomorrow night sounds cool.
And yeah, I got one.
Do you mind biting? I like to clamp my teeth
on to a strapping guy like you.

> *As long as you don't bite my little panzerfaust.*

No promises…

CLAN GANGREL

The man ran, panting, tripping, wishing he'd worn better shoes for fleeing through the wilderness. He wished he'd never left the car after it broke down. It's what the highways agency said you should do, but maybe if he'd stayed inside he would have been safe. No, he just had to run. There were lights in the distance. All he had to do was reach them.

The silent tracks on his heels didn't care for the man's fear. It was the energy, the vitality of the blood, that drew them to him. This pack of Ferals wanted to tenderize this man like he probably tenderized a steak or two in his time. They wanted him ripe and ready.

As his foot caught on a tree root and he collapsed to the mossy ground, his ankle wrenched and a scream exiting his lips, the four Gangrel stopped to loom over him.

"What... Please help me. There are wolves he-" The man's voice was cut short as one of the vampires opened his throat. The four fed as a pack, each taking a limb and biting hard. ■

Report #50 - Suburban Predators

Nearly all post-mortals make feeding grounds in the cities. We have observed all types of these infected creatures prowling in popular night spots for the meek, as we assume crowds make the acquisition of sustenance easy.

An exception to this rule are the drinkers first referred to as "Gangrel" by the Dominican inquisitor William of Baskerville. These creatures seem to dwell on the exterior of the mainstream society, preferring to feed in out-of-the-way spots where blood may be harder to find. Many frequent trucker bars, motels, and less-affluent suburbs in otherwise wealthy cities. Poorer regions (see Gary, Indiana, USA; Detroit, Michigan, USA; Middlesbrough, UK; Cádiz, Spain) draw these creatures in massive frequency.

It seems common for these feral blankbodies to pursue solitary meek through isolated regions for sport, with others launching home invasions. We have record of a roadside diner being destroyed by a pack of these beasts (see Report #51).

These "Gangrel" mix with the meek, taking a form of ownership over outsiders similar to themselves. Unlike the "Nosferats" and other breeds, the "Gangrel" do not feed from their own supply, using them as bodyguards, messengers, and distractions. It is possible they also use these meek for social company, though this school of thought only serves to humanize the blanks. ■

The Gangrel in Vampire Society

The Gangrel were once a Camarilla clan in good standing, though their departure at the end of the last century set them as independent. The Camarilla's recent position, that "anyone not Camarilla is Anarch" seemed to please the Gangrel. The Beasts proudly held the Anarch banner as the Brujah and the Ministry migrated to join them.

The Gangrel role among Kindred was always as the loyal dog, sent to strike an enemy. For centuries, the clan served as hunters and bodyguards, until the indignity grew too great. Now the clan is free of dictatorship, and claims the roads as their domain.

It is common to find vampires of the clan in Camarilla and Anarch domains alike, as few would risk insulting an Animal by asking it to leave. However, the Camarilla's Princes can no longer command them. Gangrel may perform services for cities for a fee, or because they care for the area of the local Kindred, but not because it is their responsibility. This freedom provides them with a mercenary status and outlook, which they prize in these nights.

Though the clan does not comprise many philosophical or political activists, they find their views commonly in line with those of the Brujah, causing the two to call each other kin. The Ventrue, Toreador, and Tremere eye the clan warily, waiting for a reprisal blow after years of mistreatment. For their part, the Gangrel don't appear to be planning any grand attack. The clan comprises wild vampires, and wild is how they remain. ■

Let me tell you a story about the feeding.

Once, there was a Feral by the name of Blood Claw. It was likely not her real name, but roll with it.

Blood Claw was a punk in the old sense. She styled her hair, wore her patches, pierced her face, and pounded to hard music. She threatened the norms and fought against the mainstream. The clan loved her. She was a feral in urban society. She won friends among the Rebels and the Orloks. She earned reputation for never kneeling to a Prince.

But Blood Claw had a failing. She fed from her companions.

We Gangrel never feed from our own. And by our own, I mean the mortals we place around us.

Blood Claw fed from the punks. She fed from their families. She thought it was fine — after all, they seemed to enjoy it. But the feeding weakened her pack, mortal as they were. She gorged on blood one night before a planned prison breakout led by her mortal followers.

Big mistake.

Blood Claw led her anaemic army to the prison fence and slashed open the wire. They could barely hold up their sticks, knives, and guns. It was a terrible scene. Each one fell to gunfire, fell to their knees, or fell down unconscious through exertion.

Blood Claw escaped, but she was now solo. She had no pack, and the other Ferals spat at her for the way she treated her kine.

Is there a moral to this tale? Perhaps I should tell you not to feed from your own. Maybe I should urge you use caution. Perhaps I should highlight that Blood Claw was arrogant, and our clan is fickle in its favor. Maybe I should tell you a solitary Feral is one without purpose.

No. It s just a thing that happened. Hope you learn from it. ∎

Rudi

Active Now

The Church of Caine preaches about sin. Let me tell you something of sin, little fledgling. Let me talk to you about apocalypse.

In my mortal days I was as gay as they come. I guess I still am. I guess the Church considers that a pestilence.

I was an Arab in a country with very few people of color. If there was a crime, they tried to stick it on me. Everyone thought I was so angry. War, I guess.

I never caught the bug, but damn if people didn't treat me like a leper. Plague.

My first meal as a vampire was my family. Death.

What does all this mean?

Fuck all. The Church will tell you everything you do is wrong to guilt you into service. We do not serve.

Look, we're as prone to arrogance, wrath, gluttony, and selfishness as any other vampire. We do all of them a little better because we don't fit the niche of the Camarilla, we aren't beholden to law, and no Sheriff is going to stop us draining a mortal dry.

You want to know what the Gangrel are?

We're inhuman. Our sin is that as time goes on, we resemble humans less and less, becoming bestial, which allows us to be as animalistic as our instincts tell us.

Our sin is that we're headed backwards on the evolutionary scale, and we're enjoying it. ∎

Caitiff in Vampire Society

Even when they are idolized as "the ultimate unbound" by Anarchs, clanless vampires endure a pretty harsh existence. Even if the unbound trend is towards "you are not your clan", vampires of the same Blood do share an affinity for each other, forming bonds of lineage and mutual experience, while the clanless share no such commonality. Toreador will gravitate to other Toreador, just as do the Gangrel with their own number. This kinship may not be one of friendship, so much as familiarity or Blood-borne impulse.

The Caitiff do not benefit from this association. It is rare for more than one Caitiff in a domain to display the same Disciplines, share the same sire, or emerge from the same mortal social status or profession. Their connection with each other is purely that of being outsiders. Such a bond is tight, for as long as the Caitiff tolerate each other.

In rare cases, Caitiff become Princes and Barons, but clan elitism, overt or hidden, makes other Kindred to mock Caitiff attempts at power. Derision compels some Caitiff to lofty heights, but breaks others down, turning them into bitter creatures sworn to vengeance.

All Thinblood are Caitiff, their weak 14-16th generation blood so diluted (or just different if you want to be politically correct among the unbound) that the Blood doesn't carry the traits of their forefathers. But not all Caitiff are Duskborn. The clanless have always existed, their Blood made mute by estrangement from sire and clan, from bitterness and abandonment, Embracing weak human stock, Embracing while desperately hungry, freak supernatural accidents and much more. The truth is that no-one knows why some Damned are born clanless, but everyone has a theory. In some cities like Stockholm, the link between Caitiff and thinbloods has resulted in a new burgeoning sect, one that challenges the traditions of even the radical Anarchs. These licks have co-opted the name "The Unbound" and celebrate being free from the curses and peculiar impulses of the clans. They see themselves as the next step in vampire evolution: better, more pure and the only breed able to survive the global Second Inquisition.

The Church of Caine view Caitiff and thin-blooded both as a portents of the end times and directly anathematic to their worship of the Antediluvians. In the doctrine of the Church, any vampire not of the 13 established clans are sinful in the First's eyes. This adversity brings many Caitiff and Duskborn together against the Church of Caine. Few Caitiff hold membership in the Camarilla, the exclusive sect spurning the clanless as scum lacking in the tutelage and tradition necessary to be a member, especially in an age of Inquisition. ■

From: *elterrible@sunburst.mx*
To: *clessscum@bloodspot.org*
Cc:
Subject: *Feeding*

Without a sire, you're not going to have much of a clue
about who to feed from and where to do it. Just because
you're a freedom-loving Anarch (aren't we all?) doesn't mean
you can just sink your fangs into any old mortal and start
sucking.

Excuse the vulgarity, my friend. I'll get to the point.

We benefit more from the boons of blood exoticism than any
other group. You'll have heard of the Circulatory System by
now, and the principle that some blood tastes different and
some of it even conveys an edge or two to the drinker. As
clanless vampires, we drink from anyone, and require those
edges more than any other licks. We are enthusiastic hunters,
always on the lookout for an advantage over our competition.

You're going to want to build a herd of nameless faces.
Think of an office full of cubicles, a packaging factory, or
the regulars at a nightclub. Those people are just the cover
we use to get to the best flavors in the background.

We are underestimated. Kindred think we're tasteless bores
with no clan stripe and therefore no preference. Do not be
mistaken, my friend: we need that edge and so we take it.
We catalogue the blood we need and make detailed records of
where to find it.

Keep all this in mind. Feed from the herd when you have
to, under the cover of their peers. When everyone lets their
guard down, whether it's a Prince, a Baron, the Inquisition,
or just the kine, you go hunting your true target one-on-one.
Make a meal for yourself and enjoy every drop.

One last thing: don't take this email as a good example
of how to communicate. This will have triggered any number
of flags with them upstairs, which is why I'm behind around
a dozen proxies. See this as a test and start running, new
fish. If you can survive the upcoming investigation into your
whereabouts, you're worthy of being clanless like me.

The Sins of the Caitiff

The Caitiff are prone to the arrogance exhibited by outsiders. Though their ostracism is not by their design, their resent for the mainstream forces them to take pride in any behavior that opposes vampires of other clans, or Kindred of the Camarilla.

Caitiff are prone to self-deception and the unknowing manipulation of humans. They claim to be better than other vampires due to their fringe natures, but weave webs of intrigue throughout mortal societies, form massive herds, and pursue elaborate hunts for victims of their choice. Though their abuse of mortals is not as systemic, as within clans following a rigid hierarchy, the Caitiff tendency to mistreat mortal groups and shrug it off as "them's the breaks" reveals their callousness toward life. ■

The Duskborn in Vampire Society

We thin-blooded should not be. At least that's what we've been told. Those who trace their line back to a clan founder can often count their ancestors on two hands. We need at least three to find our way back to the source. Not that most of us know about the ancient ones. If we did, we would run screaming into the nearest furnace. Our modern minds have no place for ancient blood-gods, magical thinking and eschatological bullshit. Hell, a lot of us don't even see ourselves as vampires at all.

My sources say the "Embrace" should not work beyond the 13th generation. But it does. To the monsters that made us we are a seriously bad omen, or at least worrying evidence that their precious beliefs about the origins of the Damned should be questioned. Few ancients enjoy second-guessing the laws and truths they've lived by for millennia. We have become a symbol for a strange present and a threatening future they can't understand or be a part of. For more than twenty years the Camarilla have hunted us like animals, branding us, enslaving us, feeding from us, using the new blood as pawns in their secret wars. Now that the unbound have left the Tower for good, many Movement leaders have declared that Duskborn have nothing to fear in Anarch domains, or even that we will be sheltered from Camarilla persecution in unbound cities. Color me suspicious, but it's a start.

Duskborn draw loathing from older licks and sympathy from the young. Duskborn embraces are rarely intentional, and our existence is unwelcome in most domains. Yet we are here to stay, more numerous than ever, often entirely separate from the rest of vampire society. The superstitious do not trust we even exist and the political do not know how to classify us. No other licks show such ability for enduring the sun, holding food in their dead stomachs, or can develop new powers straight from the mix of resonant blood they consume. We are not quite dead, and this scares the thickbloods shitless. No lick can masquerade as human the same way a Duskborn can. We are uniquely suited to survive this age of inquisition and we have no stakes in the eternal struggle between the Damned. Our unlife-stories are personal, gritty, and more often than not, short and bloody.

Most of us Duskborn want nothing to do with the monsters that infected us, and we don't identify as anything but a person with a strange affliction. We are an opportunity and a threat. The Camarilla do not recognise the Duskborn as Kindred and uphold the masquerade as diligently towards Mercurials as they do towards the living. This means Duskborn in Camarilla domains often know next to nothing about what we are, or about the culture of the damned in general. We're happy to keep it that way, finding our own nichés of the night-city to inhabit, taking a sip here and a sip there while we pretend they are still human, or desperately search for a way to cure this weird condition. A of us few learn the truth and aspire to full membership in the Camarilla or the Anarch Movement, the way I did, and we go out of their way to prove themselves to the very monsters that made us and discarded us.

The threat of persecution constantly hanging over us causes many Duskborn to choose the lives of nomads, passing from domain to domain in RV's or freight-ships turned into mobile Havens. Our relatively human physiology makes travel far less of a lethal proposition than to the full-blooded monsters. Most of us stay put though, and we fast become masters of the Masquerade in the inner city blocks and suburban projects we call our own. Duskborn are so good at pretending to be human that we operate unnoticed and in parallel with Kindred society, poaching from established hunting grounds without ever being discovered. We swim in the shadows of the night sharks, avoiding their attention at any cost as we hunt the same prey they do. Though we're as prone to forming attachments and allegiances as anyone, the driving force for most of us new-bloods is self-preservation and self-interest. Duskborn are individuals. We new-born children of the night are still human, ordinary people laden with a terrible condition we're trying to figure out. To us, you are the monsters - ancient horrors that have destroyed our lives and replaced them with horror and blood. We won't thank you for it. We are not you. We are something new and we will still be here when the last of your kind is ashes and bone. ■

It took me almost a month to realize I had changed. The first week I called in sick and binged Netflix and ice-cream while my body was shutting down, one vital function at a time. Johanna came over and fed me fish-soup and stroked my hair, and I couldn't understand why I kept getting turned on by her. I never liked girls before, but now my best friend suddenly made me feel all hot and bothered. I tried to hide it, but she noticed. She stopped answering my desperate messages after a while and in retrospect I'm happy she did. At the time I felt alone in the world. Usually feelings like that are self-deprecating delusions. But this time it was literally true, no one alive could have understood what I was going through. When I started shitting blood I realised this was no influenza, and I forced myself to visit a night-open free clinic. They took one quick look at me and rushed me straight to the closest major ER, my lack of insurance be damned. I was diagnosed with a terminal kidney condition and given a week tops without medical supervision. They hooked me up to a dialysis machine and kept me dosed out of my mind. I remember very little of what happened next, but as I woke up in the steam-tunnels under the hospital, covered in the blood of my fellow patients, I started to understand. I was one of the creatures I had seen in the corner of my eye all my life. The subtle ones. The cruel angels with needles for fingers and murder in their hearts had finally found me and made me their plaything. That was when I decided it was time to go back to Salt Lake City and meet my family. They would be so happy to see God had finally accepted me. They would share my blessings. Well, we both know how that went... ■

We rub shoulders with our still-living friends and family, without feeling like we're butchers chatting to the cattle. Their lives are important to us, because we're still like them! We can still experience something of mortality that the monsters just fundamentally lack.

When the nightborn ask us how we blend in with the kine, I tell them this: "it's easier to see the living with clarity when you're head isn't buried up a Prince's asshole." I used to say "your own asshole," but since we were formally accepted as an Anarch ally, I now tend to direct that kind of thing at the Tower. But the point is the same. If you stop seeing yourself as a person, as a human being, you can't blend in. You fake it. We are for real.

We mix with the living without difficulty and thumb noses at those who struggle. I mean, how hard is it to remember how to act with lovers and friends? You'd think that even though you're a bloodsucking dickhead, you'd still know how to dance without looking rigored, pretend to drink shots, eat nachos, snort lines, and deepthroat a guy in the toilets just for the hell of it. But no, for most licks that's all "going too far." I think they're all afraid of being human and settle for pretending. No wonder they become monsters.

Vampire: Prelude

For a deep dive into the perilous world of the Duskborn, get the digital visual novel "Vampire: Prelude", available for iOS, Android or Steam. The game was created to introduce new players to the world of Vampire and features a wealth of characters and ideas for you to use in any game featuring Anarchs or thin-bloods. The story is set in New York, Seattle and Los Angeles and features many characters and situations recognizable from this book.

Remember E and Lily? No? They're the clueless thin-blooded surfers you were periodically screwing in Santa Monica way back in '04. Exactly. Not your finest hour TBH. Last thing I heard of them was Lily got in trouble for ripping off the wrong blood-bank and E sunk into this deep depressive funk over being turned into a monster by his girlfriend. You know who I ran into last week? Yup. E is still around and he had this living chick on his arm. He was all winks and hush so I guess he's never told her what he is. But that's not the real kicker. No. She was seven months pregnant and E swore the kid was his. I know the thin ones are not proper dead, but come on. IF, and I say if, the child is his, I don't want to think about the possible birth complications. Like, is the little fiend going to suck mom dry from the inside? Could a thin-blood woman carry a child to term? What the hell do we call the theoretical offspring of a thinnie? Half-damned? Dhampir (that one's from Romanian folklore by the way)? Blade? I dunno. Only thing I do know is someone was following them in a black Tesla. My money is on some sick Warlock wanting to grab the kid for some blood magick retreat up in the Hills. Poor thinnies. I can see why they're scared of us. ∎

Sins of the Duskborn

Arguably, the thin-blooded are less prone to monstrous behavior than their full-blooded counterparts. They possess lower capacity for destruction and inhuman power and have the opportunity to act covertly within mortal society.

Despite this, the thin-blooded are prone to vice. They are vampires. They must drink the blood of the living to survive. As a category, their greatest sin is one of manipulation and deception. They are true to themselves, but lie to everyone for whom they ever cared out of pure necessity. Other Kindred may create a distance between their new lives and the sunlit days they abandoned with the embrace. Not so the thin-blooded, who cling to their families and loved ones, dealing unintentional harm to all those caught in the grip of their new addiction.

Aspiration is no sin, but some thin-bloods coldly eliminate rivals in their attempts to rise above their lowly status. No group of vampires ranks so poorly among the dead as the thin-blooded, creating an ever-present desire for a sliver of power that sometimes consume the Mercurians. The Camarilla use this to great effect, promising power and belonging to those that sell out their thin-blooded friends. Kindred compare it to a single loaf of bread being thrown into a mob of peasants, or a hole opening up in a cage containing hundreds of starving rats. The thin-blooded will bury friends, trample allies, and gnaw holes through other Duskborn to make their existences easier.

The Mercurials that refuse to accept what they have become either face the midday sun or try to find a way back to mortality. These reluctant leeches are no less prone to problematic behaviour than the ones that embrace what they are. Urban legend, pseudo science and pop culture lead the Duskborn to grasp at any straw to get a shot at redemption. The most common legends proclaim that to be rid of their "disease" a thin-blooded leech must end their maker, refrain from drinking blood for a year and a day, or even that they must exclusively drink the blood of virgins or some other "pure" source. While turning away from the night is a worthy goal, it's never without a high cost in heartbreak and tragedy. ∎

[Recording begins]

Reyes: Girlfriend, it is good to speak with you. How is the family?

Smythe-Jefferson: I don't know how long I can go on hiding from them. I feel like every waking night is a lie. They can't stay ignorant forever, and then what? What do I do when they find out?

Reyes: They ain't gonna find out until you want them to. The livings' talent for self-deception is stunning.

Smythe-Jefferson: Perhaps I don't want to deceive them anymore. It doesn't seem fair.

Reyes: What happened to you wasn't fair. But listen: we'll make it through this. You're still working, yes?

Smythe-Jefferson: Somehow I've managed to keep my job, yeah.

Reyes: Then you're still providing. You're keeping them fed and the roof over their heads. It's what a lot of us do. We don't have some big part of society to control, so we hide in among our families and friends. Don't feel bad. God wanted you to live, chica.

Smythe-Jefferson: You know I don't buy that. I… I've done something awful, Oscar.

[Recording ends and restarts]

Reyes: Okay, so you got to just make sure you spread the love, yeah? That's the way to end it.

Smythe-Jefferson: I can't handle the school asking questions-

Reyes: You won't have to. Sure, you got a big family. Give them all a kiss goodnight. Be mom of the year.

Smythe-Jefferson: This is sick. I hate this "life."

Reyes: The sun's that way if you wanna see it.

Smythe-Jefferson: That's not what I mean.

Reyes: You want to survive, you deal. God has a plan for us. They all said we shouldn't be here, but look at us, girlfriend. We're here. We're here and we're flourishing. This is our time. Yeah we gotta to get our hands dirty and hurt the ones we love, but God has a place for us in His heart.

Smythe-Jefferson: I guess.

[Recording ends]

CAN THE THIN-BLOODED BE CURED? How is it done? What's the price? Turning away from the curse and recapturing lost humanity is a classic story in vampire movies and literature. The key to this kind of story is making existence as a vampire seem sexy, vibrant, cool and desirable at first. Then reality hits. A loved one is killed by the player characters, the characters come face-to-face with the horror of what they have become and their addiction to blood forces them to do thinks they considered unthinkable in life. Use the Convictions and Touchstones of the player characters to get them to this moment of crisis, and then introduce the possibility of redemption. If you don't mind conflict between players a good trick is to present two ways out - regaining mortality or becoming a "real vampire" through diablerie - and watch the coterie of thin-bloods tear itself apart as they choose different paths. But after introducing redemption as an option, can it actually be achieved? We recommend that there is no single way to return to the living. Instead, the path back into the light is directly linked to the individual character and what makes for a great emotional story. A feature could be that redemption requires the Duskborn to kill their own sire, a quest that is easy to turn into an exciting multi-part chronicle, especially if the player characters decide to help each other hunt the monsters that made them. But that is seldom enough. In addition to destroying the sire, regaining mortality might also include:

■ A full blood-transfusion from a parent or sibling. The process will either kill the relative or turn them into a thin-blood themselves!

■ Achieving Humanity 10 and maintaining it for the duration of the hunt for the sire.

■ Find a way to perform the "Rite of the Red Sign", a terrifying ritual that consigns the redeemed to the fires of hell when they eventually die. Of course, the thin-blood may not believe in damnation at all, but they will soon become aware of their mistake.

■ A willing person with True Faith can give their life for the Duskborn, allowing themselves to be drained by the repentant vampire in a final act of martyrdom to secure the salvation of a monster.

■ The thin-blood sacrifices their life for a human, returning to life as a mortal in the fleeting moments before they die.

■ Whatever method the Storyteller chooses for a specific Duskborn to be redeemed, the players should never know that it works for certain.

TRAITOR CLANS

UNCHAINED Malkavians

Dearest childe,

It is with great sadness i find you affiliating with the wretched Anarch Movement. I know you have always had a loose temper, but you are no Brujah. You are better than any member of the Rabble. I am just so disappointed you elect to join a group of ruffians when your daddy is still at home, waiting for you.

I shall be leaving Milwaukee soon, so you will not find me there. Phoenix is my likely destination, but it entirely depends on that fool Esau and where he ends up. Anyhow, there is something you must know of our clan:

We were never meant for the Camarilla.

Maybe you know this already. I shall give a potted history that might act as a euphoric, should your mind be inclined.

When we attended the Convention of Thorns, our clan divided into a roughly 50/50 split. The true maniacs, those who lost control over their temperament and connection to humanity, of course drifted. But where did they drift?

The Camarilla.

Yes! Our sane ones, our oracles, they joined the Sabbat for that was our calling at the time. It is where the Blood compelled us to go. But no, half the clan resisted, and just as the poles shift, so did the sanity of our clan. Sabbat drove the sane insane and Camarilla acted as nepenthe to the madness. It is true!

So where does that leave you, my precious daughter? You are in the void. You and your sister both. It is tragic for me to say, but not a one Malkavian joined the Anarch Movement upon its formal foundation. Not a one. Why? Because it is not meant for us!

If you consider yourself one of the Unchained, you are disconnecting from the Blood, the Cobweb, the Network, and the poles of which I spoke.

It is a tragedy to me that you, and so many like you, would willingly throw yourselves into a black hole with no hope of emergence. But alas, it is your choice. I will still love you, even as you lose touch with the pull of wisdom one side or t'other.

Fare well, my glorious daughter. Send my regards to your sister. ■

Your sire,
Jacob

Gilbert Duane shook hands with the Feral, clasping his free hand over their manual grasp to reinforce his loyalty. "This has been a long time coming, Mr. Rudi, sir."

Rudi tutted and shook his head in response. They had long desired official Malkavian representation in the Anarch Movement, and now, with the tide flowing as it was, it seemed a wave of Lunatics was ready to descend on Anarch domains across the world. "A long time, maybe, but not too late." Rudi smiled at Gilbert, making to let go of his hand but finding it still gripped. He laughed. "I think it safe to say you arrived just when things started getting interesting."

Gilbert grinned at Rudi, squeezing the other vampire's hand uncomfortably tight. "I've always asked myself, 'Why aren't there more Malkavians in the Anarchs?' I mean, we're kind of meant for each other, yeah?"

Rudi looked down at Gilbert's hands and then back up to the Lunatic's face. "You can let go of my hand now, Mr. Duane."

"Oh yes, of course." Gilbert hastily extracted his hands and put them in his pockets. "I'm sorry, Mr. Rudi, sir. I'm just excited, is all. I've got all these friends coming with me, and I just know we're going to make the Anarchs a fuller, healthier, sect."

Rudi nodded, going to look out the window. "And when did you say they were arriving? There's not a huge amount of room in this hall and I understand there's somewhere between 20 and 30 Malkavians you've convinced to leave the Camarilla for us. I was hoping they might come in shifts..." He looked to the dark horizon, seeing no vehicle headlights on the approaching road.

"What do you mean, Mr. Rudi?" Gilbert looked genuinely confused.

Rudi turns to him with eyes narrowed. "As in, it might be good to handle ten at a time, or something like that. It's fine if not, it's just we'll be a little - heh - cramped. Especially with the other brothers already here."

Gilbert looked over his shoulders, left and right, turned, and then raised the ball of his hand to his forehead. "Oh God. I'm so sorry, Mr. Rudi, sir. I thought they were already here. I thought I'd invited them. It must have been a dream. A prophetic dream! Yeah, it must be something that's going to happen. I thought–"

Rudi cut him off. "It's okay, Mr. Duane. It's cool. You.. You take a seat over there. I'm going to make some calls." As Gilbert staggered off, Rudi rubbed his eyes. Malkavians in the Anarch Movement would be a huge coup, but it seemed impossible to corral more than a few at a time. For a clan supposedly possessed of a massive internal network, they seemed particularly resistant to acting as one on this matter. ■

Shh. Yes, I'm one of the Unchained. No, you're not to tell anyone.

There were far more of us once upon a time in a land of honey and wine. We shone like galaxies in this little sect, soothsayers, sage counsellors, great minds behind lesser minds.

Did you ever hear the one about Salvador Garcia's Malkavian counsellor?

Those nights are gone. In the last, oh, ten, twenty years, it's like the Unchained all drifted to one end of the spectrum or other. You were Sabbat or you were Camarilla. No room for middle ground. None at all.

So where does that leave me? All alone? Hardly. We're leaking back in from the edges, filling the center ground, just waiting for that time where we get pushed back again.

It's a little like we're iron filings. On either side of us are magnets that get turned on now and again. When they let us go, we make beautiful shapes. ■

Report #391 - Addled Anarchists

The post-mortals we call the "Addled" (who appear to go by a number of different names in their society, leading to our suspicion that they are not a family like some other blankbodies, but an infection on top of another infection), seem a natural fit for the group known as the Anarchists. Their mercurial natures and unstable bearings seem more likely to find sympathy among the Anarchists than the elitist Camarilla post-mortals. Despite this, we find they exist in truly few numbers within the former group. Whether this is due to their successfully hiding activity, or simply clinging to the Camarilla with a strange ferocity, is unknown.

We recently lost eight agents (see Report #389) in attempts to convince Addled post-mortals to join the Anarchists, just to see what would happen. The campaign (fully detailed in its own report) consisted of blackmail and enticement placed by our contacts, but failed dramatically as the Addled saw through the ploy in each instance and eliminated our representatives.

While we ascribe no mystical significance to the Anarchist Movement or the Addled prohibition from joining, our researches fail to discover any strong evidence for why they resent the sect to such a degree. It feels to this agent like these particular haemovores instinctively draw away from the Anarchist principles. Further research is required to discover the cause. ∎

RED Nosferatu

A fist to the gut with enough power to paralyze a mortal just made the malformed combatant buckle, before lashing out with a swing of his own. The two freaks, clad in shimmering boxing shorts and thick gloves, pounded the ever-living hell out of each other for the entertainment of the other Sewer Rats in attendance.

"It's the only reasonable way to settle scores." Calebros nodded at the scaled Nosferatu in the green and gold trunks. "He's mine. A true Camarilla boy." The former Prince of New York coughed loudly, before continuing. "We don't care too much about sects, but when some Anarch breaks the Traditions... Well. They have to fight if they want to survive."

The scaled vampire's opponent, a blubbery, layered Sewer Rat clad in blue and silver shorts, made several crude jabs at the midriff of Calebros' fighter. "That one is an Anarch. That was his excuse for fucking with the Masquerade so blatantly. When Traditions get breached, we fight."

The two tangled up, doing away with the rules of boxing to wrestle on the ground, pulling at limbs and smashing at each other's faces. Gumguards strapped to their mouths with iron clamps prevented either opponent from going in with fangs.

One of the two younger vampires in Calebros' company piped up with a question, his voice thin and reedy as it whistled through his bifurcated throat. "So what, you just give the Anarchs a pass until they mess up?"

Calebros laughed, his chuckle turning into a choking cough that culminating with the cough-up of a gobbet of vitae. "No. That's where the other clans have us wrong. They think Nosferatu are all alike and we see beyond sect. It's true we keep the lines of communication open, but the Traditions are more important to us than perhaps to any other clan."

A spray of blood across the ring signalled the bellringer to do his duty. Calebros' boy had pulled his opponent's right arm off and thrown it to the corner. "You can call yourself Camarilla, Anarch, Black Hand, whatever. I don't give a shit. But if you bring your sect's trash into one of our domains, as much as sneer at one of our Traditions, or peep over the Masquerade, you are going to learn the hard way that we don't tolerate it."

Calebros applauded his fighter as he exited the ring to drink from a chained-up blood doll. "We'll keep that Anarch on ice awhile. Keep him hungry. Hammer home why the Traditions are important. These Red Nosferatu think they're all that, free from law, free from the Degenerates looking down their noses, all that crap. But I tell ya - if we didn't school our own in this way, there'd be far fewer of us around."

He pointed at his two companions with each hand. "Never forget we are walking, talking, breaches. Be an Anarch. See if I care. But know that if you are, you get none of the protection the Camarilla offers, and we stick you in a ring with him."

The champion dropped the drained mortal, raising his almost-reptilian arms in victory as the other fighter cheered. ■

A lot of Kindred ask me, "why go Anarch?" They think it's a stupid think for a Nos to do. They think the Camarilla is where we're safest, right?

Well they're right. If all we wanted was safety, we'd stick to the Cam. Ben Franklin said "Those who would give up essential liberty to purchase a little temporary safety, deserve neither liberty nor safety." Old fucker was on to something. There's more to life, especially eternal life, than hiding in shadows and pretending we're weaker than the kine. Okay, so we're not looking to lord over the living, but we do acknowledge our strengths where our Camarilla brothers and sisters pretend we're weak and pitiful.

You know what made me a Red more than anything though? I was so damn sick and tired of being at the bottom of the pile. Especially after the Gangrel left the Cam, us Nos were always the shit shovelers, always the last on the invite list, and always always the last invited into the nuclear bunker whenever shit came calling. The Camarilla Nosferatu will never admit it out loud, but they will always be treated as second or third class in their own sect.

Well I say "shove that." They call us Red because it's like we had a mini revolution. I call us Red because we don't abide by their hierarchical bullshit anymore. And I don't mean the hierarchy of our clan, but the Camarilla itself. This goes beyond clan ties - this is a matter of personal liberty.

Live free or die, right? ■

Report #358 - Nosferat Anarchists

We have discovered an interesting divide in the post-mortals calling themselves "Nosferats". While it seems impossible to divide this family at a blood level - they demonstrate enormous loyalty to each other no matter their creators, sins, or appearances - it seems eminently doable at a political level.

The Nosferats claiming allegiance within the Anarchist group do so loudly enough that we have interviewed subjects from this sect who proudly tell us of their affiliation. They are then quick to disparage their similarly infected blankbodies for cowardice within the shelter of the Camarilla.

This political divide seems ripe for exploitation, either by targeting the Anarchists for their flagrant behavior, or fabricating an attack that makes it appear as if the Anarchists are lashing out at their hiding kin. Such an action will need to be practiced with subtlety, for all evidence shows the Nosferats are quick to join forces if under external attack. Any activity against them needs to appear internal to separate the otherwise close ties existing within this group. ■

From: oldisc@sunburst.uk
To: 637cx90@sunburst.us
Cc:
Subject: Need to Know

QT,

Some of our cousins have taken leadership roles in the rebel gang. This is unheard of on a large scale. Few defer to our family, as you know. It could spell a great rift between our yacht club and their gang, understand?

I need you to find out the truth behind this. If it's true, the new heads need decapitating quickly. It needs to look like an internal coup. If it doesn't, they will move their gang against our club, and a lot of unhappy employees at the low end of the club will join the gang.

Our family cannot be in command anywhere. Not in our club, not in their gang, not in the church over the way. It will shake up the status quo. Leaders breed further leaders, martyrs create martyrs. We're safe how we are.

Find out the truth. We need to know if these Reds are actively pursuing these roles. If they are, they need to be stopped.

We're only safe if we're in the shadows. ■

ABSTRACT Toreador

"It's incredibly easy to dismiss the Anarch Toreador as fad-chasing philistines," Victoria whispered to her companion, walking arm in arm with her guest as they strode through the Art Hole Gallery, "but there's something delightfully avant-garde about their artistic thrash." She cocked her head to the installation taking up a full quarter of the room, a collection of auto parts sprayed with what was assumedly a burgundy paint.

"I'm told the creator of this piece refuses to define its meaning, which is right and proper. It is up to the patron to derive meaning from art." She gently hefted an engine block from the floor, examining it carefully, tipping it slightly to hear a slosh of liquid inside. "What does this mean to you?"

The crippled Scab in her company groaned as he shuffled closer to the supposed art on display. "I don't know, do I? It looks like a car crash smeared in blood. It looks like the artist found the remains from a collision, put them on a flatbed, and drove them to this fucking gallery to take the piss out of Artistes like you." Castillo eyed the car fragments without much interest, before his scabbed over eyes widened in realization. "You do know whose car this was, right?"

Victoria shook her head with speaking, transfixed as she was with the lumps of metal. She ran a finger over the hardened rivulets of blood that had found their ways into the dents and cracks in the engine.

"This is Prince Rowlands' Merc, you bloody fool." Castillo waded into the heart of the exhibit, taking the piece in as if he was an investigator and this was a crime scene. "They found his charred body, torpid, in that fucking shop window, but someone had nicked the car. This is his! It's been dismantled, but it's his! I recognize the bloody keyring hanging off the car key, still in the bastard ignition!" The Archon pulled the key out, jangling it at Victoria Ash.

For her part, Victoria just smiled. "Then maybe we do our Anarch cousins a disservice. Perhaps the message they want their art to convey is clear, after all." ■

You may find my turn of phrase stilted. For that I apologize. English is not my first language, and drips sluggishly off the tongue or from the nib of a pen. I would rather we were corresponding in a romantic language, such as Latin, Greek, or even Italian. Alas. Such is the way of these nights that universal use of such cultured languages is dead or dying.

To the point, as you asked so kindly. We Anarch Toreador are often called the Abstracts. We didn't name ourselves that, naturally, for that would be arrogant in the extreme. Those mainstreamers who cling to the Camarilla wanted to dub us something, and Abstracts stuck. It's accurate, I suppose, in that we have many reasons for going against

the grain, but we're not just going to tell you our reasons for why. It's for you to work out why we row against the tide.

Me? I never had the option to join the Camarilla. My sire was an Anarch, I was Embraced into the Anarchs, and peering over the wall at them in their stylish outfits, exclusive clubs, and pretentious Elysia, I'm happy to be where I am.

You know, I met Toreador in St. Petersburg forbidden from producing certain styles of art. Apparently, it goes against the *Zhdanovism* principle the city still maintains, of regulating and dictating what precisely art is. I don't believe this restriction applies solely to Russian domains either, based on my journeys through Lithuania and Romania. I can

only balk at the idea of calcifying creativity in such a way.

It is a source of great sadness to me that we of the Rose are closely identified with the Camarilla. My assumption is that as with all governmental or administrative bureaus, as a sect they see art as a function, rather than an action. Such art is easy. A portrait here, a sculpture there, but nothing that might tax or change the mind.

I think we should hold the epithet of "Abstracts" closely and pursue our own paths. The Anarchs allow this. In time, I truly hope the rest of the clan sees that structure is a prison. The Movement represents complete creative freedom. ■

BUBNOV

Report #414 – Toreador Anarchists

Following our interviews with Subject #91 and #93, it becomes apparent that while the post-mortals identifying as "Toreador" experience a schism within their family, this fracture in philosophy does not lead to violence. This is an unfortunate revelation, as we were seeking a way of disuniting this group, who otherwise seem ill-disposed to conflict. We do not believe they abhor internal fighting as much as view it as vulgar (see Subject #91 interview), preferring to joust in other ways.

Concerningly, these other ways include the subjugation of the meek. Whether affiliated with the Camarilla or Anarchists, it seems the blankbodies of this family will settle conflicts using meek servants and unwilling victims. Sometimes these fights are of the physical variety, but other times the victims are forced into "talent contests," for want of a better term. Made to perform for post-mortals in a number of fashions - creating artworks, singing, dancing, performing comedy routines, etc. - these Toreador settle disagreement by virtue of their servants' talents. This unusual display makes them hard to push further.

We are currently discussing the ethical quandary of disabling these pet performers, placing false evidence for their injury or death on a rival Toreador. Our ambition is to sow seeds of dissent by implying breakage of etiquette rules. If we can plunge this ostensibly refined family into chaos by making them doubt their own rules, we may find them to be easier targets in future. ∎

I d expected something a little more inventive than Checkpoint Charlie for our meeting point." Rosa's coterie met with that of her sister, Mascha, the two women hugging without anxiety over their audiences. Mascha quirked the corner of her mouth in a smile. "You've always been the innovative one."

The siblings had been divided by the war and then the wall, one in West Berlin, one in the East. Their upbringings had proven entirely different. One had a nurturing, encouraging sire, the other had a cruel and tempestuous mentor. One had been gifted an Elysium to run in their sire's absence. The other had to carve out power for herself. One was a member of the Camarilla by invitation of her sire. The other fell into the Anarch Movement and decided to stay there. And yet, they were still sisters and both Toreador. They still felt love for each other.

"What do you have for us, tonight?" Mascha's coterie surveyed the scene while she spoke softly to her sister. "We've been looking forward to this for a long while."

Rosa, typically cold as ice to her fellow Anarchs, could barely suppress her grin. "A fresh batch straight from the frozen wasteland out east. Russia. They call them combat enhancers. Luke, get the box from the car." She gestured toward the coterie-mate standing at the side of the road, and off he went. "You'll find they pack a punch. If you're still having Lupine problems, have your blood dolls take them before feeding, or just dose up your ghouls. I know you fuckers don't care much for them anyway."

Masha rolled her eyes. "You think we just use and abuse the kine? Stop buying all the Anarch propaganda you write, for God's sake." She clicked her fingers and a sharp-suited Kindred was at her side carrying two briefcases. "This is all the money you asked for, in all the denominations you asked for."

Rosa allowed one of her friends to take the cases, leaving the two alone for a minute. "I'm guessing you've still not told the Prince where you get this supply?" She already knew the answer, but wanted to hear it from her sister.

"No... She doesn't think well of Anarchs. But hey, you don't think well of her, so no big deal, right?" Mascha put a hand on her sister's upper arm in a stiff, but comforting gesture. "It really makes no difference to me though. You could be Sabbat for all I care. We're both of the same blood in more ways than one. We're family."

Rosa went in for another hug with her sister. "We are. None of this shit will ever drive us apart." ∎

IPSISSIMUS TREMERE

"**F**orget all you knew before." The Adeptus Exemptus' voice emerged from a speaker in the north-east corner of the room, while the Kindred adherents sat on mats, their eyes closed, legs crossed, foreheads daubed with the vitae of their companions. "The pyramid you knew is gone. Enslavement is finished. You are free. Free to ascend as individuals and advance to your perfect states."

The coterie of Warlocks each smiled to the sound of the commanding voice, broadcasted from another world for all they cared. The bond was severed. The voice was correct: the enslavement was finished. They were free to become whatever they wanted to be. They could forge their own destiny now.

"Only through perfect balance between activity and inactivity, waking and resting, life and death, might you achieve the state of Ipsissimus. When you are harmonized to the center of the world, you-" The voice cut off abruptly, the transmission failed. One of the Warlocks opened her eyes, one after the other, sneaking a look around the room. She saw her fellow adherents doing the same.

"Can you hear that?" Roland, the Neophyte of the group, asked the question without opening his eyes.

"Nothing." Beatrice answered. "Nothing at all. No crackle of static. No air condition. No... Hum of electricity. The compound has been cut off." The five acolytes stood, quickly clothing themselves. This was the moment they'd been warned about, when the House came back to claim them.

They would not go down without a fight. ∎

We are unusual, even for blood magicians. I will concede that. The fact is, when the bond shattered, our master magus became a three-eyed worm - if rumors are true - and Vienna later detonated Well, I m surprised more factionalism didn t occur.

House Carna claims to have Anarch sympathies, but those witches are Camarilla through and through. Schrekt claims to represent the core of the clan, the traditionalist faction, but how can he make such a claim when the pyramid s peak was shorn clean off? And then there are the Goratrix freaks Ugh.

It seemed natural to me that we would cling to the magic we knew in life. Without the enforced order of Clan Tremere, we explored blood magic and ascension of spirit and body in ways we could build, not in imitation of previous failures.

But yes, we are unusual. We are the only House of Tremere who belong exclusively to the Anarch Movement, but we do not stay here through hatred for the Camarilla or love of the kine. We stay here because we will never meet our highest states while existing in a cage.

We of House Ipsissimus believe in the efforts of our forebears, Crowley, Harris, Regardie, and others. We can all achieve enlightenment, but no-one should make the journey alone. ∎

Report #260 - A Fourth House

Recent investigation leads us to believe that our initial supposition in Report #139 was incorrect. Where in that report we stated the post-mortals known as "Warlocks" aligned within three separate "Houses," our studies into the Anarchists reveal a fourth house known as "Ipsissimus" (see *Crowley, Aleister* in Report #L32AC for further information regarding this term).

An apparently new development, these apolitical blankbodies seem more concerned with spiritual matters than political gamesmanship, but disturbingly, practice violent bloodletting and sacrificial rituals that cause other haemovores concern. While they seem to lack any outward sadism, the ease with which they murder, maim, and indulge in carnal acts, implies a strict disconnect from normal, human behavior.

House Ipsissimus is on our radar for immediate targeting and destruction, unless we can find a purpose for keeping them as unknowing spies or instigators. At this time, we are unconcerned by their internal activity. ∎

[Start: print-out of IRC Channel 'The_Lodge', set to private]

<DrMagus added Xbor5>

DrMagus: OK. Stay frosty.

Xbor5: Got it. Thanks for inviting me.

Devlin: np

Xbor5: Got some intel on HS activity in Vienna. Looking to re-build.

DrMagus: BS!!

Xbor5: No. True. We gotta ride this momentum we got now in the A and act against them or take Vienna for ourselves.

DrMagus: No way we're going back there. No way. You said this was good intel. What are we supposed to do with this? It'll put us right under the I's nose.

Xbor5: We already there. They watching us now. Not here, but we stick out like a sore thumb. Look, we use that to our advantage. Lure them to the rats.

Devlin: This isn't as stupid as it sounds. Do you know where they're planting their new tree?

Xbor5: I can get you coordinates. But on a different channel. I swear this is truth. They're too worried about all the unclaimed goodies scattered around the city and want to reclaim it.

Devlin: Okay okay I believe you. You text me coordinates, okay?

DrMagus: If you want the Ips in on this, you're going to have to send us down payment, understand? We aren't doing this for free.

Xbor5: Sure. I got a whole bevy of vgins and fresh vtay just for your house. Make it in the style old man Trembly used to like.

DrMagus: You know where to drop the container?

Xbor5: I do indeed. It's gonna be fun doing business.

<Devlin logged out>

<Xbor5 logged out>

<DrMagus logged out>

VENTRUE

"There's no such thing as an Anarch Ventrue." Upton Rowlands kept his hands on the wheel, his eyes straight ahead, only his lips moving. He was tired of this kind of backchat from his childe. "You need to put the thought from your head. A Blue Blood who abandons the Camarilla is no Blue Blood at all. More of a clanless wretch, if you ask me." The car came to rest at a red light, puttering as the driver waited for the lights to change."

"So you're saying we can leave the Camarilla if we choose to?" The voice was from the backseat. Upton's childe, Tasha, was lounging back there without a seatbelt on and not dressed in the formal get-up her sire had requested the night before. She was a wild one. Upton almost regretted her Embrace, but for her valuable connections in the sports entertainment business of Connecticut.

"No." The older Ventrue put his foot down as the lights flicked from red to amber, conscious of the time and when they were due to meet Warwick and his fellow Leper. This was an important meeting and they were not to be late. "If you leave, it is our responsibility to put you down or bring you back. We will do one or the other. Probably the first. You wouldn't be the only one of our clan to tire of the hierarchy, but I promise you, give it more than a few decades and you'll understand why we've pinned our colors to the Camarilla." Despite his undead nature, Upton sighed. "Ventrue do not exist within the Anarchs because our Blood rebels against such freedom. Our lineage is one of nobility, law, and loyalty. The Anarchs respect none of these things."

"I respect loyalty." Tasha's voice trembled a little as she leaned forward, one hand on the door handle to her right. "It's just I've realized who I should be loyal to in these nights."

With her left hand she thrust a blade between the headrest and the seat, piercing her sire's spine and throat. With her right, she opened the door and tumbled to the road, watching as the car careened into the window of a furniture store, flames swiftly bursting from the vehicle.

She couldn't help but think that went better than expected as she fled Hartford to meet with her new friends in the Anarch Movement. ■

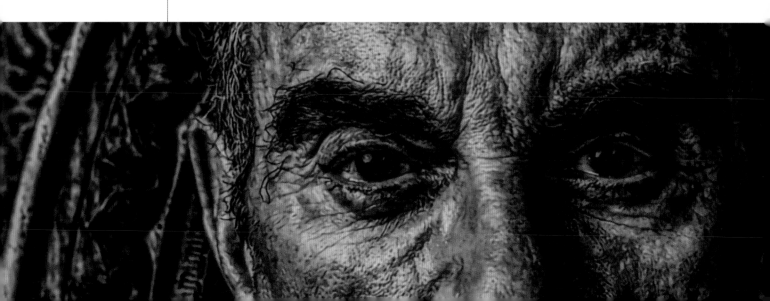

I am a Free Ventrue.

Free from worshiping my dead great-great-great-grandsire, free from having to recite the names of my ancestors all the way back to fucking Adam, free from having to curtsey to some Prince I should respect just because he's family, and free from all the forced deference to my goddamned sire. God. We Ventrue have a rod stuck up our assess. It's no wonder the other clans despise us. We wouldn't grab freedom if it was offered on a silver platter.

You know, a lot of Kindred point at the Tremere and say "those poor bastards are stuck in a pyramid scheme that lasts an eternity." Poor bastards? Try having to scrape and grovel before the same old prick for centuries, just because he came before you. At least the Warlocks respect merit. In Clan Ventrue, it's age, age, age.

There are not a lot of us Free Ventrue, but I have to say, it's quite the life. Without even trying, we become Barons over domains, get our pick of vessels and retainers, acquire the choicest territories. I guess we're just talented like that and the Anarchs respect our skill and hard work.

Just don't make a big deal of your clan, or if you do, show your contempt towards your kin openly and clearly.

That's the biggest difference between the Anarch Movement and the Camarilla when it comes to Ventrue neonates. If you're a Ventrue in the Camarilla, you're waiting to fill a dead man's shoes. Until your superior falls, you're never going to climb the ladder. Here in the Anarchs, we climb and climb. The sect appreciates power, and we're made of it. ■

Report #412 – Venture Anarchists

Despite our best efforts, we have been unable to instigate or discover an existing schism within the post-mortal group known as the "Venture" (assumedly named after venture capitalists, according to Report #115). This is unfortunate, due to the apparent leadership role these haemovores occupy among their infectious species. It appears many defer to them no matter their political or philosophical affiliation, from a meek and post-mortal standpoint alike.

We have discovered several Venture post-mortals among the Anarchist Movement in commanding positions, typically of the militaristic variety. According to our research, it is uncommon for these individuals to take on political power within the Anarchists, due to a lack of trust regarding their motives. Instead, they lead assault parties on a localized, paramilitary scale, harassing post-mortals not of the Anarchist group or attacking the meek in order to accumulate power.

Of interest are the Venture Anarchists recruited specifically for the purposes of obliterating memory of haemovore presence in an area. We have only interviewed two subjects who recall any of the details surrounding these operations, but it is apparent the Anarchists utilize these Venture as hypnotists and thugs, intimidating or brainwashing victims into forgetting facts surrounding haemovore activity. These actions go some way to explaining the lack of meek knowledge concerning these people. ■

Free Ventrue? Hardcore Ventrue? True Ventrue? There's no difference. Look, Kindred here don't trust us, but they sure as shit respect us. They really shouldn't. We broke free from the Grade-A Camarilla clan. Big whoop. We have the greatest number of Princes out there. Why should that make a difference to the Anarchs?

Being here in the Movement is a little like being an exiled king. You've done very little to earn the respect of others, but because of who you are, you get it anyway. It's sick and twisted, and it shows just how easy the Ventrue have it. We say jump, they ask "how high," before they realize they're supposed to be Anarchs.

There aren't many clans in the Anarchs who can twist wills like we do. Find me a King who hasn't mastered the art of getting into the heads of victims and commanding them to "forget" or "run." You won't. You know why? We Ventrue are all alike. You can't cut out the cancer when we are the cancer. This is who we are, and the sooner we stop acting like we're in any way like the freedom-loving Kindred in this sect, the sooner we can stop this mass delusion. ■

Hunt Called

Prince Jackson has authorized a Blood Hunt on all Illinois Ventrue found to have voluntarily abandoned the Camarilla. All Kindred are hereby entitled and encouraged to destroy Ventrue affiliated with:

■ The Anarch Movement
■ The Sabbat
■ The Cainite Heresy

Exceptions are to be made for fledglings and neonates never invited into the Camarilla.

In all cases, proof of treachery such as recorded confessions, five or more individual witness statements, or similar, will be required in order for completion of said Blood Hunt to be considered as more than opportunistic murder. Any such murders will be punished under the fullness of the Traditions.

As the eminent Prince in the State of Illinois, Prince Jackson agrees to award all faithful Camarilla Kindred who pursue this hunt to completion with territory to call their own carved from Joliet, Rockford, or Naperville. Bringing said quarry intact to the Prince Jackson's court, suitable for questioning, is rewardable with territory from the city of Chicago itself.

Prince Jackson wants it known that the Clan of Kings is a clan of the Camarilla, and the Camarilla alone. All who rebel against this edict will be considered Caitiff. ■

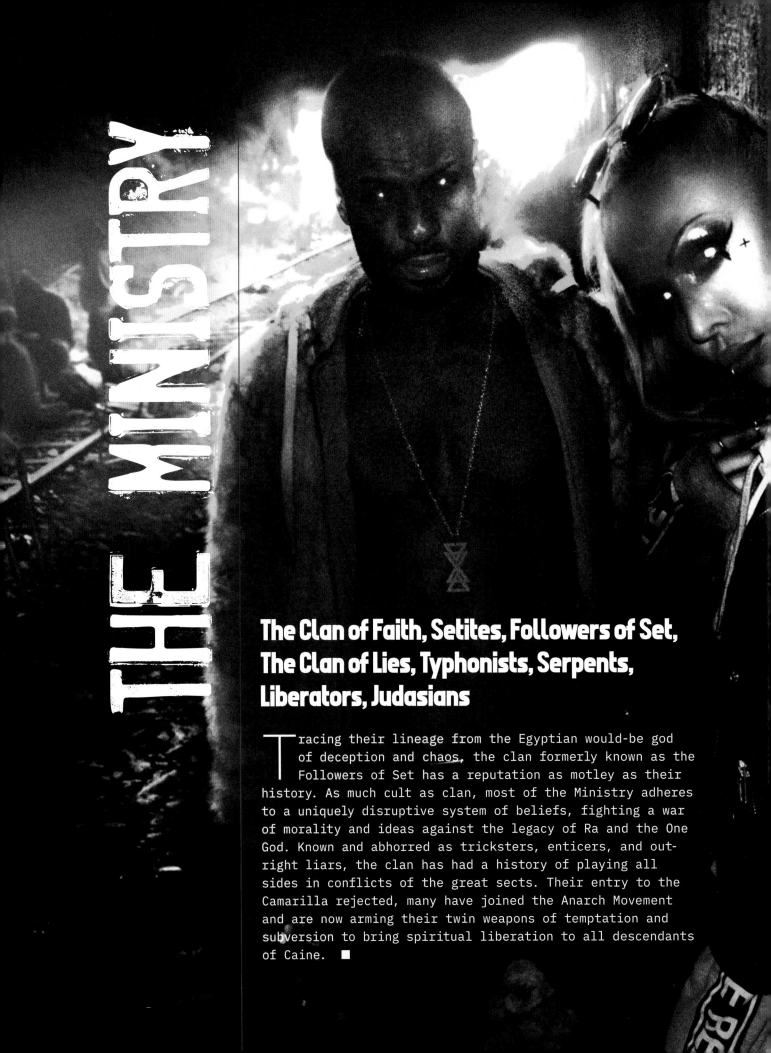

THE MINISTRY

The Clan of Faith, Setites, Followers of Set, The Clan of Lies, Typhonists, Serpents, Liberators, Judasians

Tracing their lineage from the Egyptian would-be god of deception and chaos, the clan formerly known as the Followers of Set has a reputation as motley as their history. As much cult as clan, most of the Ministry adheres to a uniquely disruptive system of beliefs, fighting a war of morality and ideas against the legacy of Ra and the One God. Known and abhorred as tricksters, enticers, and outright liars, the clan has had a history of playing all sides in conflicts of the great sects. Their entry to the Camarilla rejected, many have joined the Anarch Movement and are now arming their twin weapons of temptation and subversion to bring spiritual liberation to all descendants of Caine. ■

F71: Tell me about what you call "the rebrand."

Subject 363: It's not just me. A whole bunch of us do. Stupid thing.

F71: Take your time.

F71: None of us is going anywhere-

Subject 363: So you probably got records, right? They call us the "Followers of Set"?

Subject 363: Okay, keep writing. Yeah, that's what they called us.

F71: And this name changed when?

Subject 363: Different times in different places. The only ones who still use that name are in Africa, or of Egyptian descent. Now we're… I guess we're like the opening sequence of that TV show. You know, the one with the smiling Buddhas and floating pills, worship of sleek guns, sports cars, anything addictive.

F71: Why are you called the "Ministry?"

Subject 363: We're part blood, part religion. We got it in our heads that we've always been close to our god. Why not deliver his word to others?

F71: You mean Caine's word?

Subject 363: Followers of Set. We followed Set.

F71: Who is Set?

Subject 363: Who- who is Set? Are you kidding me? The father of vampires?

F71: Your peers seem to claim differently.

Subject 363: They would. They're wrong.

F71: So why do you no longer "follow Set?"

Subject 363: You can't follow something inside of you. We are Set, now. We are his living church. His temple. All of our bodies belong to him. He can hear you now.

Subject 363: Oh, he doesn't like you.

Subject 363: He says you do not believe.

F71: The subject appears to be talking-

Subject 363: Set dislikes ignorance.

F71: What does Set like?

Subject 363: The shrouded parts of your soul. The things you like to hide. Like what you did to your neighbour's brother.

Subject 363: I'm sorry. Did I upset you?

F71: Why the "Ministry"?

Subject 363: We are now the church for all our kind. Our faith speaks through any faith. We are in all faiths. Once, we were the clan of faith. We are now that clan again. Your neighbour's brother is very angry. He is trapped in Duat. He waits for you.

F71: This interview is now-

Subject 363: He doesn't forgive you.

Subject 363: He asked you to stop.

Subject 363: But he knew you couldn't. He could see it in your eyes. You have a beast in you t-

Who are the Ministry?

Every tale of the Serpent is true. Every tale of the Serpent is a lie. Set-Apep, Loki, Kali, Lucifer, Ahura Mazda. Satan. No matter their name, they are the eternal enemy of the divine. They are the noble devil, seeking to liberate mankind from the tyranny of God. In this tale he is Set, and it is he, not Caine who is first among the hungry dead. This is a true lie that most Serpents believe. In their own minds they are not cursed by God, but the blessed children of a slumbering Anti-God.

In black-paved Annu, the great First City of ages past, the god-king Ra was growing old and weak and needed to choose a successor to the seat of godhood. Noble Set, scarred by a lifetime of war against the serpent Apep, listened in dismay as Ra named Set's brother Osiris the future lord of earth and heaven. How could God choose a weak scholar over the mightiest of warriors? How could God be omniscient if he couldn't see the weakness in Osiris? In a fit of jealous rage, Set's eyes were opened to the truth.

"Every man and woman is a star, a god trapped in mortal flesh. We are not lesser than Him and we don't need His tyrannical law!" spoke Set to his disciples, twelve in number. "We will slay Osiris and claim godhood for ourselves."

Freedom, power and the death of your enemies – Set knew how to make a tempting offer right from the start. Soon he was standing over the dismembered body of his brother, jawbone of an ass in hand. Triumphant, Set spread the body parts all over Egypt, but in his pride he had forgotten Isis, wife of Osiris, and her Magick. She searched out the pieces of her dead lover and stitched them back together. When she was done, he rose. Isis disrobed, loving him like he was still alive. From this posthumous union sprung Horus, and Ra named him rightful king and God.

Set's plot had failed. He in turn was captured, slain and exiled to Duat, the land of the restless dead. To his final dismay he was greeted by his victim, Osiris risen as the lord of the underworld. It should have been the end, but for Set, death was just the beginning. Some say he made a deal with his old enemy, the devourer serpent Apep, others that he killed the snake in single combat. No matter how he achieved it, he gained great powers from consuming the heart of the great enemy, and fought his way back out of hell. Not dead, nor alive, Set was cursed to eternally hunger for living blood and to wither at the sight of God's burning eye. One by one he liberated his old allies from their various punishments and fed them the Blood of the Serpent. They

died and rose as servants of sin, tasked to lure mankind away from the blinding light that hid God's tyranny and to make war on heaven: Set and his army against Horus, the tyrant-lord of creation, a demiurge born from dead seed. It's a war that will never end.

Vampires of the Ministry typically Embrace from the ranks of the irreligious, the heretical, and the corrupt. Criminals are common targets, as are con artists, stage fraudsters and self-help gurus. Likewise, the clan approaches those who seek to destroy or subvert religion. Proselytizing atheists, iconoclasts, professors and students of philosophy, and historians who seek truth behind myth are all desired by the Ministry. The clan are drawn to those who know their way around human desires and falsehoods. The Ministry does not seek to corrupt them – this is a common misnomer – but they do seek out those who know how to handle debasement, fraud, and erosion of blind belief.

As they're inducted into the vampiric condition (or often before), clan recruits are brought into the cult of Set. To the Ministry, the clan and their secret belief are intimately entwined, though their faith takes many forms. Equal part religion and memetic instrument, it can insert itself into any creed, organised or personal, and bring it down from within. Usually taking the shape of a subtle alternative to, or outright heresy against, its parent belief system, its ultimate purpose is to erode whatever faith it clings to, liberating (as the Ministry tells it) the believer from their former chains. It is no coincidence that the rise of the Cainite Heresy follow the growing Ministry presence in vampire domains. Many of the clan keep vast libraries of philosophical and theological tracts for this very purpose, in some cases making it a nightly occupation to hunt for ancient writings and artifacts to bring home to the cult. Others take a more improvisational route, seeking out to liberate subjects, vampires and mortals alike, on a more personal level, not limited to the breaking of strictly religious convictions. Many months can be sunk into simply observing their mark, in order to deduce exactly what forbidden vices will yield the greatest temptation. ∎

The Ministry in Vampire Society

Rudi: I'll be straight with you, Agata. I don't like it when the Serpents starts an operation in my city. Copenhagen and its inhabitants will be happier without them.

Agata: When you say that they start an operation, are you referring to my boyfriend?

Rudi: Please, be serious. This is a real issue. The Serpents are parasites who prey on people's desperation, fear of death and yearning to belong.

Agata: I am serious. When we first met, Rahim brought me three things. The name and address of the mortal lover of a Camarilla Sheriff I'd been looking to kill, a wonderful young man with an exquisite flavor of fear in his blood, and a bouquet of red roses.

If you ask me, that's an operation.

Rudi: A bouquet?

Agata: Don't judge. It's been centuries since it was last the norm for men to be romantic.

Rudi: You're seriously letting one of the Ministry seduce you with flowers?

Agata: ...Thanks to the Ministry, the Anarch Movement is spreading to places it would never have accessed otherwise. Besides, they're not a monolith. There are so many groups and they all give us strength. The Witches of Echidna, who demonstrate that a good cult will never truly go extinct. Hall of Jörmungandr here in the Nordics. Khay'tall's Edenic Serpents...

Rudi: Jörmungandr? Isn't that a metal band?

Agata: Yes. True Black. Fanatical fans. Effectively a doomsday cult. You saw them in action at the last protest. ...Are you so confident, Rudi, that you think you don't need any help? The Ministry is everywhere, from the Americas to the Indian subcontinent. Personally, I like knowing there's a temple waiting for me if I ever get it in my head to go to Delhi.

Rudi: Since when did you become such an expert? You've never been interested in questions of the occult. You're just a killer.

Agata: You would say that, wouldn't you? That's the difference between you and Rahim. He actually makes me feel alive again.

Rudi: Okay, so you're saying we should make common cause with these slithering creeps… For emotional support? What's their endgame? What kind of a world do they want?

Agata: I'm not sure...

Rudi: Can't you ask your boyfriend?

Agata: He's mad at me. I killed his childe. But I couldn't help it, he was talking about "reincarnation in the Blood" and I thought he could use a little push to get to the next life. ∎

In vampire domains, the Ministry comfortably serves two purposes. On one hand they are suppliers unafraid to dirty their hands with drugs, vessels, and anything else on the desperate side of the tracks. On the other, they are the spiritual core of many coteries. This dichotomy does not pass the Ministry by. They dance with the devil and preach spiritual purity. Though some licks consider them hypocrites for this mixed message, the Ministers claim the role of martyrs: They fraternize with sin so others need not. In this way, they retain plausible deniability. Most vampire accept this explanation, as the Ministers' usefulness outweigh lingering most suspicions.

Internally, the clan is often organised around a "temple," with larger cities harboring multiple shrines. These are rarely overt places of worship, but rather areas of seclusion, discretion, and convenience. The spacious back rooms of a lingering pornographic retailer, the abandoned warehouse serving as shelter for the city's homeless, or the top levels of a local esoteric order – all are suited for the congregations of Set. This does not mean that all members of the clan adhere to its teachings. Many Embraced into the clan abandon its ways, or are never taught them. These vampires are rarely sought for re-recruitment by their peers, and are in most cases allowed to do as they please. Unless caught revealing Ministry secrets, for which the punishment is usually merciless, long, and creative, the clan does not force its creed on its children. Still, in keeping with their Blood's propensity for subterfuge and attraction, most Ministers gravitate to similar roles in vampire and mortal society, consciously or not. Another reason for the persistence of the clan culture is the way many vampires of the bloodline claim to hear the very voice of Set, or Sutekh, in the Blood. Some spend a considerable time in meditation, hoping to receive some inkling to the will of their creator. Those who manage to convince others of their connection to him gain considerable respect within the clan and often act as high priests within the local temple. Proving such communication is another matter, and as is often the case among licks, it comes down to who has the strength to make these claims unchallenged. The ire of Set seems mostly directed toward the Abrahamic faiths, claiming them to be descendants of Ra and Aton of their native lands. It might be for this reason that the clan has become associated with the serpent of the Garden of Eden. Officially, the clan ostensibly considers its Egyptian holdouts as anachronisms tied to a past that has moved ahead of them, loudly decrying the "Setites" who dwell in temples and consort with mummies. All the while, a regular line of communication runs to and from the Egyptian clan bases, where the Ministry never truly lost control. ■

The Ministry in Mortal Society

The Serpent swam through the river of humanity like a fish following the current. She bobbed and wove, smiling at some, tipping her head in deference to others, finding a new friend with every glance. Her grin cut through the crowd as her gaze found the teen straggling behind his parent. They must have been on a late-night shopping trip, with the boy an unwilling participant. Despite himself, the adolescent smiled back at the enigmatic woman, the crowd shifting to let her pass. "Your eyes tell me you do not wish to be here."

The teenager put his phone away, looked around, then smirked from beneath his hood. "Who are you, mall security? Hold on, do I know you?" His brow furrowed, the Serpent still smiling.

"I know you. I know the gang you run with. The deals you do. In the dark. I heard about what you did to your friend." The Serpent's eyes narrowed. The smile remained. Her threat was welcoming an answer.

"Look, we couldn't help her. We didn't know she was going to take it all at once." The boy's voice came out shaky. His mother was now out of sight, but he couldn't take his eyes off the Serpent.

"No, you couldn't help poor Philippa. She died, yes, but that wasn't your fault. Hiding her body though? Making sure her parents would never know what became of her? That took a certain boldness. A certain vacancy. Now, you don't want your mom to know about this, do you? Or your principal? Or the... police?"

"No. No I don't."

"Then come with me. Come to my congregation. We will find a way to set things right. For you to make amends." The two walked away from the mall, the boy never taking his eyes off the Serpent.

The vampires of the Ministry are often found Masquerading within the mortal night society, as drug lords, club owners, or simple pimps. Others climb a few rungs, ending up as movie executives, self-help lecturers, and the occasional therapist, assuming that they can balance the mask requirements with their nocturnal dependencies. No matter the disguise they wear, Ministers are rarely without a following. Whether a gang, a sect, or an informal posse, the lost flock to Serpents like the proverbial moths to the flame. Seldom bothering with bureaucracies or complicated conspiracies, the network spun by the Serpents are more personal, held together by desperation, need, or fear. Most Serpents hold themselves above licks who hunt kine and feed in alleys, or who groom herds in an emulation of family. Their herds are congregations. Their vessels give up their blood willingly, because they know the consequences of not doing so. They come to love the vampires feeding from their veins, because ultimately, they're the only creatures that can understand the moral void within their souls. ∎

The Camarilla Betrayal

AS TOLD BY "M-Z", SELF-PROCLAIMED HIGH MINISTER OF ROTTERDAM

That's what you all want to hear about, isn't it? How we went from independent, to Camarilla hopeful, to Anarch. I mean, what a slope into muck. I'll tell you the short version. I'm sure you'll hear the longer one with all the adornments from one of the "ordained" Ministers.

Our clan was once upon a time the Followers of Set. Before that, we were something different. Keep going back and you'll find we changed names like they were going out of fashion. Fact is, we always latched on to faith, picking a new one to emulate as soon as we had sucked one dry.

Nobody liked us. They all knew we were a corrupting influence on other licks. But we were useful. You wanted something, we could get it. But one thing nobody ever understood about us was we were once mortal, just like everyone else. And we still had our morals. Yes, there were some who pushed it a little close, or went over the edge, but that was the minority. It was frankly easier for most of us to wash our hands of crimes two steps removed than to hand over pink flesh to some Ventrue pervert.

So, we were hated in our time, but everyone wanted what we had.

Way back before your grandsire was made, the Camarilla was formed. All the bigwigs came together and asked "Who's gonna sit at the top table?" There were the Ventrue, the Tremere, the Toreador... You get the picture. Rumor has it, we got an invite too.

So, we had this invite, examined the way the wind was blowing, and said we'd take a rain check. The founders were surprisingly calm to our faces, but I understand Rafael de Corazon blew a fuse once our Hierophants left the room.

500 years or so later, and things have gone to shit. The Beckoning is happening, our territories are being invaded, and the Sabbat is clearly up to something more than simply biting down on the big buffet in the Middle East. It's not a good time to be independent.

So, we organized a sit-down with the Camarilla. They sent some of their leaders, we sent some of ours, and we made a big deal of the ceremony in some upper class Paris hotel. Wanted to let everyone see we were back and not to be fucked with!

...it didn't go to plan. Word is, our gifts to the Camarilla were lavish. A bunch of supposed ancients in sarcophagi were handed over and we made a massive investment in Ventrue portfolios. We shook hands with the founders, signed the scrolls not touched since Henry VIII, or whoever the fuck was king back then, sat down, and then... Boom.

I'm sure it wasn't the Camarilla's fault that the most high-profile terrorist incident since 9/11 happened that night. That hotel, and all the buildings around it, levelled as if – I don't know – some Haqimites had snuck in and wired the whole fucking place with explosives. Were there any survivors? A few, but they weren't in the mood for another pow wow. They got the hell out of Paris.

If you listen to the rumor mill, you'll be told we got our ball and went to play with the Anarchs at that point. No, my friend. We waited. We waited for the call. "So guys, we signed the docs. I'm sure one of you scanned them on, uploaded them, or something. When are we getting Primogen seats?" Nothing. No call from the Camarilla. In the meantime, the Banu Haqim rebels got admitted with no fuss at all. If that wasn't the crowning insult, what happened next was.

Hesha Ruhadze – you might have heard of him? Pretty influential Setite, now Minister, reached out to some high-up Camarilla contacts a month or so after Paris. "What gives?" he asks, adjusting his stupid monocle.

"You're off the team, you scaly pricks," says his contact. "Since time immemorial you've brought the heat down wherever you go. You should be the Clan of the Albatross. You're a bad omen. You'd be hanging around our necks like a dumbbell. In short, get stuffed, and go suck Tutankhamun's mummified cock while you're at it."

I made some of that up, but you get the picture. Someone or some clan made it clear to the Camarilla we were persona non grata. I blame the Haqimites, because why not? But it could have been any of those fuckers. They found the perfect opportunity to get our strongest clan members into that hotel and pressed the big red button.

If I believed in conspiracies, I'd blame the Degenerates not wanting us to muscle in on their act, and say they were prepared to sacrifice their Justicar to get at us. I don't though. For all I know, it was mortals behind the bomb. They certainly took credit. What I do know is the Camarilla built us up and knocked us down. They betrayed our hopes and our offer of alliance.

So yeah, now we're with the Anarchs. It's not so bad. At least we don't have to serve some decrepit old Haqimite Prince. ■

Sins of the Ministry

Susanne
Active Now

    I'm at the club.
    Where are you?

    I'm so so sorry S.
    I was heading to Asylum and passed one of those Bible bashing street preachers around the pier. Just moved on by until I saw he was doing some of that faith healing shite. I took a look and realized he was cracking their necks back and biting their throats!!
    There was fucking blood all over the sidewalk but nobody batted an eyelid.
    He had a queue of people waiting to just give it up!!
    I'm heading to my car now because I think the preacher noticed I wasn't drawn in.
    Some of them seem to be coming after me.

All clans struggle with vice, whether urged on by the Blood, or acting on depravities they possessed as mortals. The Ministry make a habit of cultivating those vices, but they are not out-of-control monsters. They carefully lure or lead other vampires into transgressive behavior to help them break out of patterns. They are enablers and promoters. Ministers claim not to take the drugs they deal, at least, not if they wish to remain in high standing within their clan.

The sin that comes most easily to the clan is deception. Most Ministers lie to themselves about their self-control, and lie to those who come to them seeking spiritual guidance about the chances of success. It can be hard for a vampire encouraging others in vice to remain clear of it. The Beast is not silent, despite all the Ministry's claims of mastery over it. It snarls in their ear to indulge, to manipulate, to despoil. Ministers cannot help but ruin beliefs, even those built after their own specifications. ■

Ministry Archetypes:

- **FAITH HEALER.** This Minister has always found it easiest to heal people through the power of words and faith. As a mortal, they were an evangelist, therapist, or homeopath convincing others with their kindness and strength of conviction that all ills can be believed away. As one of the Damned, they aren't too different. Now, the sin they preach against is the Beast instead of simple mortal urges. This kind of Minister acts as the spiritual guide for other members of their coterie.

- **LIFETIME FRAUD.** The Ministry prizes its frauds, con artists, and charlatans, both as the front of house for the clan and for their aptitude for relieving other vampires of burdensome guilt and deviancies. As a mortal this Minister likely had a fake name, a job for which they weren't qualified, and told more lies to their partner than truths. A real enigma who found it easy to move from city to city with just a suitcase in hand.

- **CONSPIRACY DEBUNKER.** Considering they are the Clan of Lies, the Ministry has an unkind opinion of others who would deceive the masses. This Minister was dedicated to removing the veil from over the eyes of the people by debunking fake mediums, blowing holes in conspiracy theories, or using reason to combat the logical fallacies of religion. The Ministry values such a lick for their perception, and prizes them highly when they buy the clan line.

- **MOUTH OF THE GODS.** This Minister was able to hear the voice of God before the Embrace. Ardent in their belief and skilled in channeling visions into action, they succeeded in life, raising a family, running a business, and were well-regarded throughout their hometown. Now Embraced, the voice of God has multiplied. Maybe it's schizophrenia, maybe it's the Beast and the Blood, perhaps it's Sutekh and his family; this vampire believes all of them can be heard.

- **ENTREPRENEURIAL ARCHAEOLOGIST.** Genuine archaeologists seldom get much money out of their profession. This Minister was once one, or at least an amateur enthusiast, and stumbled upon a trove of history they kept for themselves, leading their future sire to their doorstep. While they still pursue their passion for archeology to keep up a legitimate front, many pieces go missing for study, trade with other enthusiasts, or just to be added to their personal collection. ∎

Disciplines

OBFUSCATE: The ability to melt into shadows, craft an illusory appearance, or vanish from plain sight. The Ministry use this to discover the beliefs, creeds, and vices of vampires and mortals alike, to facilitate their exploitation and liberation. Powerful Ministers also often wear the faces of trustworthy figures and friends to better lure prey to into their shrines and temples, or just to the nearest secluded spot.

PRESENCE: The ability to sway the emotions of others, both to attract and repel. In these nights, this is the Ministry's favored ability. They use it subtly, but with great prowess, with majestic gestures and resounding speeches cutting to the hearts of a congregation assembled in worship or to the lone junkie in need of a new fix.

PROTEAN: The ability to change the body's form, whether to extend monstrous fangs or take the shape of animals. Sometimes known as Serpentis within the clan, the Ministers use this ability to awe observers but also have use of its many novel ways of escaping harm. They will often adopt the form of a snake over that of a wolf, but can meld with the earth to avoid the sun alongside any Gangrel. ∎

Bane

The Blood of a Minister abhors the light. When exposed to direct illumination – whether natural or artificial – members of the clan recoil. Ministers receive a penalty equal to their Bane Severity to all dice pools when subjected to bright light directed straight at them. Also, add their Bane Severity to Aggravated damage taken from sunlight. ∎

Clan Compulsion

MINISTRY: TRANSGRESSION

Set teaches that everyone's mind and spirit are bound by invisible chains of their own making. Their Blood chafing at these bindings, the Minister suffers a burning need to break them. The vampire receives a two-dice penalty to all dice pools not relating to enticing someone (including themselves) to break a Chronicle Tenet or personal Conviction, causing at least one Stain and ending this Compulsion. ■

New Powers

Presence

Level 1

Eyes of the Serpent

AMALGAM: Protean 1

The eyes of the vampire turn into slitted, serpent-like orbs able to freeze a mortal meeting the vampire's gaze in place. The user can even mesmerize other vampires with this power, though the effect is short-lived and likely to rouse the victim's ire.

COST: Free

Dice Pools: Charisma + Presence vs. Wits + Composure

SYSTEM: By catching the eye of a mortal (see avoiding eye contact on p. 255 in the Core book for victims actively trying to avoid it) the vampire can immobilize a victim, keeping them frozen in place as long as they themselves maintain eye contact. The effect can only be maintained on a single victim at a time, and ends if they suffer damage or are forcibly removed. Speech is still possible, though shouting is not. In order to paralyze a vampire in the same way, the user must win a contest of Charisma + Presence vs. Wits + Composure. The vampire victim can escape paralysis on any turn after the first by spending a point of Willpower.

DURATION: Until eye contact is broken or the scene ends. ■

RESPONSE ALGORITHM

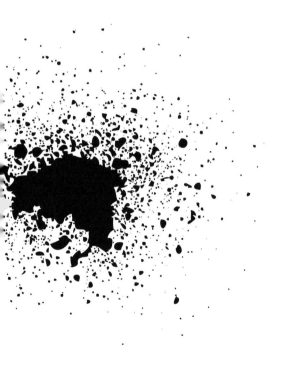

The player characters act, possibly unwisely. They have attracted the attention of the powerful, possibly unfavorably. What happens next?

The Storyteller may not always have that answer right to hand. This response algorithm provides a guide and, if need be, the next step in the dance. While no substitute for a hand-crafted personal drama, it can provide the skeleton of such a thing for the Storyteller to clothe as they see fit. Use it constantly to drive story, or just as an idea mine. The Storyteller can always change the responses up to fit their chronicle.

This algorithm uses the term Organization to refer to whichever criminal network, Camarilla court, Anarch soviet, or Second Inquisition district the player characters have disturbed. The Storyteller can adjust the responses as they see fit depending on the Organization's precise nature, but as a general rule the Organization defaults to the next most severe response in the tree. For example, once an Organization has tried Pay them Off, they most likely try Erase the Enemy or Lure them Away.

Although the writeups below refer to "the coterie" for simplicity's sake, almost all of these options can be carried out against either one vampire or the characters as a group. In chronicles with lots of inter-character drama and suspicion, a clever Organization almost certainly approaches different characters with different methods. ■

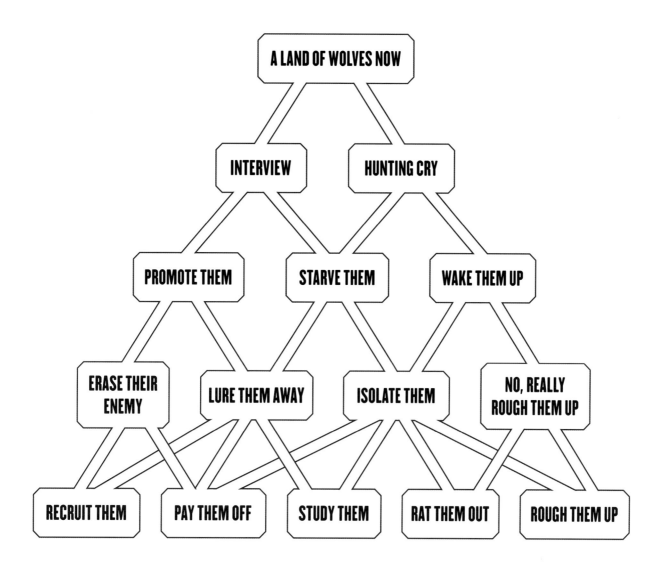

Swatting Flies

The coterie have disturbed the outer fringes, the lower tiers. Local underbosses, ancillae childer of the Primogen, Anarch vigilantes, activist priests, deniable contractors for the Second Inquisition, or similar mid-tier figures decide to do something.

RECRUIT THEM: The Organization can use just this kind of murderous monster team in their own operation. They expect loyalty, of course. Primogens of very rich domains use this tactic and the next more than you might think. This offer does depend on the coterie having been impressively successful and discreet at the same time, which is a big ask. The Second Inquisition is unlikely to use this tactic, even on the lowest levels.

PAY THEM OFF: A representative soldier of the Organization offers to direct the coterie's irritating efforts somewhere else, for a fair price. This negotiation may not even include a veiled threat.

RAT THEM OUT: The Organization's tools in the police department, city government, archdiocese, or other troublesome entity drop a dime on the coterie. When the mortals move on them, the coterie might be able to find out who fingered them.

STUDY THEM: The Organization sends a reliable agent to study the coterie and analyze any threat they may pose. They likely spot a hunt, though they may not recognize it as such. If the coterie is sloppy, the Organization may find their haven or Touchstones.

ROUGH THEM UP: The Organization sends low-level goons to knock some respect into the troublemakers. They don't want them killed, just out of their domain or off their turf or not poking their noses where they don't belong.

Killing Rats

The coterie has persisted, or changed course decisively. The Organization has been inconvenienced or impressed. They have come briefly to the Prince's notice, or shown up as chatter on the local Second Inquisition briefing. A higher-level official takes over the case, and they know the coterie's names or m.o.

ERASE THEIR ENEMY: The Organization eliminates one of the coterie's other foes, as a reward or as a veiled warning or as a way to frame them for a killing the Organization wanted for other reasons. The Second Inquisition loves to do this to set Kindred at each others' throats.

LURE THEM AWAY: The Organization creates a crisis (or offers a reward) somewhere else and maneuvers to send the coterie there. This might include a move against someone or something the coterie values outside the domain, if only by accident. It's hard to straight-up ignore a Princely commission to "carry a letter to the Prince of Cleveland for me," even if you suspect the Prince never saw or wrote the letter.

ISOLATE THEM: The Organization begins moving against the coterie's friends, family, childer, or other connections on their relationship map. This probably involves at least one messy death. If the coterie has been sloppy, the Organization begins with a threat or near-miss hit on a Touchstone.

NO, REALLY ROUGH THEM UP: The Organization finds a heavy hitter and sends them after the coterie, with all the information needed for an ambush. This might be a satellite gang, a rival coterie, or an unusually effective local hunter team. The Organization still doesn't want to expose its own killers, either to preserve plausible deniability or the Masquerade, because they have limited manpower (the SI suffers from this), or because they still underestimate the coterie.

Next Up At Bat

The coterie have definitely gotten on the Organization's radar. The Prince recognizes their names, the Anarchs know their sign, their blurry pictures are pinned to some shadow government cork board. The Sheriff adds the coterie to their work load. At this stage, they have the luxury of being one of many real problems to deal with – here's a good spot to cut a deal or turtle up. Players being players, of course, when the pressure eases a bit they usually jump for the jugular instead.

PROMOTE THEM: If the coterie still loyally serve the Organization, they get tasked to deal with some other coterie that's causing problems. If they fail, that other coterie's damage is on their heads now.

STARVE THEM: The Organization starts moving against their Turf or poaching on their hunting grounds. With a mortal Organization, it's just adding protection: cops or capos. With a vampire organization, it might involve deniable Caitiffs startling all the quail.

WAKE THEM UP: The Organization finds and attacks their haven. This doesn't have to be a daylight SI raid – it can be a highway re-route or a quick sale to a condo developer. Again, a Touchstone or other relationship map figure might be exposed by this attack.

Setting the Hounds

The coterie are a real threat now, and what's worse the Organization believes it. The Prince has tasked the Primogen to deal with it, Washington wants action, shit is about to get real.

INTERVIEW: The loyal coterie must square off with their biggest rival: compete to complete a crucial mission, with all the backstabbing that involves. Or perhaps just a throwdown for all the marbles in Elysium or a council meeting.

HUNTING CRY: The Prince hasn't called a Blood Hunt because it's undignified and against the code and might be dangerous in itself if the coterie has been at all careful to cultivate other factions in the domain. But someone is after the coterie now, someone more powerful than they are, who has the Prince's nod. The Second Inquisition just orders them killed and deploys a hunter team to do it.

A Land of Wolves Now

The coterie has to come to some agreement with their foe, or they have to destroy them. There is no other alternative. Of course, some other Organization may have noticed all the ruckus and put both the coterie and their enemies on a watch list – there's always a bigger flea to bite 'em. ■

SALVADOR GARCIA

Salvador Garcia is not famous as a killer of Camarilla Kindred or a reckless Masquerade breaker, yet many Princes fear his coming to their city more than any violent troublemaker. Garcia fights the war of ideas, traveling from city to city rousing up the local Anarch underclass to fight for their rights.

Garcia's role is like that of a union agitator: He talks to young licks, helps them see that they don't have to accept their miserable role in undead society and carries news from other domains. One single visit can leave ideas germinating in the mind of a city's disenfranchised, leading to the birth of a new Anarch Movement.

Originally famous as the chief ideologue of the Anarch Free States in California and the killer of the old Prince of Los Angeles, Garcia now visits his home city only rarely. Instead, he uses his extensive contacts in the Movement to travel from domain to domain, spreading the revolution and evading Camarilla forces keen to see the "undead Che Guevara" executed.

Lore

● **A Way With Words:** You've studied the thoughts of not just Salvador Garcia, but all well-known Anarch political ideologues. You're a veteran of the Movement's political debates and can hold your own. For this reason, you get two extra dice in any roll involving a political debate where you invoke Anarch principles.

●● **Old School:** You've met Garcia and advocated the ideas of abolishing Princes and establishing domains with decentralized power. This gives you cred among old school Anarchs of the California Free States generation, who kept the Movement going through the lean years before the current explosion of activity. Because of this, you have the equivalent of a three dot Mawla representing older Anarchs

who like you, though they will help you only in matters of the Movement.

●●● **Enemy of the State:** The Camarilla despises you because of your open advocacy of Anarch ideas. They attempt to discredit you by spreading bizarre rumors: You sold out your domain to strange Chinese vampires, you didn't really do the heroic acts ascribed to you, you're actually a Sabbat infiltrator, and so on. As an unintended consequence of these rumors, all attempts to find real facts about you are made at a two dice penalty to the relevant roll, and any information gained is tainted by falsehoods unless the roll is a critical win.

●●●● **The War of Ideas:** Garcia teaches many young licks about the ideas of the Anarch Movement. Some of those ideas were formulated by him, but not all. Indeed, you once wrote down a vision of how undead society

should be organized and that text has become part of Garcia's standard spiel. Because of this, you're known all across the Anarch territories and can use this fame as the equivalent of three dots of Allies in any Anarch domain.

●●●●● **Rise Up:** You know how to talk to your fellow Anarchs, and they know what you stand for. When you call for a revolution, things will happen. Unfortunately, you have no control over what exactly will happen. Once per story you can make make a politics roll to rile the local Anarchs into action. Gauge the scale of the effect to the number of successes rolled. (three can give you a spontaneous raid on the Prince's Haven while six might starts a revolt encompassing most of the city's Anarch population).

AGATA STAREK

For a Ventrue ancilla, the name Agata Starek summons images of nihilistic, gleeful terror, Anarchs as a wave of destruction demolishing everything in its path. But for the neonate anarchs living under the arbitrary and cruel rules imposed by that same Ventrue, she's the very personification of revolution as revenge. Who cares if we're going to live another night? Let's tear these bastards down right now.

More ideological and principled Anarch leaders tend to despise Starek because of her practice of diablerie and lack of interest in any utopian cause. For them, she's nothing but a monster, little better than the creatures of the Camarilla. Yet their perspective might be tainted by the power they wield, because Starek does have one single principle: She always punches up, usually literally. She's famous for turning on her friends and allies in favor of a mistreated ghoul or suffering human.

For all their dislike of Starek, few Anarch leaders really want to make a move against her. Deep in their unbeating hearts, they too appreciate the idea of a monster of their own, a joyous terror giving the Camarilla something to be afraid of.

The less power you have, the more hope Agata Starek gives you.

 **Lore**

● **Terrorizing the Powerful:** Like Agata, you have an uncanny ability to strike terror in the hearts of licks more powerful and influential than you. Once per story, you can reroll an Intimidation test when confronted with a lick of greater means than yourself. This can mean age, resources or Sect status, but the final call on whether your ability applies is up to the Storyteller

●● **Apprentice:** You've met Agata Starek personally, and something in you caught her interest. Sometimes she sends you little tidbits of information about the weaknesses and private vices of the powerful licks in your city, often with the aim of allowing you to taste their sweet, sweet blood. Once per story you gain the equivalent of a four-dot contact for the purpose deducing a weakness in a stronger enemy. This could be anything from their feeding habit, their Touchstones or the flaw in their haven's security.

●●● **A Favor Owed:** You've met Agata Starek once or twice, perhaps in a delicate situation involving murder and the spilling of Camarilla blood. Because of your shared history, once per story you can cash in a boon someone in your city owes her. A known appreciator of vitae, the boons owed to Starek always involve gaining access to particular type of vampiric Blood. You explain what kind of Blood you need, and the Storyteller tells you who owes the boon to acquire it, limited by what's possible in the domain. For example, methuselah Blood is probably not possible, but the Blood of the Prince might be.

●●●● **Unlikely Allies:** Starek is a figure of hope for many who no longer believe that a better world is possible. They are content to yearn for revenge, and like her, you've become to seem like someone who could make things difficult for the powerful. Because of this, once per story an oppressed servant or minion of your undead enemies will help you in a tight spot as long as they can do it without getting caught. The Storyteller can make this happen, or you can appeal to a minion with a Persuasion roll with four additional dice.

●●●●● **The Joy of Transgression:** Agata Starek argues that diablerizing powerful Camarilla vampires is not only an Anarch responsibility, it's also one of the chief joys of the revolution. You've taken her words to heart and no longer suffer an automatic loss of a point of Humanity when diablerizing someone with more Sect status than yourself. However, the potential Humanity loss from when you roll the effects of the diablerie can still apply.

HESHA RUHADZE

Though the Ministry have largely aligned with the Anarchs in these turbulent nights, Hesha Ruhadze stands like an old rock in a stream. When asked about sectarian allegiances, the Nubian archaeologist rolls his eyes and mutters to himself. He spurns politics, referring to it as a wasted focus for creatures that might live for an eternity. His dedication is to history, the mysteries of vampire origins, and importantly, discerning their fates. All the while, he sits in at Anarch moots and listens attentively.

Hesha is a willing servant of the Blood, and believes he can understand the voice of Sutekh calling from his vitae. Where this might be a mark of insanity for some vampires, Hesha's standing among Kindred far and wide lends credence to his claims. He is still the same coolly charming man, and every word he speaks feels heavy with gravitas, but now he speaks as the herald of his god's will. Every time he does so, it is with a smile.

 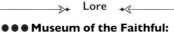 Lore

● **One of Hesha's Works:** You own one of Hesha's treatises on the history of Kindred existence. While the work may be controversial, and oppose the traditional Cainite mythology, it conveys one additional die on Occult-based dice pools, or pools relating to vampire origins. This work may be sold in exchange for one dot of the Resources Background.

●● **Something Hesha Wants:** You know what Hesha currently seeks, and can access it, or already own it. This item can be used to bargain with, blackmail, or threaten Hesha, or even present to him as a gift for future favor. This artifact or piece of information conveys an additional three dice to Persuasion or Intimidation dice pools involving Hesha or his cult. It can also be sold, adding three dots to your Resources (up to five) for the duration of the story.

●●● **Museum of the Faithful:** You possess the rare privilege of membership in one of the Ministry's museums of vampire history. These underground treasure troves are securely guarded but contain a plethora of accessible information about legendary Cainites. You must submit a new treasure to the museum every year for continued membership and will have your access denied if you fail to do so, or ever steal from one of these Setite hoards. You gain three additional dice to all tests involving the research of vampires and vampire history for as long as you keep you membership.

●●●● **Blood Cult** (Ministry characters only)**:** Hesha has taught you the old ways of the Followers of Set, in which mortals and ghouls perform more than a servile role. Your cult encompasses a warrior, a priest, and a scholar, as well as willing vessels from which you feed. Three Background dots can be split between these specialzed cultists, who can count as Herd or Retainers. They possess more knowledge and ability of your kind than typical servants and ghouls, giving them an additional die in all interactions with vampires.

●●●●● **Hear the Blood Sing** (Ministry characters only)**:** Maybe Hesha taught you how to hear the words, or perhaps you accomplished the feat yourself. You hear the voice of Sutekh more loudly than you do your Beast. Through riddles, visions, and musical refrain, the Storyteller will occasionally offer you guidance from the godlike voice issuing from your vitae. Once per session, you are also able to automatically resist Frenzy, treating it as a Ministry Compulsion instead

THE CHURCH OF SET

Most Ministers have rediscovered their cosmopolitan, multi-faith routes. While they still revere Set as their founder and the first vampire, it is less common for a Setite of the Ministry to cling only to the worship of Sutekh. This is not the case among those Setites who claim membership in the very Church of Set. Dedicated to the rites of Setite Orthodoxy, the Church of Set's members believe they must conspire to weaken all other clans and their founders in order to pave the way for the resurrection of their founder. Your membership in the Church of Set may be as a new adherent, desperate to find meaning and mentorship in a hostile world, or you may be one of the dedicated faithful, rejecting the idea of enslavement to other Antediluvians and seeking freedom from all chains by following Set's holy guidance.

Lore

● Congregation: You have access to a herd of kine, but these mortals are a unified religious flock you can manipulate. This congregation can belong to any mainstream of fringe religion, and whether they see you as their leader, or just another parishioner, you can feed from them easily. This lore is equivalent to a two-dot Herd, though it requires you to show up and uphold the faith regularly.

●● Tap the Secret Vein: Through the method of a simple interview, you can analyze whether a mortal or Kindred has a secret they're trying to hide. You gain a two-dice bonus to Insight-based tests to find whether someone is keeping a secret.

●●● Freedom from the Aeons: Set despises his fellow clan founders, or so the legend says. The Setites consider the other founders Aeons, and demonstrate a resistance to their power. You gain two additional dice on rolls resisting Dominate and Presence attempts from vampires of other clans.

●●●● Degenerative Process: The Church of Set teaches its adherents that a man must be brought to his lowest before he can rise to meet glorious Sutekh. You can push any being, mortal or immortal, to indulge in degenerative corruption only to come out clean on the other side. With a successful Manipulation + Persuasion roll, you can persuade any individual to break a Tenet or Conviction, gaining at least one Stain. When it is done, they feel purified. The targeted character restores up to three Superficial or one Aggravated Willpower damage.

●●●●● Body of Set: You possess a fragment of Set's skeleton, sarcophagus, or burial robes. Though the implication of Set's Final Death is debatable, the holy (or unholy, depending on your perspective) artifact gives you drive to succeed and impressive influence over other Followers of Set, conveying a four-dot Status among other Ministers. The relic also helps you to touch the mind of Set through meditation, and once per story you are able to reduce Stains gained from breaking a Tenet by one, if following what you and the Storyteller perceive as the will of your god.

DESCENDANT OF XAVIAR

(GANGREL CHARACTERS ONLY)

Nobody, even fellow Gangrel, listened to Xaviar the first time he spoke. It took marching into a convocation of the Camarilla's biggest players for other Kindred to take notice of him. He spoke of interacting with one of the Antediluvians and seeing his entire coterie eaten alive by this mythological creature. He accused the Camarilla of perfidy against its members and cast aside his role of Gangrel Justicar.

News travels slowly among the Gangrel, as a clan with little hierarchy and lacking an effective communication network. Slowly, Gangrel followed Xaviar out of the Camarilla, some becoming Autarkis, while more ultimately joined the Anarchs.

Gangrel now share a communal guilt for their initial disbelief of Xaviar's claims and slow reaction to his proclamation, as he met Final Death soon after. Few know if the Camarilla or some other agency slew the mighty Gangrel, but all know their ancestor was wronged. Now they take up his torch and attempt to bring the Gangrel into truth's flickering light.

  Lore

● Martyred Ancestor: Other Gangrel treat you with the respect they took too long to afford Xaviar. Despite any personal grievances, you can always find sanctuary with other Gangrel, if any are present in your current domain, at least until you insult them grievously. With them, you have two dots of Status (● ●).

● ● Where the Bodies Are Buried: Xaviar's experiences with melding through earth, blood, and vitae left a mark on his lineage. Gangrel of his line can make a Resolve + Awareness test to detect whether a vampire has merged with the earth or lays torpid beneath the soil. Difficulty depends on the area you have to search.

● ● ● Loyal Hound: You resisted the winds of change, remaining with the Camarilla despite your clan's actions. For your loyalty, the local Camarilla Prince awarded you status, feeding rights, and territory, amounting to four dots you can distribute among Domain, Herd, and Status. Non-Camarilla Gangrel despise you, and even Camarilla vampires of other clans pity your solitude, but you guarantee yourself a voice among the Primogen, should any rebel Gangrel pass through your domain.

● ● ● ● Monstrous Bat: Xaviar's preferred bestial form was once that of a bat, but following his encounter with the Antediluvian, he found his form capable of changing into a hybrid between human and bat. Once per story when the moon is just right, you can take the same form. This man-sized bat has an extra dot in all Physical Attributes and can glide in the air from any height. Biting in this form adds +1 Aggravated damage to mortals and vampires alike.

● ● ● ● Experienced the Antediluvian: Xaviar was not the only Gangrel to sink into the ground and find himself inside his clan founder's vast, inhuman form. You have done the same, and the experience changed you. You are now a little mad, likely suffering from paranoia or claustrophobia. Whenever you call your encounter to mind, you feel your veins rooted to the ground, connecting to every other Gangrel in the world. Once per story, you can sense any Gangrel's location and drain a thimbleful of vitae from them to reset your Hunger level to 2. You must be touching open ground, not concrete, to use this ability.

DESCENDANT OF TYLER

(BRUJAH CHARACTERS ONLY)

Every aspiring Brujah rebel worships Tyler – once known as Patricia of Bollingbroke – and going by many names since. Her revolutionary violence against tyrant elders and insidious methuselahs irrevocably changed Kindred society and inspired the Anarch Movement. Tyler herself doubts that her actions led to effective praxis, but her childer and clanmates compare her to everyone from Robin Hood, to Malcolm X, to Che Guevara, to Gavrilo Princip.

Tyler still exists: a quiet, studious rebel in these nights. With centuries of reflection, she struggles to reconcile her actions with the results of modern nights. Her descendants continue the fight with the hopes of uplifting her to her destined greatness one night.

Lore

● **Instigator:** Once per story, whenever you attempt to persuade a mortal crowd into violent action, your hot-blooded nature adds two dice to your dice pool to do so.

●● **Champion of the Cause:** When vampires want a leader for a rebellion, large or small scale, they come to you for advice or leadership. They might even listen to your words, and providing your advice is not completely ridiculous, might even defer to your authority. You add two dots to your Status with them during such rebellions, but you might find the numerous contacts gained before a rebellion more valuable and certainly less dangerous.

●●● **Tyler's Mercy:** You know when to stop. Tyler recognized when the Sabbat went too far with her Anarch ideals, and you likewise recognize the limits of violent revolution. Once

per story, when frenzying, you may at any point take a Brujah Compulsion (p. 210) to immediately cease the outburst. You do not suffer any confusion or tiredness after an interrupted frenzy, abruptly snapping back to Humanity.

●●●● **The Furores:** Tyler's philosophies first emerged among a historic vampire group known as the Furores, dedicated to the destruction of all Kindred tyrants. This group still exists in secret, and you claim membership. When the time is right (once per chronicle), the Furores arm you, provide you with sanctuary in a regnum where they have influence, and activate assets in the target domain as surprise Allies (available within one scene). The Allies add up to five dots of Effectiveness; the rest depends on your collaboration with the Storyteller. Furore assets can only

be used when attempting to take down a Prince, unfit Baron, or vampire of higher station. Misuse makes you a target of the Furores and their unknown operatives.

●●●●● **Permanent Revolution:** You have already taken down one sect figurehead. You now lead an army of revolutionaries to sweep the board in the neighboring regnae. For as long as you keep fighting and are not found to be indulging in the luxuries of station, Anarchs stop to listen to your every word, and Brujah Anarchs do exactly as you say, including embarking on suicide missions. No rolls are required if your speech is strong and argument convincing enough.

RUINS OF CARTHAGE

You are a vampire who traces their line back to the height of Carthage, or an attempt to rebuild the great empire that opposed Ventrue and Malkavian-controlled Rome. Likely of Clan Brujah or the Banu Haqim, you were taught the words of your ancestors, carry the fire of hatred for tyranny, and crave the nights when you can establish a domain where mortals and vampires alike can relax the need for the Masquerade.

Knowledge of the principles of vampiric Carthage is both enlightening and damning, for once a vampire tastes the freedom of this fallen empire, they struggle within the Camarilla's strictures. Licks who obsess over the Ruins of Carthage often get caught in webs of intrigue, paying for their curiosity with the formation of inescapable pacts.

  Lore

● **Clan Historian:** You have studied the path of Clans Brujah, Lasombra, and the Children of Haqim from pre-Carthage nights through to the formation of the Camarilla. You know their rises and their falls, their constant battles with the Ventrue, Malkavians, and Toreador, and can recite names and dates with ease. This lore impresses other Kindred historians and rebels looking for a cause, giving you a bonus die on social tests where you can put this knowledge to use.

●● **Punic Pride:** To this night, Brujah still look back on Carthage as the ultimate symbol of rebellion. They believe Carthage was the most successful domain to successfully resist Ventrue-controlled Rome, until its calamitous end. You take great pride in your Carthaginian ancestry, whether through mortal links, or immortal bloodline. When invoking this ancestry, you speak with increased confidence and draw the attentions of fellow rebels. Gain two dice in Leadership-based tests to lead others against perceived oppression.

●●● **Death to Tyrants:** If Carthage taught the Brujah and Children of Haqim

anything, it's that it's always worth fighting until the end. Never since – even when considering the Anarch Revolt – have the pillars of the establishment been so shaken. You harness the strength of the vampires who fell fighting Rome whenever taking the fight to a figure in power. Gain a bonus dice to all contests against someone who can claim authority over you.

●●●● **Moloch's Will:** At its height, vampiric Carthage was led by the Brujah Antediluvian and her consort, a methuselah known as Moloch. This pair indulged in thousands of human sacrifices, bathing in the blood of the young, hosting orgies of primal decadence, and yet somehow never succumbing to the Beast. You have inverted your own Beast, finding that by performing gross actions and inhumane rituals, you are able to feed it, and never lose control. Your mastery over the monster inside somehow grants you a hellish charm that you can use to lure young vampires and innocent mortals into service.

●●●● **Troile's Wish!:** AMany Brujah claim the damning tales of Carthage

are simply Ventrue propaganda spread from Rome, and extant to this night. Brujah and Banu Haqim scholars alike claim Troile was a benevolent ruler, treating both Kindred and kine fairly, and ensuring every soul in the empire remained fed, educated, and loved. You believe in this credo, and exude a reassurance that convinces others to trust you, supplicate before you, and help you in whatever schemes you have to mind. You gain a two bonus dice to all social tests involving vampiric servants, yours and others, whether they are retainers or just part of a herd.

●●●●● **Carthage Anew:** You are an advocate of Carthage anew. Plans have been set in motion and you already have an Anarch city selected where the Masquerade will soon fall without being targeted by mortal agencies. (The deals and pacts you had to make for this to happen are left to you and the Storyteller.) Up until that time, you are able to break the Masquerade and get away with it in that city once per story, no matter the severity of the breach.

BLOOD PLAGUED

Vampires are immune to most diseases, but some plagues make their way into the vitae and transfer from vampire to vessel with ease, while others fester and mutate, becoming something threatening only to the vampire hosts.

A Blood plague, sometimes known as the Curse, swept through the undead society in the late 20th century, decimating domains and striking down vampires no matter their clan or status. Gustav Breidenstein, former Prince of Berlin and powerful elder, was one of the highest profile victims of the contagion that brought countless Damned to frenzy and forced vitae to escape from every orifice until the victim withered and died.

It is said the Blood plague died out, or was cured through a great ritual sacrifice. Unfortunately, the plague may just be torpid, like so many of its victims. These infections rise again and again across the centuriest.

Lore

● **Detection:** The Blood plague manifests in vampires in a variety of ways, depending on the incarnation of the disease. As the curse afflicting vampires evolves, so must the experts who seek to study and eradicate it. You are one such vampire, who knows all associated symptoms of the Blood plague. You can use this lore to easily determine if someone carries infection, or more malignantly, you can sow rumors in a domain of the plague's existence, by using facts about the disease's course. Add two dice to any Medicine or Occult roll involving the plague.

●● **The Science of the Blood:** You believe the Blood plague to be largely medical in genesis, possibly even started among mortals before it infected Kindred. Your thorough study of the Blood plague enables you to simply detect the plague's recent paths and patterns, analyzing where an infected host may have been, who they might have been infected by, and when. Such information can be incredibly useful when attempting to quarantine all infected subjects. Add two dice to all Investigation rolls and other tests to track active victims of the plague.

●●● **Trace the Torpid Victims:** You see the strains of Blood plague wind through the earth. Your interest in this condition goes further than just quarantine and healing of the infected; you can follow the plague's stench and unholy aura to its torpid victims. You already know where many of the bodies are buried. By making a Resolve + Occult roll (Difficulty 4, modified depending on the vampire population and the history of the Blood plague in the area) you can locate the body of an infected victim still in torpor. Who they are and whether they are still contagious is up to the Storyteller.

●●●● **Curative Vitae:** TYou believe any disease is curable, with the correct research, and the willingness to sacrifice. Your vitae is clean of the Blood plague, and you show no symptoms despite your proximity to many victims. You believe your Blood may hold the cure, but scientists of other clans require a lot of your vitae to test this idea. By giving enough Blood to force a Rouse Check you can add two dice to any attempt to manufacture a cure, temporary or even permanent (Storyteller's discretion).

●●●●● **Vector:** You have a secret. You carry the Blood plague, and can even infect others with it, but you display none of the symptoms. This dangerous lore allows you to spill your vitae in an Elysium or feed a mouthful of it to a popular vessel, and watch the terrible effects as the other Kindred succumb to the Blood plague. If you feel more altruistic, you may volunteer for thorough tests on your vitae, and how it may be applied by your sect as a weapon, or by those looking for a cure. The specific effects of your strain of plague are up to you and the Storyteller.

ANARCH REVOLT

You claim lineage to a vampire important to the Anarch Revolt of the 14th and 15th centuries, or perhaps you possess records chronicling the fall of tyrannical Princes, or rise of upstart Barons. You know the time and place Tyler murdered Hardestadt the Elder, and the participants in the diablerie of the Tzimisce Antediluvian. Maybe you've even spoken with Lugoj or Lambach, two of the Fiends present during that incident.

Your knowledge of the Anarch Revolt is such that you can see the waves and eddies of time repeating itself in the society of the Damned tonight. You recognize the exact same crimes of the past repeated now, and can predict, and perhaps control, the way the young will rise up to smash the old.

  Lore

● **Critical Ancestor:** Vampires largely of Clans Brujah, the Banu Haqim, and Lasombra led the Anarch Revolt across Europe, with power-hungry Tzimisce taking part to eliminate the greatest monsters in their own clan. However, Anarchs rose from all clans, as most elders manipulated their young to disastrous ends. You can name one of your ancestors as critical to the Anarch Revolt, either as an instigator, chronicler, or opponent. Your ties to this ancestor give you credibility in discussions regarding the Revolt, and a passion for its analysis. Gain a point of Anarch status as well as the Suspect (Camarilla) flaw, or vice versa.

●● **Speak the Words:** TThe Anarch Revolt was driven more by words and energy than flashing blades and spilling blood, at least at first. You possess the same ambition as the Anarchs of the past, and can accurately pinpoint where oppression occurs, and where revolt is necessary. When vampires listen to you, they feel more inclined to seize power from their masters. Add two dice to social tests involving the instigation of Anarch activism.

●●● **Enemy of the Establishment:** You consider yourself an Old Anarch, not necessarily by age, but by ethos. The new Anarch Movement has its strengths, but also many weaknesses. Your views put you in direct opposition to the Camarilla and its Victorian methods of subjugation. The Camarilla has marked you as an enemy, which only draws more listless Anarchs to your banner. You gain the equivalent of a four-dot Mawla, representing your comrades among the Anarchs, as well as a one-dot Adversary, representing someone tasked with keeping tabs on you and, if necessary, bring you down.

●●●● **Icon:** You have taken the name of one of the Anarch Revolt's original participants, and act as that vampire's successor. This would be disrespectful, if you had not performed many of the same actions as your forebears. Many Anarchs see you as the next great leader of the Revolt, whether or not that is your intent. You may have seized an historic identity

for the cult status and easy access to herd, but now the sect puts increasing pressure on you to act in their interest. Gain two dots of Status, two dots in Herd and two dots in Resources for as long as you put the Anarch cause before anything else. Any misstep and they are lost until you redeem yourself.

●●●●● **Reignite the Revolt:** The time has come. You know how the Anarch Revolt took place half a millennium ago, and know how it needs to take place tonight. You know the weakness of your city, the greatest threats, and the Camarilla positions direly in need of removal. You can threaten your enemies with the prospect of war for extortion purposes, or to prevent the Camarilla taking more liberties with the Anarchs than they have already. Once per story you can use this leverage to gain four dice in any Social conflict against a member of the Camarilla establishment. If you fail the roll you either need to make good on your threat or lose this Advantage permanently.